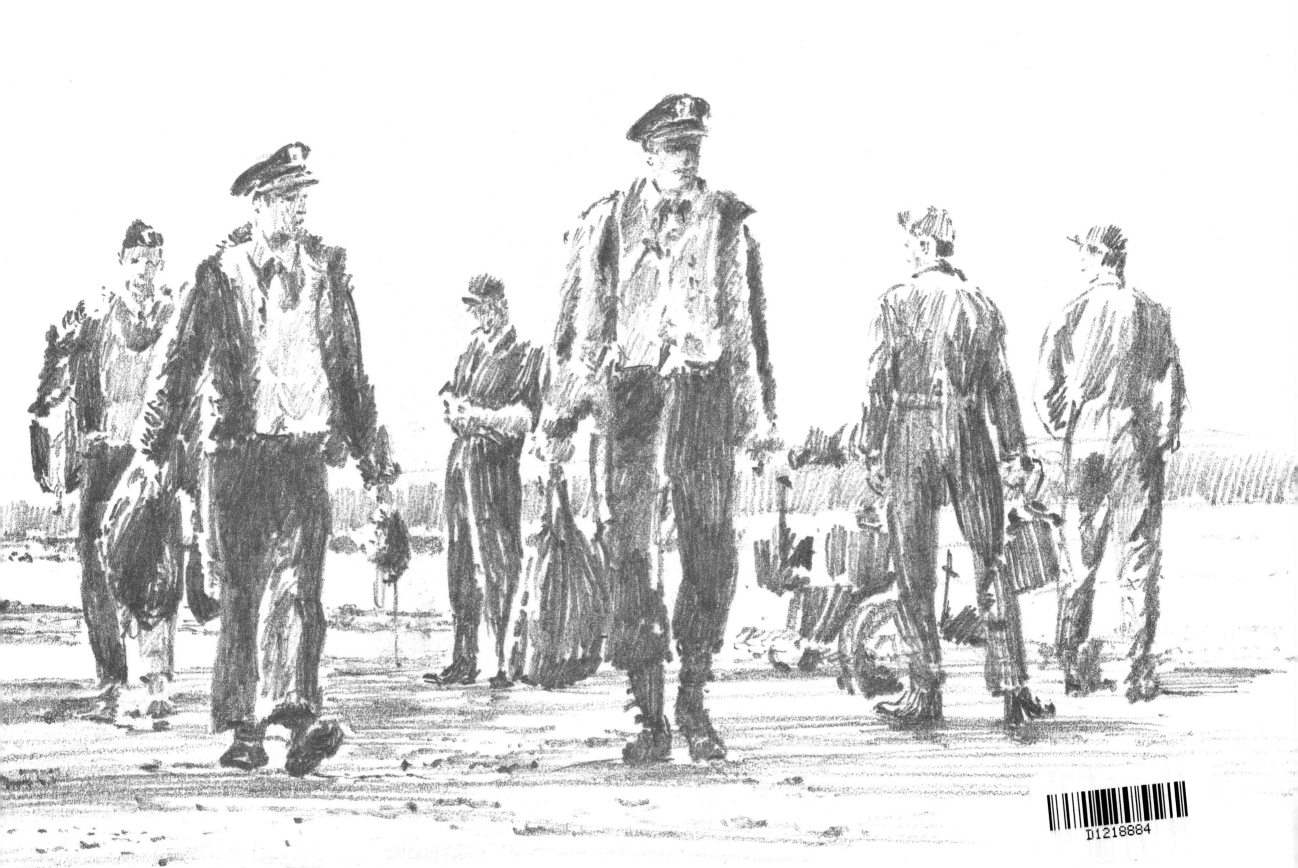

ROBERT TAYLOR
AIR COMBAT PAINTINGS VOLUME II

For Charlie ~
with best wishes ~

Robert Taylor

13ᵗʰ Sept 9J.

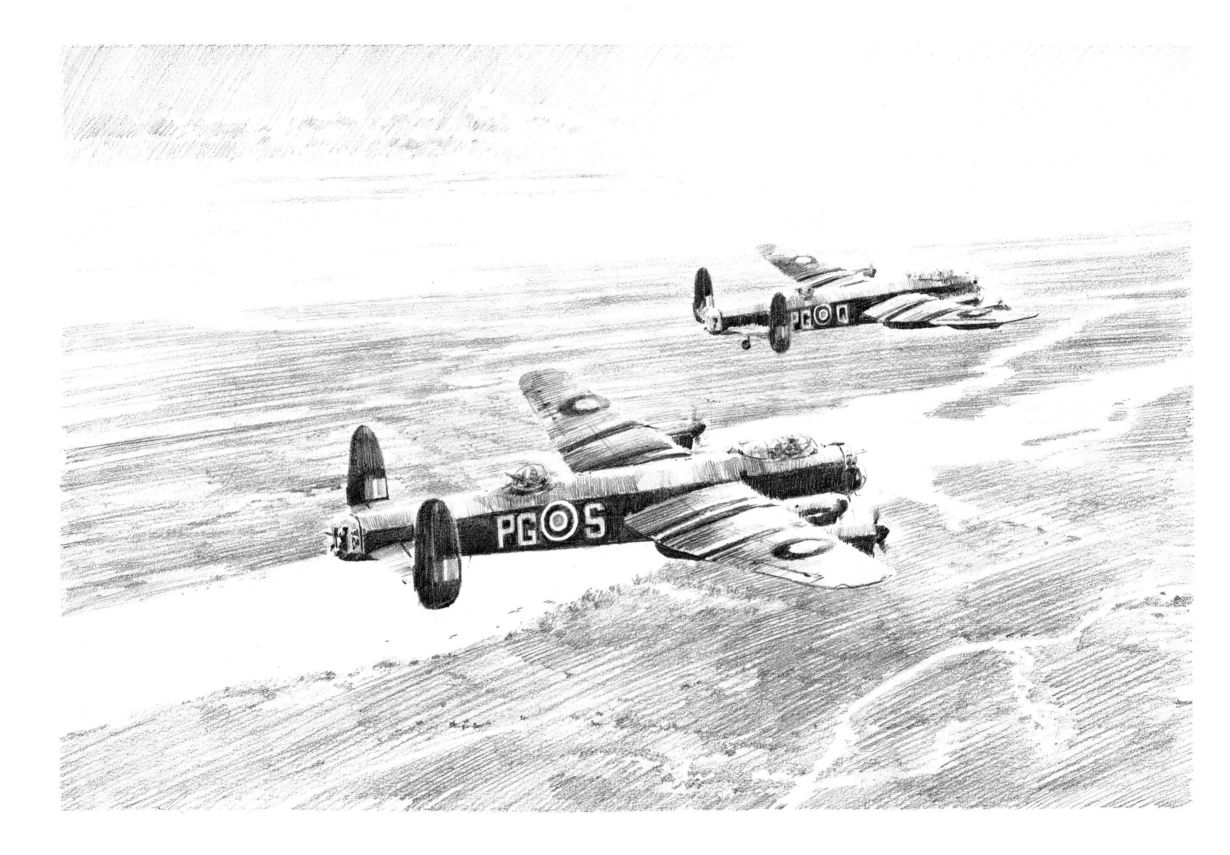

ROBERT TAYLOR
AIR COMBAT PAINTINGS VOLUME II

Charles Walker and Robert Taylor

FOREWORD BY

Group Captain Peter Townsend
CVO, DSO, DFC

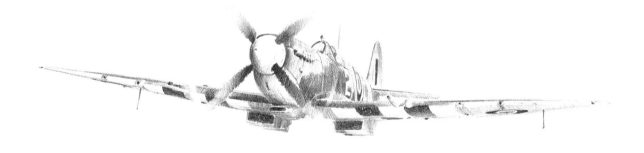

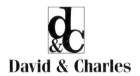

David & Charles

To my wife and family, and to my collectors,
many of whom have become my friends.

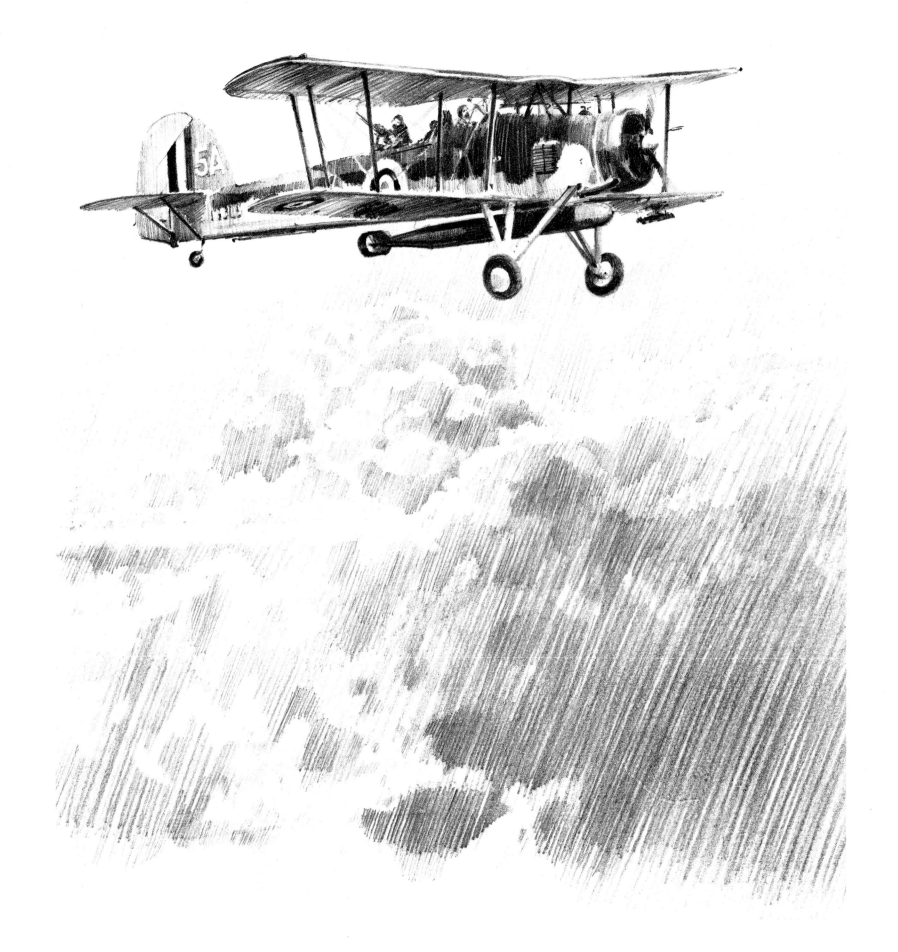

British Library Cataloguing in Publication Data
Taylor, Robert
 Robert Taylor: air combat paintings: Vol 2.
 I. Title
758

 ISBN 0–7153–9889–X

First published 1991
Reprinted 1992, 1995

Designed and edited by Pat Barnard

Typeset by ABM Typographics Ltd, Hull
Printed by Saik Wah Press Pte Ltd, Singapore
for David & Charles plc
Brunel House   Newton Abbot   Devon

CONTENTS

THE PAINTINGS
Introduced by the Artist

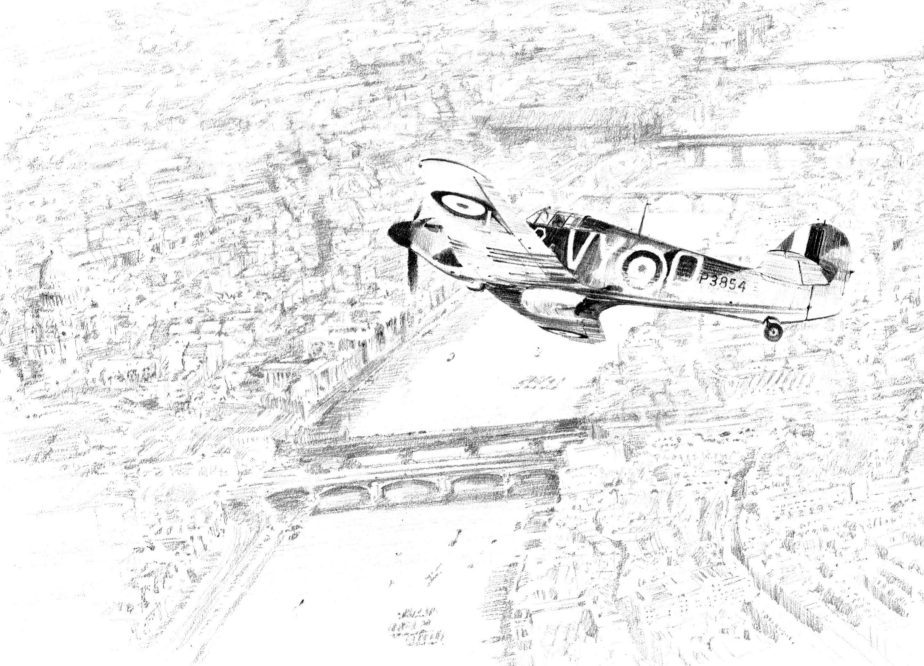

FOREWORD

Dear Robert,

You have received thousands of admiring letters during your brilliant career and here, if you will allow me, comes another, just as your second volume of Air Combat Paintings is to be published.

Thanks to Pat Barnard and his prestigious Military Gallery in Bath, we have known each other for some years. Like so many others who meet you for the first time I was touched by your shyness (despite all that you have achieved) and the soft West Country burr in your voice. I, too, am from the West Country; places like Bideford, Westward Ho!, Falmouth and Plymouth were all part of my boyhood. Which means that you and I have the smell of the briny in our nostrils, the sea-salt in our veins.

I say this only to prove my intense feeling and admiration for your work. When I was a kid at Bideford I was crazy about ships, like you a generation or so later. But while I would spend hours carving and shaping their hulls out of some old block of wood and sewing their sails cut from an odd piece of cloth you, when your time came, expressed your passion in a manner far more sophisticated: you sketched and painted your ships in their element, placid or the raging sea. No doubt, too, the years you spent restoring pictures helped you to master your art. Was not Rembrandt, in his youth, apprenticed in the same way?

The comparison of our boyhood continues: one day a small aeroplane, a Gypsy Moth, whizzed overhead, banking steeply so that I could see the pilot, his scarf trailing in the slipstream. That day a new passion was born in me – flying. Not that I forgot ships and the sea; sailors and airmen have much in common in their experience of the elements and of wide and distant horizons.

You, in time, and after convincing Pat of your talent with that famous picture of a tiger (which still snarls menacingly from a wall in Pat's home), were to turn from the sea and ships to the air and aeroplanes.

In my case the new passion was so strong that it carried me on beyond the carving of model aeroplanes to – believe it or not – drawing them! And here comparisons end. You, lucky chap, had talent. I had none. Despite my efforts, my aeroplanes often had one wing longer than the other; the wheels, in perspective, gave no impression that they were really round and the tail plane was nearly always out of joint with the fuselage.

Both of us had and still have a passion for the sea and the air. While yours, aided by your marvellous talent, led you to your studio, there to take up palette and paintbrush, mine carried me up and into the cockpit, there to grasp the throttle-lever and 'stick' – the 'joy-stick' as it was called, and with reason, for it was a true and emotional nick-name. Joy is the essence of flying.

You have said that people occasionally reproach you for 'glorifying war'. I do not agree (knowing you well). While you depict so vividly those fearful, heroic moments of combat when young men, for whom flying was a common passion were trying their utmost to kill each other; when elsewhere youthful aviators are flying on through a storm of bursting shells to send down their bombs upon blazing cities or launch their torpedoes into some doomed battleship, it does not occur to me that you are giving an aura of glory to war. Rather, you are recording, with extreme realism the dramatic moments of the war in the air and down below.

Part of your genius is to create, around and beyond the violent scenes of battle, a decor of immeasurable beauty which proves, even to the most barbarous soul, how sublimely wonderful is our planet and the heavens above it.

As I study your paintings I marvel at the skill and subtlety with which you manage to portray, on your blank and static canvas, the grace and the motion of flight and the mortal dangers of wartime flying – fighters whirling in combat, stricken bombers pressing on to the target or staggering back to base above the English countryside where wondering haymakers look up in awe and admiration; drifting clouds brushed with the soft colours of the setting sun or the sombre grey of an approaching storm, while from the pilot's cockpit we look down and through a break in the clouds, get a glimpse of our well-beloved English countryside, the fields and hills, the villages and towns which so inspired us to defend our island. With your meticulous care for detail, (be it an aircraft fitting, a ship's pennant, a farm dog or a startled pheasant), with your feeling for colour and form you evoke the hellish thrill, the piercing agony, felt by those young men who fought in the air and of those who watched from below.

And finally you leave us convinced how much happier the human race would be without war, just left to enjoy the glories – and caprices – of nature which you paint with such a sensitive brush – I would even dare to say with a genius similar to that of Constable and Turner.

Thank you, dear Robert, for giving us such profoundly moving impressions of the air war of some fifty years ago, and through them bringing together in friendship airmen who, erstwhile, were bitter foes.

And again, all praise to you for contributing so much, through your work, to the relief of war victims. Hasten the day when war will be no more. When that day comes your painting will still stand as a testimony to the skill and sacrifice of airmen at war, as they fought, paradoxically, for peace.

Peter Townsend

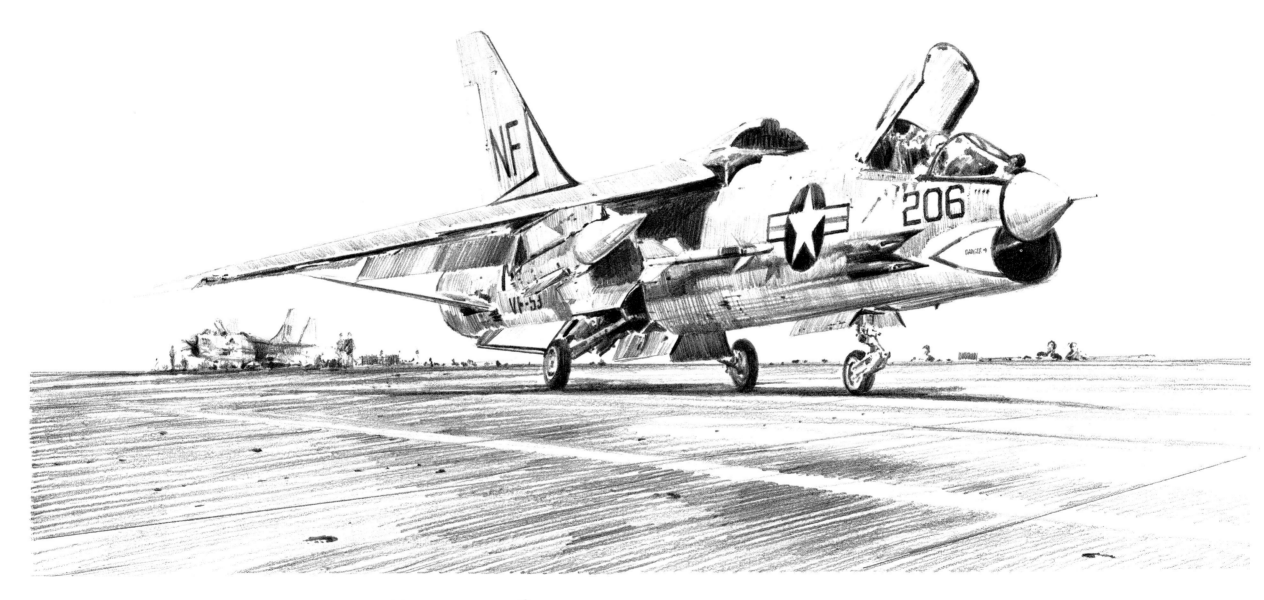

Vought F-8E Crusader operating from USS Hancock. March 67.

INTRODUCTION

Most of the old aviation photographs that were taken during the period which I cover with my paintings were in monochrome, and were made without any artistic thought, by people who had no purpose beyond recording what they saw. Few depicted combat scenes, for obvious reasons – people shooting and being shot at don't have much time or inclination to take photographs. My job is to recreate scenes which were not, indeed mostly could not, be recorded by the camera, and to do so using the most colourful medium I know, which is oil paint.

Much goes into trying to recreate a scene from the past, including a great deal of research and planning, and all the imagination which I can muster. Much of the planning is to ensure that what is painted is accurate, because – hoping not to sound too pompous – I try to recreate little cameos from our aviation history. Perhaps what I paint is not all that important in a truly historical sense – I don't really know; I suppose that only time will reveal the answer to that question. What I do try to do is to avoid becoming too obsessed with all the detail of this huge subject, and to leave the making of out-and-out historical

statements to the historians so as to concentrate on trying to recreate the atmosphere of the era and the arena.

The historians and writers of technical literature provide an abundance of facts; photographers and technical illustrators provide a plethora of highly detailed graphics showing the aircraft from the era I paint. I try to translate all this information, aided by the help of many friends who were there, into something which I hope gives my audience a realistic feeling for what it was like to live and fly in combat some fifty years ago.

All the paintings in this book depict aircraft which were designed, built and flown in what for me was the golden age of aviation. I suppose we all look back at things past with some affection, usually conveniently forgetting the unpleasant parts, remembering only the best, and sometimes longing for those days to reappear.

Living a life of nostalgia suits me. I count myself sublimely fortunate to be able to spend my days painting the classic machines of the past, and the great natural arena in which they flew through

history. As I work I am easily transported back into their heady epoch-making world, reliving events over and over again. Involvement with each picture is an intense affair.

Paintings are a little like one's offspring: the day comes when they leave home – but they are never forgotten. Often it is difficult to part with a painting, and sometimes it is only the knowledge that it is going to a 'good home' that allows me to let it go – that and the bills that drop through the letter box! But when they go they have always brought me friendship. I have had the good fortune to get to know personally many collectors who have acquired my paintings and prints. All of us without exception have in common a great enthusiasm for aviation, together with a deep admiration for the courage and skill of the men who flew these historic aircraft.

I am continually inspired by this enthusiasm and friendship, which increasingly spurs me on, and it is to my collectors, therefore, that I would like to dedicate this book.

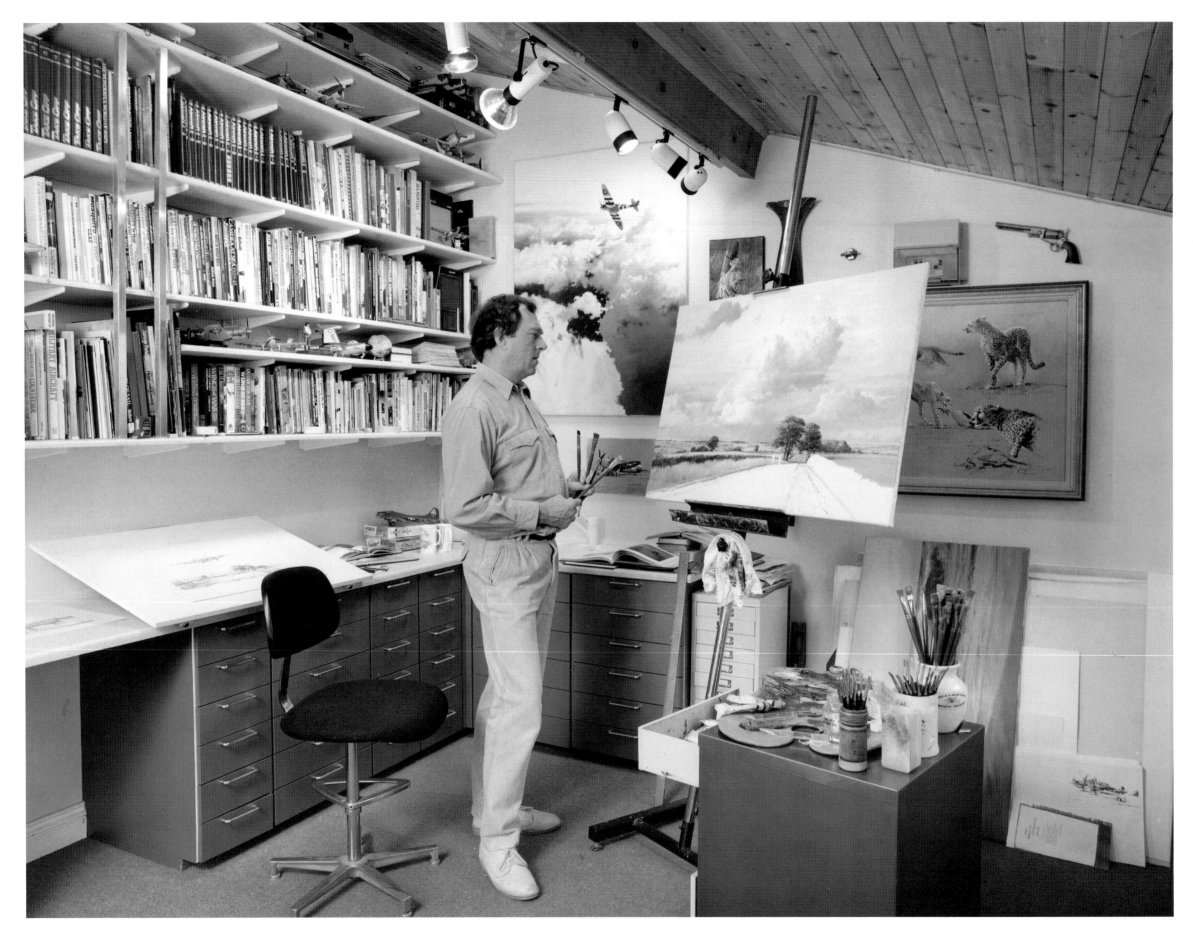

ROBERT TAYLOR

It has been a great pleasure over the years to observe the development of Robert Taylor's career. In the time that I have known him, he has graduated from being a keen, extremely gifted, but little-known artist to the status of an internationally sought-after and celebrated master of his profession. Without doubt, the most satisfying aspect of this progression has been the one constant in an otherwise rapidly changing picture – Robert Taylor himself. It is an enlightening experience to sit and talk with Robert in his studio, knowing that the painting on his easel could, perhaps, end up in some royal residence or in an internationally acclaimed museum collection. One then notices that he is talking as if nothing had changed since those early days when he was producing paintings which, if he sold them at all, would be handed over for little more than the price of the paints and the canvas he had paid for and used.

There is an interesting paradox at work here. Robert Taylor, as a young man, never had any stronger wish than to be able to draw and paint for his living. But he did not foresee, nor did he have dreams of, becoming a painter whose work might be so popular that it would be bargained over by anxious collectors. Had he been the sort of person who dedicates his time to such thoughts and ambitions it is unlikely that he would ever have achieved the recognition he now enjoys. The fact is that almost all his efforts since he was a boy were given over to the one subject which occupied his mind above all others – his art.

Robert's choice of aviation and marine art as his medium of expression is not one which surprised those who know him well. Perhaps the only fact which did surprise those people is that he has been able, at least in recent years, to confine his painting to just one area, since his versatility and range of interests are both so great. One half expects him to break out in some new and exciting direction at any moment, taking the subject by storm, then asking in his quiet and unassuming manner what all the fuss is about.

Born in 1946, Robert grew up in the shadow of World War II. England had just come through six years of harrowing conflict and was only beginning to readjust to the pleasures of peace and freedom. But an austerity which is difficult to imagine today was the norm in the post-war period when the young Robert Taylor romped around the school playground in his home city of Bath, deep in the English West Country. The abundance of toys which is taken for granted by today's small children did not exist in the 1940s and early 1950s. Youngsters made up their own games to play and the most fun was often enjoyed by those with the greatest imagination. Playthings were invented and, where practical, constructed with whatever materials were to hand.

There was little money in the Taylor household and whatever luxuries there were at that time were not available to the three small Taylor children; life was a struggle for the devoted mother and stepfather who brought them up in the small but happy household. But it was the young Robert who could always be relied upon to fashion something out of nothing, his creative and practical talents already showing before he could properly read or write.

Like most young boys of the era, Robert quickly developed a fascination for aeroplanes. In those early days after the war, his native West Country was scattered with active service airfields and the sky always seemed to be busy with aircraft carrying out their daily activities. Robert could easily recognise all of them, and some of them simply by their sound alone.

By the time that Robert was five or six, his models of ships and aircraft – mostly fashioned in those days out of lumps of solid wood – were better constructed than those made by boys twice his age, and it was not long before he was drawing them with a flair and accuracy that amazed his family and fascinated his young friends.

The first aircraft Robert Taylor ever sat in was a Spitfire. Having as a boy heard tales of heroism of the legendary fighter aces, and seen the classic fighters of the day wheel and turn in the sky above the Somerset countryside, he day-dreamed of being at the controls himself, and, like the fictional character Biggles, he had already won many a battle on high against the dreaded enemy. At the local airshow at RAF Colerne one year, the six-year old Robert spotted a battle-worn Spitfire standing alone on display, being ignored by the crowds who thronged around the exciting new jets of the era. Drawn to this legendary aircraft Robert asked its solitary attendant if he could sit in the cockpit, and, eagerly anticipating briefly reliving one of his heroic fantasies, he was unceremoniously dropped down into the cockpit. He completely disappeared from view! His eyes lined up, not with the gun-sight atop the instrument panel, but with the firing button on the control column. He couldn't see out at all.

So the long wait to fly a real Spitfire into an imaginary air combat came to an abrupt and disappointing end. He fought no great aerial battle that day but his close encounter with a real fighter served to heighten his developing imagination and further fuelled his enthusiasm for aeroplanes. Robert recalls that he produced masses of drawings of aircraft after the visit to the cockpit and reflects that it probably created a more lasting impression upon him than he realised at the time.

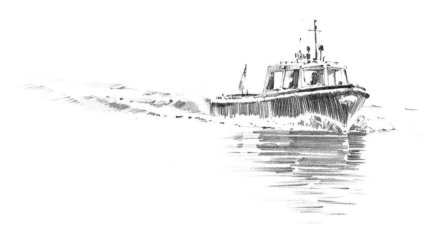

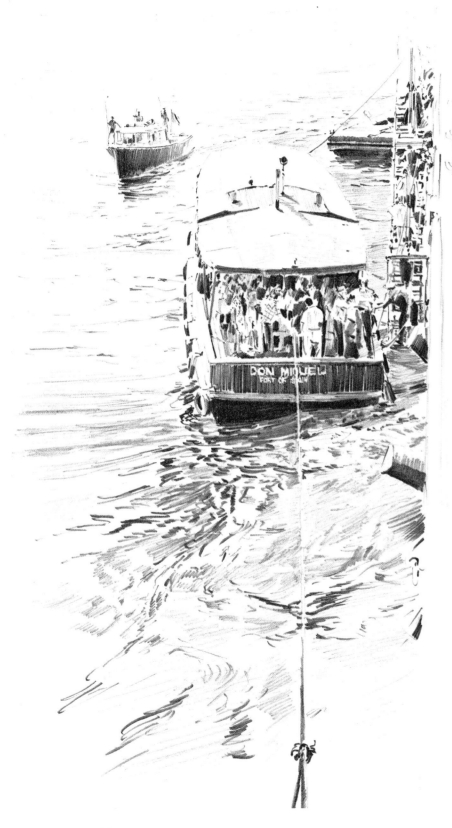

Robert has extraordinary powers of observation and retention and can easily recreate in sketch form subjects that he has seen hours or even days before. This can often involve a considerable amount of detail which the ordinary person may not have even noticed in the first place. This remarkable ability, combined with his patience and a practical understanding of technical matters, gives his paintings an authority which gains the respect of those who fully understand his subject.

Like many artists, Robert is an eminently practical person. After leaving school at the earliest legal age of 15 to help contribute to the family income, he went to work in a local art gallery as a trainee picture-framer. His natural aptitude for working with his hands, and his in-built obsession with getting things done properly, immediately stood him in good stead and enabled him to master this exacting trade within a short time.

It was his quick mastery of the craft of picture-framing, together with the obvious talent which the 15-year-old demonstrated in his weekend watercolour paintings, that prompted his employer to introduce the enthusiastic youngster to the art of picture restoring, the profession which gave Robert the first real opportunity to develop his talents as a painter. By the time he left the gallery to begin life as a professional artist, Robert had become one of the most sought-after picture restorers in the West of England.

It is impossible to judge whether Robert Taylor would be a better artist today had he had the opportunity to attend the Royal Academy or another such venerable art establishment. No doubt there are some who would say that he would, but to what extent might his prodigious talent have become redirected, or perhaps even 'over-coached'? The fact is that apart from spending four years at the Bath School of Art between the ages of 11 and 15, he is entirely self-taught.

So few artists who have become internationally well-known, their work being widely acquired by prestigious collectors, have achieved their success without an academic art training that it is worthwhile looking at how Robert Taylor's phenomenal success has been achieved, and analysing how he trained himself to paint to a standard that is the envy of many academically trained artists.

Circumstances prevented any possibility of Robert going on to art college after he left school. His income, even as an apprentice picture-framer, was sorely needed in the Taylor household, and although his natural talent at this young age would certainly have gained him a place at almost any art college in the country, his growing responsibility to the family would probably have dictated that he turn down the opportunity had it arisen.

None of this, however, deterred him from his ultimate goal and he conscientiously set about studying the works of other artists. He was ideally placed to do this. The art gallery was full of original paintings, prints and books about artists, covering several centuries, and his day-time environment was perfect for the initial stages of his intended career. In the evening and at weekends he made drawings and painted watercolours on subjects ranging from local scenes to copies of some of the famous works which he had seen in print.

Recognising his determined ambition, his employer, Cedric Harris, himself an accomplished watercolourist, took Robert under his wing and taught him all he knew about painting and picture restoring. Soon Robert was producing work of a standard high enough to sell in the gallery.

Encouraged by this and the obvious improvement that he could see in his own work, Robert determined that he should make the difficult transition from watercolour to oil. His first attempts, he recalls, filled him with such frustration and disappointment that initially he felt the technique was beyond his capabilities. He says that had it not been for the fact that other artists before him had demonstrated that indeed it was possible, he would have concluded that painting in oil was an impossibility.

Cedric Harris was a watercolour painter and could not help the young student. Robert simply had to get on with the task of finding out for himself how the great oil–painters had mixed their colours and applied them with such apparently magical skill. He devoted every available minute he had to the project. He read everything he could obtain on the subject, visited every art exhibition in the area, studied every oil painting that entered the gallery, and painted endlessly. Gradually, his perseverance and will to learn started to pay dividends and he began to master the technique of oil painting.

Robert was determined from the outset that he would take no shortcuts. He used no acrylics, no mixed media; he always painted on canvas, and he never gave up on a painting. Cedric Harris noticed

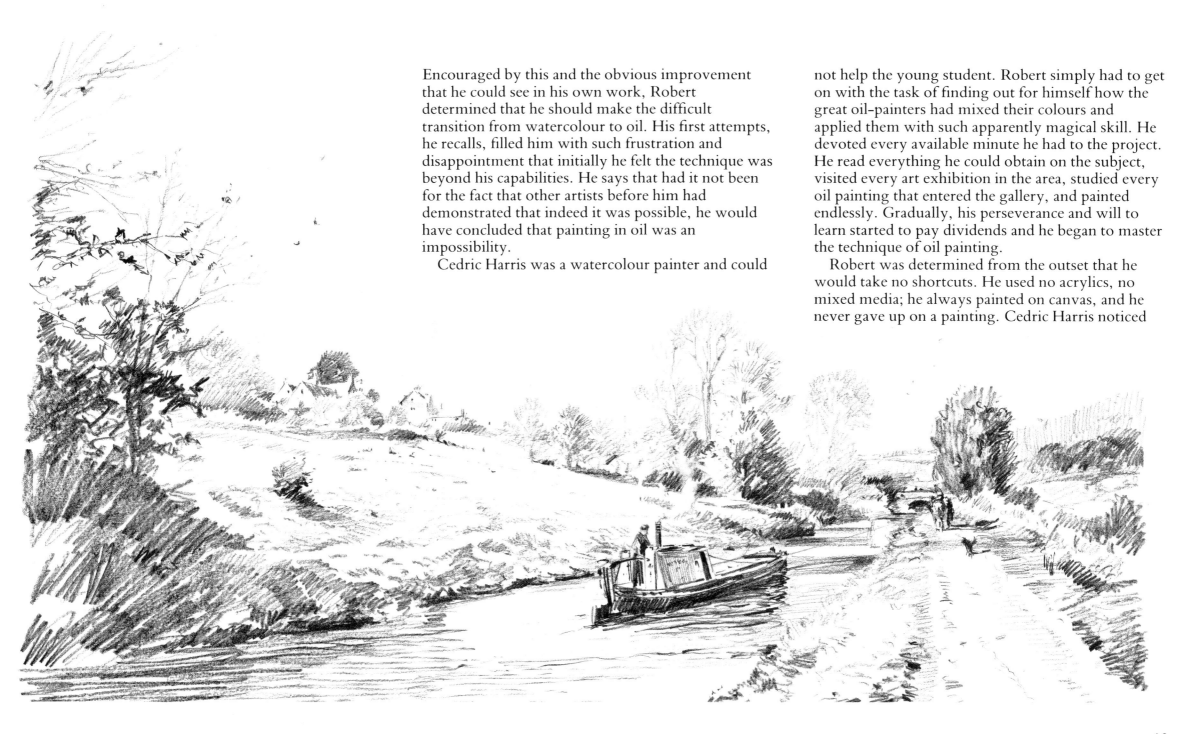

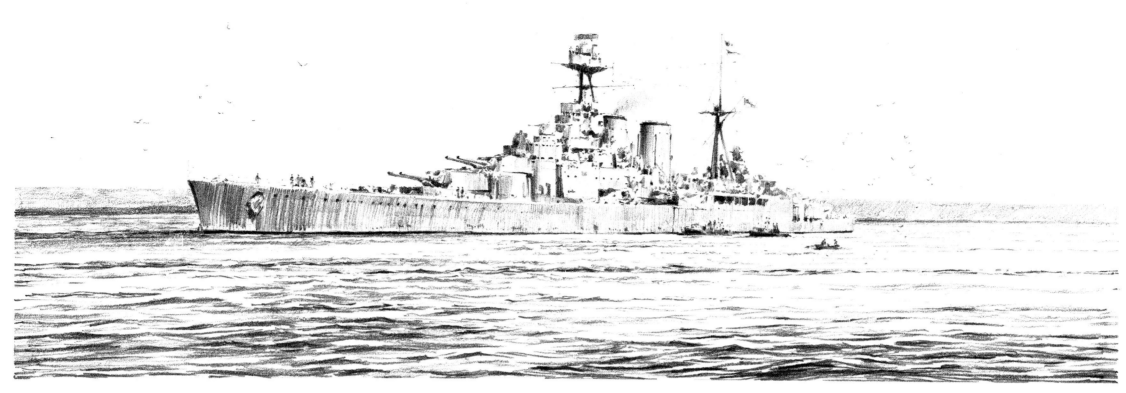

The Battle-Cruiser HMS HOOD at Scapa Flow prior sailing to meet the Bismarck, May 1941.

the improving standard of Robert's oil paintings and entrusted him with more and more of the restoration work on valuable oil paintings which had become damaged. This was just the opportunity Robert was looking for. Now his entire day involved working on original oils, and he quickly demonstrated a unique talent for the art of picture restoring.

It is probably due to the many years that Robert spent as a restorer of other artists' paintings that he acquired his great quality of versatility. Each artist has a different style, a different way of painting and obtains a different effect. One artist may apply paint very thickly, using the Impasto technique, while another paints using a series of thin glazes. Careful analysis of the style and method is necessary before a restorer can even think of starting work. When repairing the damaged area of the canvas he must try to imitate the brush or palette knife in as close a way as possible to the method employed by the original artist.

Restoring paintings is a painstaking art and one that requires a deep understanding of the mechanics of painting, the application of paint, and the ability to mix required colours precisely. Only one who has tried to paint in oil will know that to obtain the precise colour required at any moment during the

painting of a picture is one of the most difficult operations an artist faces, and the ability to mix the exact colour required on the palette comes only with experience. During a decade of restoring paintings, ranging from the works of the unknown to the great Masters, Robert mastered this difficult aspect of art. It amounted to a ten year apprenticeship, perhaps three times longer than he might have spent at an art college, but in retrospect it can be seen as a critical phase of his career and a period to which he owes much of his success today.

After nearly fifteen years at the Harris Gallery, Robert felt that it was time to move on with his career, and he often discussed his prospects with his wife Mary. Robert had met Mary at the gallery, where both worked. They had married and set up home together, and by now were the proud parents of three children. With all the commitments that accompany family life, both knew that it would not be easy if Robert were to try to fulfil his dreams and leave the gallery to become a full-time painter.

Mary then, as today, always had her feet firmly planted on the ground, and she offered sound, practical advice, although she was always sympathetic and supportive of Robert's dream to

one day paint for a living. Indeed, without Mary's support it is doubtful that Robert would have taken the plunge when the big opportunity finally presented itself. The usual calm that pervades the Taylor household is due in no small measure to the quiet home-loving way that Mary organises and supervises her family, never once allowing herself or any of the five Taylor children to become remotely intoxicated by the fame and success of their father.

At about the time that Robert and Mary were wrestling with the problem of how to take the next step in Robert's career to become a professional artist, he met Pat Barnard. It was a fortuitous meeting because Pat, a print publisher who was also based in the city of Bath, was at the time looking for a new artist to paint pictures for a particular art project, and the two took an instant liking to each other. This period of Robert's career and the circumstances which brought him and Pat together are covered in his first book, *The Air Combat Paintings of Robert Taylor*; suffice it to say the two have worked together ever since that meeting in the mid-seventies. Pat's company, The Military Gallery, has been responsible for the publishing and marketing of every Robert Taylor print ever since, and Pat is personally involved with all Robert's clients for his original paintings. It is one of those rare unions between artist and businessman that has never faltered. Each complements the other perfectly. I have often heard Robert explain their relationship in his usual modest and succinct way: 'I paint and Pat does everything else.' That, of course, is very much an oversimplification, but it serves well to explain a happy association between two people who have a high regard for each other.

Robert sometimes describes himself as a 'marine artist who is painting aircraft'. Most of the paintings that he completed during the early years of his association with The Military Gallery, and, indeed, many of Robert's early prints, featured ships and the

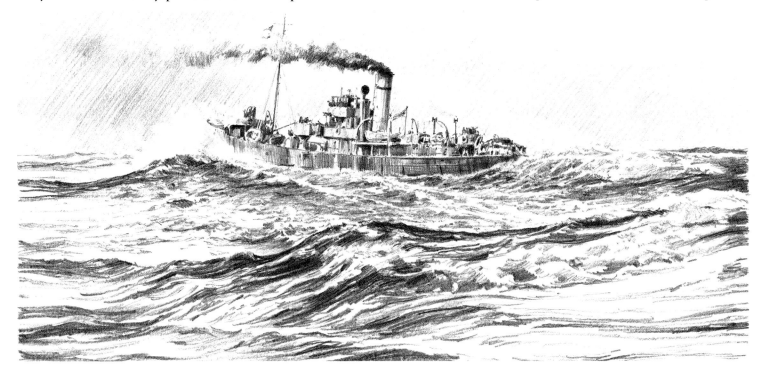

sea. Although he never lost his boyhood enthusiasm for aircraft, his interest in and ability to paint the old sailing ships held him in good stead during his first years as a professional artist.

In his usual diligent way, over a period of many years, Robert had set about understanding the old sailing ships and had collected what has since become a substantial private maritime reference library, covering the period from the Napoleonic Wars to the early twentieth century. Also over a long period he made endless visits to the various maritime museums, clambered over Nelson's flagship *Victory*, the *Cutty Sark*, and countless other relics of the maritime past, and rushed off to the coast every time that some interesting event occurred involving sail.

His ability to teach himself a subject astonished many people who, impressed not just by his marine paintings but also by his knowledge of ships and the sea, took it for granted that he had either served at sea, or at least had come from a sea-faring family.

Such was the standard of the new professional artist's first maritime paintings that Robert's submissions were immediately accepted by the Royal Society of Marine Artists for their annual exhibition in London. When his large painting of the famous clipper ship *Pamir* was bought by a well-known patron on the opening day of the exhibition, more than a few eyebrows were raised in this respected establishment, and the question buzzing around the gallery was: 'Who is this new artist, Robert Taylor?'

There is no doubt that the standard of Robert's painting, even at this early stage of his new career, had a special quality about it. People admired the power and movement that he achieved in his work and, more importantly, they started to buy his paintings. It was not long before Robert was accepting commissions, which was a new experience for him; up to this point in his career he had produced paintings speculatively and without the constraints of a client's brief. He recalls to this day the fear and trepidation with which he handed over his first commission. When a client buys a painting in a gallery he has the opportunity to see and evaluate it before committing himself to the purchase, but when a commissioned painting is delivered that is usually the first glimpse the client gets of his new acquisition, and it is often a close-run thing as to who is the more nervous, the client or the artist.

On one occasion Robert delivered a large painting to a client at an exclusive club in London. It had been commissioned by Commander Sam MacDonald-

Hall, and, great benefactor that he was, the painting was to be donated by him to the Royal Navy's Aviation Museum. The subject of the painting was a particular jungle airstrip in the Far East where the Commander had been based during World War II, flying F4U Corsairs. When Commander MacDonald-Hall came into the room he stood in front of the painting for several agonising minutes, motionless and speechless. Robert was convinced that the Commander did not like the painting and that he was thinking up a kind way of telling the hapless artist without hurting his feelings too badly. After what to Robert seemed like an eternity, the veteran fighter pilot turned and said: 'Robert, I could walk right into that picture it is so lifelike. You have literally taken me right back forty years. It is quite breathtaking.' The painting is called *Puttalam Elephants*, and it hangs today in the Fleet Air Arm Museum at Yeovilton. Even today Robert confesses to a nervous twinge at the handing-over ceremony of a commissioned painting, his modesty not allowing his reputation to play any part in the transaction.

Robert's maritime paintings were becoming noticed by a widening circle of people and in 1979 he was asked to paint two pictures of World War II destroyers as part of an important fund-raising programme. One of these ships, HMS *Cavalier*, was the last surviving example of its type and was on the point of a final voyage to the scrapyard. A group of ex-Royal Navy sailors who had served aboard destroyers during the war had mounted a large-scale operation to raise sufficient funds to save her from an ignominious fate. Leading the campaign was no less a person than Admiral of the Fleet, Lord Louis Mountbatten, and accordingly it had been decided that the second painting should feature his old wartime command, HMS *Kelly*. Lord Mountbatten

had already seen some of Robert's paintings and, having been suitably impressed, it was no surprise when Robert was nominated as the artist to complete the task. When the two paintings were completed, Lord Mountbatten paid Robert the compliment that

they were 'fine pieces of work in the mould of the marine artist Montague Dawson'.

For this young professional artist it was praise indeed to be compared with one of his boyhood idols. Almost immediately one of Britain's largest

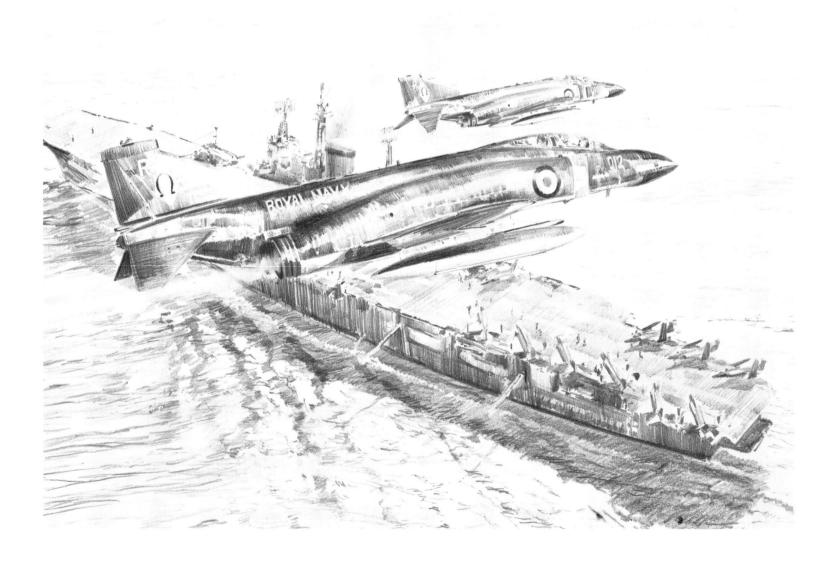

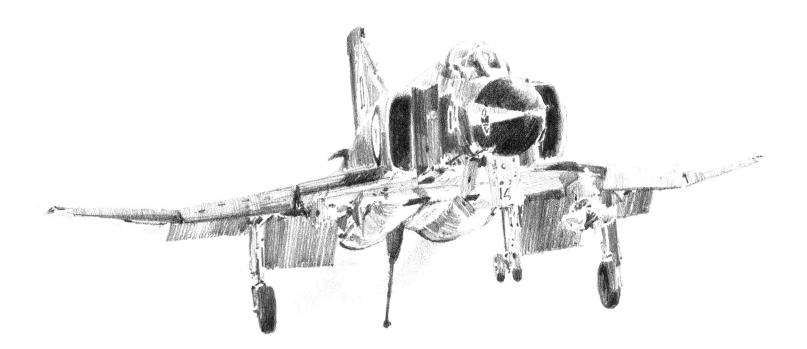

circulation daily newspapers, the *Daily Express*, picked up the story and illustrated Robert's paintings in an unprecedented two-page feature article. Suddenly the name Robert Taylor was in print right across the country and the phone started to ring with a variety of interesting offers. One telephone call was from the BBC who asked Robert to appear in a TV programme to discuss his two now famous destroyer paintings together with a selection of his other maritime pictures. Several million people saw the telecast and, to Robert's astonishment, the phones at the studios were ringing before the programme had finished.

In the short space of a few months Robert had emerged from relative obscurity to become a name familiar to people throughout the length and breadth of Britain. The demand for his paintings steadily increased, as did the invitations for him to exhibit his paintings and to make public appearances. Becoming a celebrity in a short space of time can bring pressure on people, sometimes with adverse effects. It was not so with Robert, however. Thrown into the limelight with such little warning, Robert simply took it in his stride and went about his work, and his life, much as if nothing out of the ordinary had happened.

It is not within Robert's nature to be complacent and although he has felt an increasing obligation to meet the high standards expected of him, he is able not to let these pressures affect him, thus enabling him to sail along with the tide, enjoying his work more and more as his career has flourished. I believe this relaxed approach to his work is reflected in the steady advances Robert has made in technique and style during the years I have been acquainted with his paintings.

Not long after his two naval destroyer paintings had raised £20,000 for the HMS *Cavalier* Trust (she

was saved and today is a museum ship) Robert was commissioned to paint HMS *Ark Royal*, the last of the Royal Navy's great angled-deck aircraft carriers. Prints made from the painting sold in huge numbers and this led to a further commission featuring an F-4 Phantom making the Royal Navy's last arrester-wire deck landing. The painting was reproduced as Robert's very first aviation print and, as Robert often puts it, 'The Royal Navy's last recovery was what catapulted me into aviation art'.

When Robert first started to paint aircraft in the late seventies, there was no aviation art market as we know it today. Although artists have painted aircraft since the Wright brothers first took to the air, for a long time pictures of aeroplanes were never considered by the art establishment to be *real* art, and consequently there were few good aviation paintings to be found. This was perhaps due to the newness of the subject. Paintings of the early forms of transport – ships and the sea, and horses and coaches – had long been accepted in the art fraternity, as had paintings of sea and land battles, presumably because the subjects themselves dated back to the time when artists mixed up their first pigments; but these new forms of transport, powered by the revolutionary internal combustion engine, were far too novel and sophisticated to be thought of as legitimate subjects for artists.

Much of this has to do with nostalgia. Indeed, a great deal of representational art has to do with nostalgia. Many paintings provide a link with, and an

appreciation of, the past, and it is therefore understandable that until subjects start to slip away into history, they hold less attraction for either the artist or his viewer. This is, of course, only half the story. There is another interesting facet which has influenced the development of the aviation art market during the last decade or so. This is the ever-expanding number of people who, by actually experiencing flight themselves, become drawn to the subject. Most people today take to the air, albeit perhaps by courtesy of one of the world's airlines, but if one goes back fifteen or twenty years, such was not the case. There is no doubt that the extent of commercial air travel today has had much to do with the appreciation of flight, and this accessibility has made aviation enthusiasts out of tens of thousands of hitherto ordinary travellers.

This widening interest in aircraft is further fuelled by the development and expansion of aviation museums around the world, and the increasing number of air shows, aeronautical symposia, tours and other events staged for the growing number of aviation enthusiasts.

So today there is what the pundits would call an established aviation 'market' and once such a phenomenon is established the more traditional institutions sit up and take note. The result is that in the space of about fifteen years aviation paintings have become an accepted area of the art world, and today we see the great auction houses like Sotheby's and Christie's holding regular sales of a wide

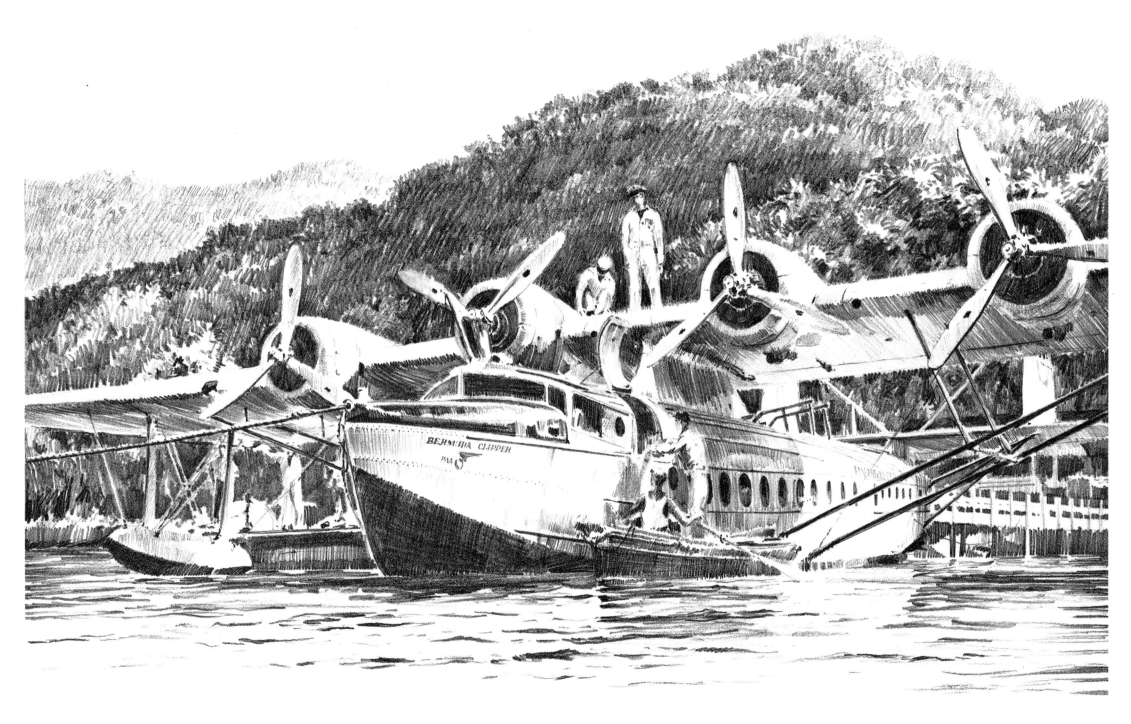

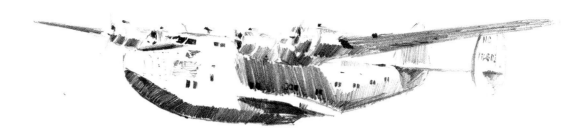

collection of aviation paintings and prints, and fine art galleries all over the world giving wall space to the works of the leading aviation artists.

For a variety of reasons, there has been considerable debate over the years as to whether aviation art is fine art in the true sense. It is easy to understand those who feel that it is not. The art establishment often does not regard any particular type of painting as fine art unless it has a long pedigree. This obviously cannot apply in the case of aviation since the subject depicted has existed since the beginning of this century.

One exception to this rule is the group of painting styles broadly classified as 'abstract'. Here, it is difficult for anyone to specify any ground rules by means of which we can determine what is fine art and what is not. All too often, perhaps, critics are unwilling to pass negative judgements on a particular piece of work for fear of seeming ignorant or philistine when others whose opinions are respected declare that it is to be regarded as 'important' or 'meaningful'. In short, incomprehensibility seems to provide a useful escape from any objective assessment of value.

For anyone who sees it, Robert Taylor's art is far from incomprehensible. He paints subjects which are important to him and which he understands very well. For the great majority of his collectors, these subjects are equally important and equally well understood. For this reason, Robert brings into his work a considerable amount of detail and authenticity. Those who are most interested in

Robert's prints and paintings not only appreciate this, but they would not expect anything less.

Another criticism of aviation art, however, hinges upon this very fact. To give this much attention to accuracy and detail, it is often said, is to be a technical illustrator rather than a fine art painter. Again, this attitude is an understandable one. Technical illustrators are required to produce highly accurate renditions of their subjects and not to detract from the central theme with superfluous backdrops or artist's licence of any kind. There are many aviation artists painting today whose work clearly demonstrates the influence of technical illustration.

In Robert's case, however, this certainly does not apply. Essential though they are to him, the technical details of the ships and aircraft he paints are by no means the whole story. The settings in which he places these machines are at least as important. The human element, too, is an integral part of the emotional response his work arouses. His pictures have a wholeness which compares more than adequately with that contained in almost any creative work in any field.

Even though the aviation art market was yet to become established when Robert's first aircraft paintings were issued as prints, they were a mild sensation and they propelled him into a new area of painting which, within a decade, he was to make his own. There were two reasons for this success: the first was that aviation enthusiasts at large were ready for something more sophisticated than the photographic posters and technical illustrations of aircraft which for the most part were all that was available. The second was, that they recognised in Robert's paintings a quality that treated their subject in the same way as the great painters had portrayed the more traditional subjects of the past, taking aviation painting into the realms of fine art.

Since the time that he first started to paint aircraft, Robert has developed his technique and style to such effect that his works are now instantly recognisable as 'Robert Taylor's' and today one can see his influence right across the spectrum of aviation art on both sides of the Atlantic.

Recently, when Robert was visiting a famous aviation museum, the curator showed him a newly published print from a painting by another aviation artist. It so closely resembled a well-known Robert Taylor painting that the curator was convinced that it was a deliberate attempt to copy and suggested to Robert that he should take the matter up with the artist. Far from being irritated by what the curator saw as a deliberate attempt to plagiarise his work, Robert later said that he felt mildly flattered and, though he contained it at the time, quite amused that the curator was so disturbed about it.

The episode demonstrates not just the measure of Robert's confidence in his own art but, more significantly, his feeling towards the whole subject of aviation art. He does not appear to see himself in a competitive situation with other artists of the genre, being of the sensible belief that the collecting public should be offered the widest possible selection of types and styles of aviation art. Every artist at the top of his profession will have his style copied, and such leading artists are usually philosophical about this; as Robert often says, he spent many years as an amateur making copies of the great marine artists' paintings, pointing out that most painters begin this way – even those who attend the great art academies which, as part of their syllabus, often despatch students to leading galleries to make copies of the Masters' works.

Developing a unique recognisable style, as Robert has done, is a natural progression within an artist's

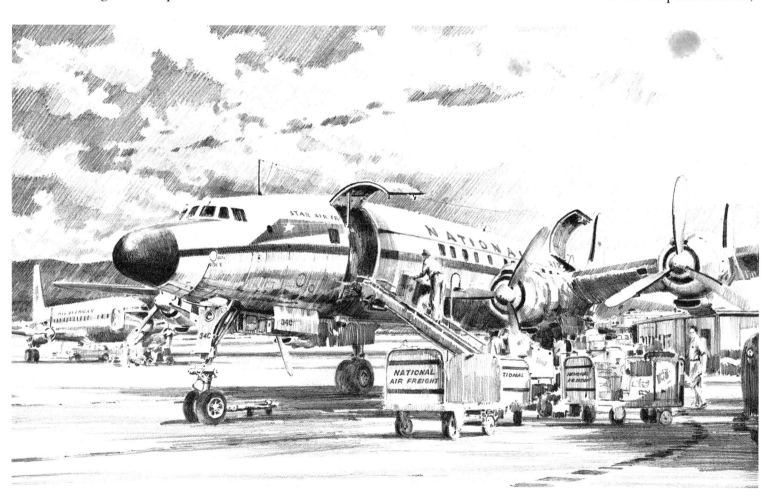

career, the style itself evolving gradually and naturally. I have often heard Robert say that what aviation art needs is for more and more good artists to appear and to introduce their own individual styles. He is, of course, right. Aviation art has now 'arrived' as an accepted part of the art scene and, as the genre develops and expands, we shall see new artists with their own ideas and styles becoming established. If in the process of becoming established a young aspiring artist should look to Robert's work for influence and inspiration, then he will be flattered rather than offended.

Virginia Bader, a long-time friend of Robert's and one of his staunchest supporters in the USA, tells of a visit she made with Robert to his show midway through the term of his Washington exhibition.

"He slipped unnoticed into the gallery at the Smithsonian and circulated for about an hour with the crowds looking at his paintings. When he emerged he said, 'Now I know what they *really* think', indicating how difficult it is for an artist to know what people genuinely mean when they tell them that their painting is wonderful. I noticed he was smiling so I am sure he heard nothing uncomplimentary. But, then, who could ever say anything but nice things about a Robert Taylor painting?"

The influence of artists upon other artists is an on-going part of the art scene. It always has been and it always will be. I have talked at length to Robert about the artists who have influenced him during his life and interestingly he tells me that people he meets often ask him which other artists he admires. There is no doubt that the answers to such questions provide an intriguing insight into how the 'Taylor' style and

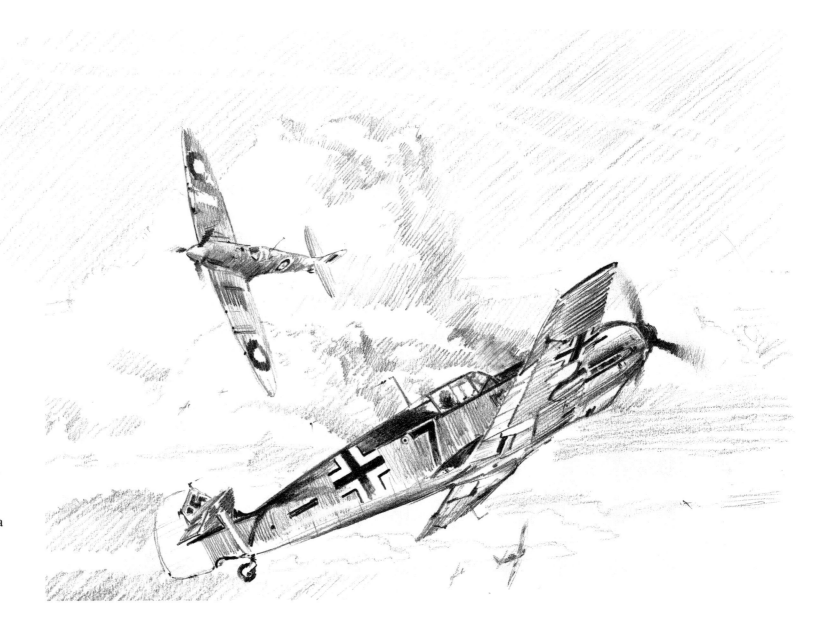

technique have developed during the time since he first started to paint in oil.

Robert's earliest recollections of paintings which both fascinated him and left a lasting impression were those of the seventeenth-century Dutch Maritime School, and later he became greatly influenced by the immortal landscape painter John Constable. From both these different traditions we can identify an impact on Robert's style and technique.

Dutch marine painting in the seventeenth century mirrored life in what was then the most powerful maritime nation in the world. Dutch artists above all understood the sea they painted – powerful, possessive, ever-changing. After all, not only did their nation make its livelihood from the sea but they, like their descendants today, almost lived in it!

Commissions for Dutch artists came not from the large powerful royal dynasties, eager for self-gratification and glory, but from down-to-earth, hard-headed merchants and corporations who wanted to portray their own trades in a serious businesslike way. Whether we see their fishing boats buffeted by the tide, their barges bustling along crowded waterways, or solid ocean-going vessels traversing the high seas, they are all statements of accuracy and reality.

Like most contemporary marine painters, the influence of the late Montague Dawson has also played a part in Robert's art. Although he had a much freer style than the Dutch School, Dawson's ability to project atmosphere, mood and movement into his paintings, which were also technically correct, is a

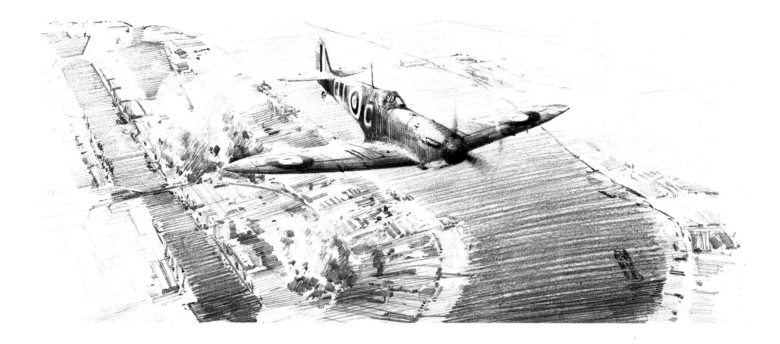

quality that is also to be found in Robert's work. His ships, like those of Dawson and the Dutch marine painters, rise and fall with the swell, and Robert's aircraft glide across his canvas in realistic movement, their configurations properly portrayed. He makes no attempt to glorify or idealise the perception of how his ships or aircraft should look – he simply paints them as they are.

It was later, however, from the works of the great master of landscape, John Constable, that Robert drew inspiration about the techniques of sketching nature *en plein air*, and in particular learned how to draw the sky. Constable, more than any other artist before him, accurately recorded the movement of the sky. His numerous cloud sketches and drawings were littered with jottings and close observations, such as the time of day, the date and season, wind speed and direction, humidity and temperature – all of which are critical to the formation of cloud. This unique way of looking at air impressed Robert, who also began to observe the sky and landscape more closely for himself, making drawings and notes as Constable had done. His sketchpads are full of comments concerning the weather and the change of mood brought about by the change of light, the refraction of light and luminance of the clouds, and even when he is in an aeroplane at 30,000 feet, Robert is constantly peering out of the window, making notes and taking photographs, often to the amusement of other passengers.

If ever there was a school of painting whose artists need to understand fully the sky under which we live,

it is that of aviation art. Yet how often do we see this aspect of a painting ignored, the artist intent upon painting every rivet of his aircraft? In reality – and ask any flier – it is the shape, the movement, the density, even the feel of the air upon which he is borne, that provides the very sensation of flight. The ability to convey this sensation comes only from a true understanding of what it comprises.

Whether it is a great billowing cumulo-nimbus sweeping across the landscape or a wisp of cirrus on the edge of the stratosphere, a Taylor sky is full of interest and fascination, and, like a Constable sky, instantly recognisable. The years of hard endeavour have given Robert a complete understanding of the great canopy under which we live, and his ability to bring the beauty of it all to his canvases is a wonder to behold.

Of contemporaries, there are three artists whom Robert greatly admires. They are all British, but since Robert too is British, this is not surprising, for their inspiration and influence came mostly in his formative years when as an amateur painter he was seeking direction. One of these is the wildlife artist, David Shepherd:

"I used to see David Shepherd's wildlife prints in the gallery. His paintings of elephants and tigers were so terrific I used to dash home after work and sit up half the night trying to emulate him. I never was able to, of course, but his paintings always had that effect on me."

Another artist whose work has always fascinated and inspired Robert is the great elder statesman of British representational art, Terence Cuneo:

"His brushwork is unbelievable, and he is capable of painting almost any subject you care to mention, all with an incredible feeling of life about them. As a young painter I almost wore all the ink off the pages of his book by the number of times I went through it."

Some years ago, the publication of one of Robert's maritime prints prompted Terence Cuneo to write a note to Robert:

"*My congratulations on your splendid painting of* Hornblower and the Atropos. *This is truly a delightful and beautifully constructed piece of work and one of the most satisfying examples of marine art that I have seen for many a moon!*"

Terence

The spontaneous commendation from the doyen of representational art was received by Robert with complete surprise at the time and did as much for the confidence of this young painter as any of the many accolades that he has received before or since. The handwritten note is still one of his treasured possessions.

The modern-day artist who has perhaps influenced Robert more than any other is the British maritime painter John Stobart. Stobart, who has lived and painted in America for many years, is a painter in the classic style, and, like Robert, he acknowledges the inspiration and influence of the great English landscape painter, John Constable.

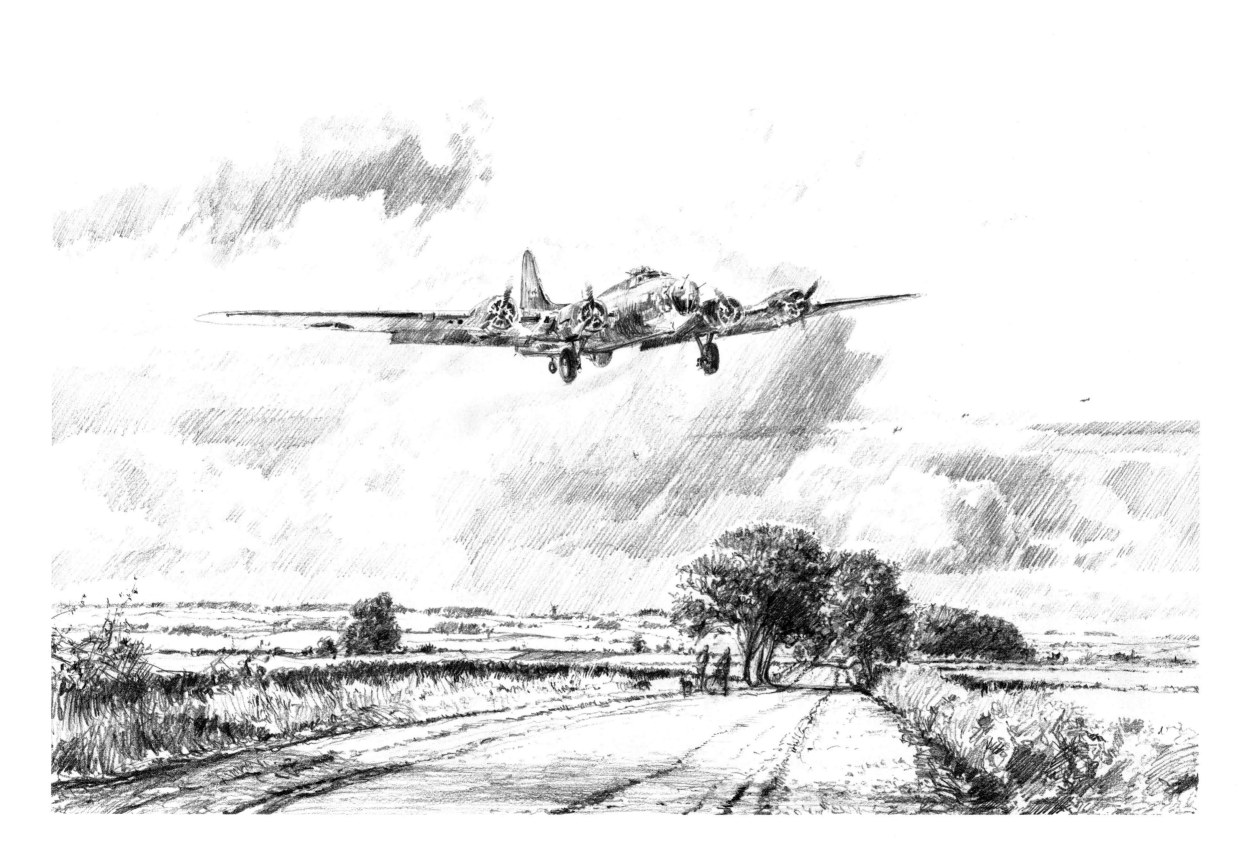

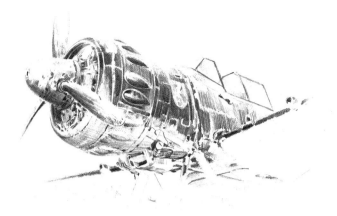

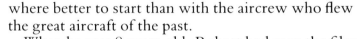

"I admire John Stobart not just for his art but also for what he has achieved in art. I have met John a number of times, and he is always ready with sound advice. I think he has influenced far more young representational artists than he would ever believe. His paintings have a classic quality that, in my humble opinion and for my personal taste, surpass the works of most other artists painting today."

What is interesting when one listens to Robert talking about the styles of artists whom he acknowledges have influenced his own work is that when I compare his paintings with theirs, there appears to be no apparent hint of this influence. The now well-known Taylor style is completely his own.

With the shift in direction towards painting aviation art, it became necessary for Robert to set about a thorough research of his new subject, and

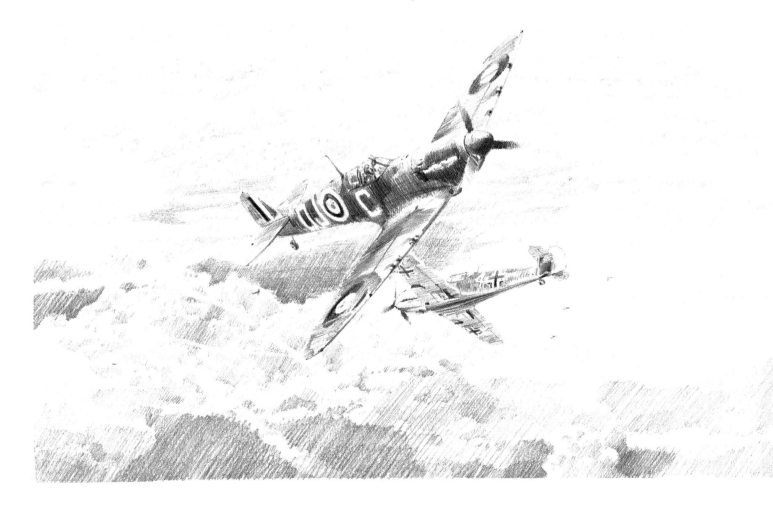

where better to start than with the aircrew who flew the great aircraft of the past.

When he was 8 years old, Robert had seen the film *Reach For The Sky*, which told the epic story of the famous legless fighter ace Douglas Bader. It had left an indelible impression on him, but never did he imagine that one day he might meet the great aviator in person. It was therefore with some trepidation that the young, relatively unknown, Robert Taylor went to visit the legendary fighter leader. By this time he was 'Sir' Douglas Bader, a knight of the realm and a famous public figure with a reputation for having strong likes and dislikes and for speaking his mind. Robert need not have worried. The two hit it off right away and with such good effect that in no time Sir Douglas had appointed himself, ex-officio, Robert's publicist. So impressed with this budding aviation artist's paintings was the great man that he volunteered introductions and meetings with all manner of leading people in the world of aviation.

Robert found himself writing names for appointments into his diary that included most of his boyhood heroes: Johnnie Johnson, Alan Deere, Bob Stanford-Tuck, John Cunningham, Cocky Dundas, Leonard Cheshire, Peter Townsend and a host of other legendary aces whom hitherto he had only read about. He was invited to the RAF Club and other exclusive places where old aviators meet, and was generally introduced and accepted into some of the most exclusive 'circles' in the aviation world.

Recognising an unusual talent in the emerging artist, and perhaps too, an uncommon degree of integrity in the way that he set about his research, Douglas Bader and other great names from aviation quickly became Robert's mentors, friends and ultimately his devoted fans. I recall a few years ago observing a cameo at an aviation symposium at Long

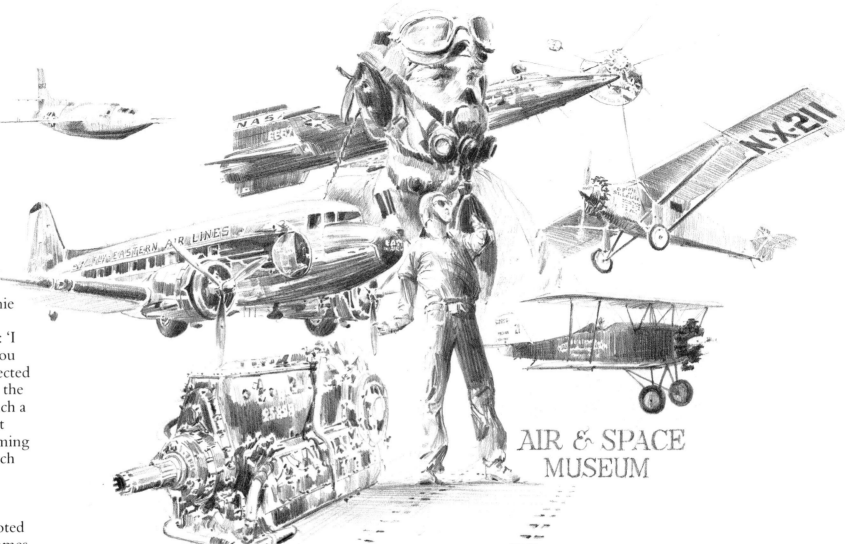

Beach, California, when Air-Vice Marshal Johnnie Johnson pushed in front of the artist a copy of Robert's newly published first book of paintings: 'I say, old boy' said the great fighter ace, 'Would you mind signing a copy of your book for me?' I reflected at the time upon the curious reversal of roles and the odds Robert might have given himself against such a happening, a mere half-a-dozen years earlier. But there again, I mused, I don't suppose the unassuming Robert Taylor would have given the episode much further thought.

Robert has been defined as the 'pilot's artist'. During the dozen or so years that he has been painting aviation subjects, he has gained the devoted admiration and respect of some of the greatest names in aviation history. His paintings instil in pilots an uncanny sense of 'being there'. The feeling his paintings evoke for those who took part in the great aerial campaigns is perhaps summarised best by the legendary Dambuster pilot, Air Marshal Sir 'Mick' Martin, who, when confronted with his first sight of Robert's painting depicting that epic raid said: 'You have captured exactly the atmosphere of the situation, Robert. That is just how I remember it was on that night in May 1943.'

The admiration and esteem which many of the great legends in aviation history have for Robert's art was demonstrated in full measure in 1988, when his one-man exhibition opened at the National Air and Space Museum in Washington DC. Aboard the Pan Am 747 which climbed out of London's Heathrow with Robert, en route for the opening ceremony, was a collection of aviators whose names read like a history book. As the Jumbo flew out over south-west Britain, by prior arrangement an RAF Harrier, no doubt flown by another of Robert's fans, formated off the starboard wing to escort the mighty airliner

out of British airspace.

It was a fitting send-off for the distinguished group of pilots and the artist who had, within the space of a decade, taken himself to the very top of his profession – and one that was not without its amusing side. Almost all the passengers aboard moved out of their seats and over to the starboard windows to peer at the extraordinary sight of an RAF jet fighter a few feet off the wing-tip. This took the weight of almost the entire passenger list to one side of the aircraft, causing the captain to make some hasty adjustment to the trim! As the Harrier dipped its wings in salute and peeled off, one famous Battle of Britain pilot was heard to chuckle to Robert: 'I think the RAF want to make sure we are actually leaving.' A little later, when the 747's captain visited the cabin to meet Robert and the group of pilots accompanying him, he commented that in twenty years of flying he had never had so many back-seat drivers on his aircraft!

During the twelve months of Robert's much

talked-about exhibition in Washington DC, over 10 million people visited the museum, and after the close, Colonel Don Lopez, the Deputy Director, reported that Robert's was the most popular art exhibition they had ever staged. The exhibition received wide acclaim in the press from art critics, many of whom were not familiar with the aviation genre but who were nevertheless suitably impressed by the painterly style of Robert's treatment of the subject. Many Taylor fans flew great distances to view the exhibition, taking the unique opportunity to see so many of his original works on show under one roof. Many also wrote to Robert afterwards saying how much they had enjoyed seeing his paintings, and one enthusiast claimed to have visited the show six times. More than one collector flew the Atlantic just to see the show, saying afterwards, 'I just couldn't pass up the opportunity to see so much of Robert's work all together at one time. It was a feast!'.

It was a major milestone in the career of a truly gifted painter and the importance of the occasion was not lost on the artist. Robert is not a person who

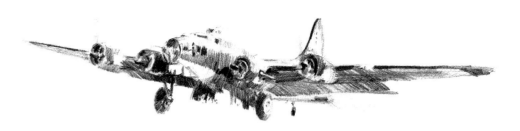

visibly gives much away about his feelings and his placid nature prevents him from making the demonstrations of emotion that are usually associated with artists, but he was clearly deeply moved by the welcome he was given at the opening ceremony held in his honour. Later at the hotel when it was over he confided 'That was some event!'.

Part of the exhibition in Washington included a collection of drawings made by Robert in preparation for the paintings on view. Any appraisal of the art of Robert Taylor would be incomplete without some discussion about his pencil sketches and drawings.

The study of an artist's drawings are said to reveal not only a better understanding of that artist's approach to his work, but also an interesting insight into his mind. The recognition of this is not lost on the art world: recently a sketch by Raphael was sold for over £3½ million at Christie's of London; even anonymous drawings of reasonable quality sell today

for many thousands of pounds. The acquisition of artists' drawings is considered by some to be the pursuit of the true connoisseur.

A look at Robert's drawings in this volume reveal a special empathy with his subject, draughtsmanship of inordinate skill, and a free and fluid touch that does more than simply record: all these bring his subjects to life.

Robert started sketching almost before he could write. At school he was constantly in trouble for making drawings when he should otherwise have been writing or reading. While other pupils would be making notes about Nelson's great victory at Trafalgar, Robert would be sketching a raging sea battle, his imagination translating the history teacher's words into vivid graphics. Throughout his childhood he made drawings of ships, aircraft, steam trains and all the subjects which appeal to growing lads, and it was clear to all who knew him in his early

years, even if frustrating to his teachers, that here was an unusual talent.

Today, many of the notes that Robert makes when he is reading research material are studded with small sketches (he calls them scribbles), his vivid imagination translating words into pictures, although often he does not realise that he is doing it! When he is 'working-up' for a painting, he prepares so many sketches and drawings that sometimes one fears that he may disappear totally from view beneath them, but miraculously, when his mind has fully assimilated them all, a master drawing emerges and a painting is born.

In evaluating Robert's drawings, a fascinating story unfolds that provides a wonderful insight into how a picture was created. Adding to the fascination of his working drawings are cryptic notes, sometimes little drawings within drawings, perhaps a diagram or two in which perspective angles are worked out,

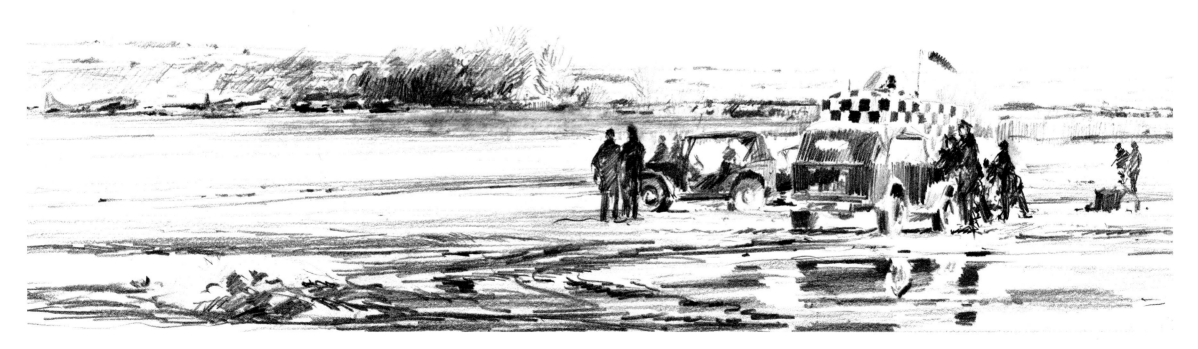

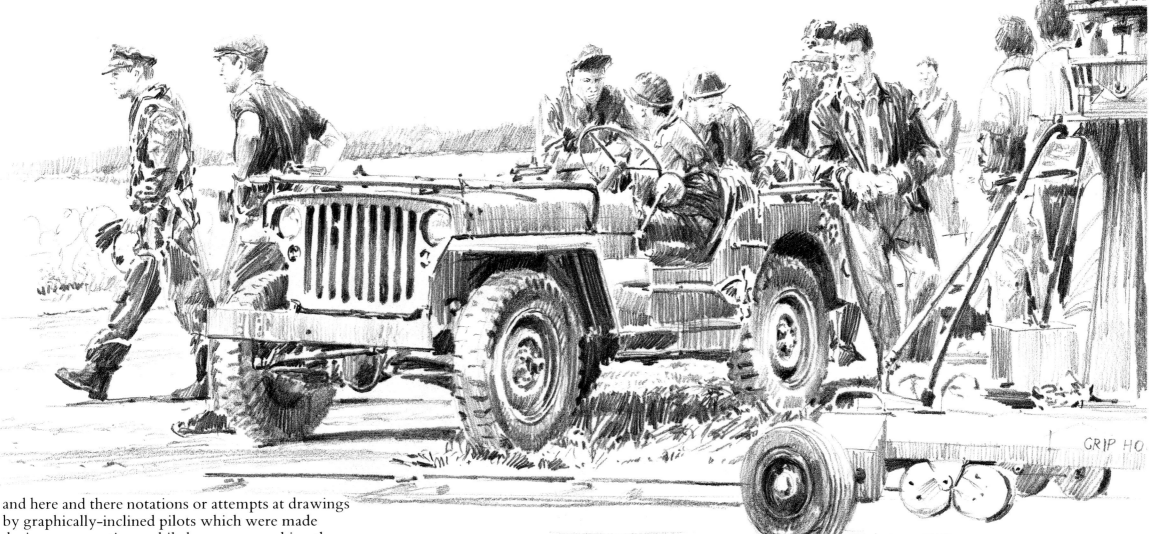

and here and there notations or attempts at drawings by graphically-inclined pilots which were made during conversations while he was researching the final painting.

Robert's finished drawings are delightful, having the same feeling of special quality that is present in his paintings. In his exhibition in Washington the communication between artist and audience that his paintings evoked was heightened in no small way by the outstanding collection of drawings which supported them.

For all his qualities of determination, Robert is a man with interminable patience. He is never in a hurry. He has a naturally relaxed personality and it is not difficult when you are with him to slide out of the usual high-speed, non-stop pace of life, into his gently turning easy-going world. Not that Robert is old-fashioned – he's not. His studio and indeed family home are filled with modern gadgetry, and even his easel is of a hi-tech design: 'Not so quaint as the old easels which most artists like to acquire, but infinitely more practical'. But his demeanour is one of a bygone age when people had the time to stop and pass the time of day, and went about their business in an unhurried way.

In many ways Robert fits the popular image of the artist: a little vague sometimes, nearly always forgetful and almost completely without a sense of time. Yet in spite of all these outwardly apparent tendencies that are normally expected and accepted in an artist, he is deceptively well-organised and self-disciplined when it comes to the actual painting process. For all his forgetfulness – he has been known to turn up for a publisher's briefing having left his drawings behind – he has a remarkable memory for detail and is often able to rattle off technical statistics to everyone's astonishment.

At a recent meeting of fighter pilots during the signing of an edition of prints, a lively discussion took place as to whether all Me109s had a gun positioned in the centre of the propeller hub. After much talk on the subject, these veterans, all of whom had flown combat against the Me109, were unable to come to a satisfactory conclusion. After listening quietly to the discussion for some time while he continued to sign and number prints, Robert waited until they had all had their say, then quietly and

without interrupting his flow of signatures, gave them the precise answer to their dilemma. 'We ought to have known that you would know!' muttered one of them quietly, winking at the others.

Robert's relaxed, mostly unflappable outlook, is another quality which has enabled him to develop his powers of concentration, and his patience allows him, in his own mind, all the time in the world to complete his observation and investigation into his subjects. He is a man who likes to travel through life at his own speed. With his mind on the business of research, he disappears into a timeless world of his own, becoming almost oblivious to everything unconnected that is going on around him, and usually giving no thought to the normal inhibitions that would constrain most of us.

During one of the many intervals between shooting scenes for the film *The Memphis Belle* at RAF Binbrook, hundreds of people were milling about on the set, including Robert who was busy with sketchpad in hand. Ready to resume filming, the

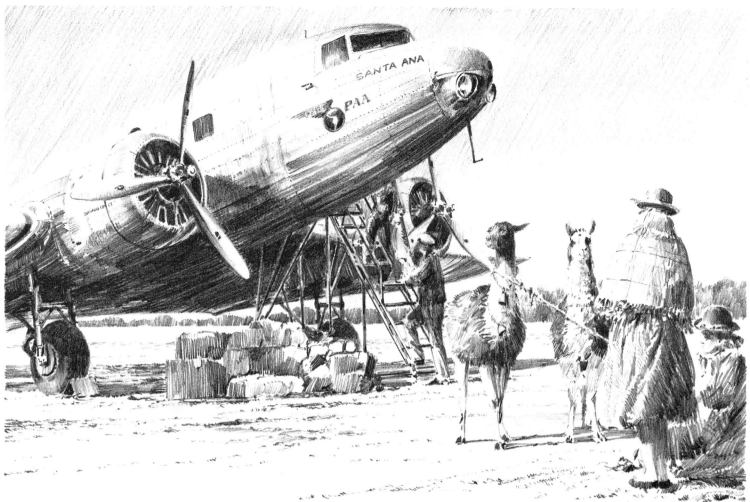

director called through his loud-hailer for the set to be cleared. Gradually everybody moved out of camera leaving just one person standing by the B-17, busily focusing his undivided attention on some part of the nose of the aircraft. Again the director called for the set to be cleared. The lone figure didn't move, clearly totally absorbed with whatever he was doing. 'Would the man in the green striped shirt kindly allow us to make this damn film,' he boomed a third time. Startled, Robert turned around to find himself alone on the set, facing a red-faced director and an amused audience of several hundred actors, extras and film people.

But it is this total absorption in what he is doing that is part of Robert's success. He approaches each painting in much the same way as an actor might prepare to play a role. He begins always with a detailed and thorough research of his subject, then starts experimenting with ideas, as an actor might in looking for his 'character'. Then, when all the preparation is done, he totally immerses himself in what he is painting, playing the part as it were, thinking himself into his subject. Robert almost never works on more than one painting at a time. His

involvement with each particular work is too deep to allow this. As he works at the canvas his concentration is such that he becomes almost oblivious to the world around him.

I do believe that Robert could paint almost anything he put his mind to – even portraits, which he professes are outside his scope. I have seen Robert's wildlife paintings; they compare with the best. I know his marine paintings and am convinced that if he made this his primary subject he would quickly achieve eminence in this field, too. Where architecture appears in his paintings, the line, form, colour and perspective have an exceptional flair that is not always present in the works of some who make it their subject. His landscapes, which sometimes appear in his aviation paintings, have all the hallmarks of a modern-day Constable.

He has the ability to delve into the very innermost nature of real subjects and this characterises his art. He is not an illustrator illustrating only the obvious. His art seeks out and portrays the things no camera would see.

If Robert Taylor's paintings stand the test of time – and I believe they will – he will bequeath to future

generations a true feeling of reality in the subjects he paints, enabling his audience to look back at the great military aircraft of the twentieth century with a clarity and understanding. He, perhaps above all aviation artists, will be able to transport them back in time to that glamorous era when the classic shapes and noises of piston engines roamed the sky, when men fought in chivalrous combat that shaped our civilisation perhaps for centuries.

It takes a great deal to upset Robert, but there is one question that always tests his powers of self-control. An encounter with a press reporter in Los Angeles was not the first time that Robert has been asked the question 'Do you not think that your art helps glorify war?'. After a brief moment to retain his composure, his reply to the pressman went something like this:

"I am an artist, a painter of pictures. I paint aircraft and ships and the sky and the sea because those are the subjects I love to paint. Sad though it may be, the way we live today has been to a large extent shaped by the events of wars we have fought. Whatever one's views about war – and I hate war – they are part of our history. The men and machines that fought the wars of this century are all a part of this history. I see myself as just one artist who, at this moment in time, has the opportunity to record some of these historic events with the benefit of having first-hand information from the participants. To me this is important and I believe that artists of my generation painting the types of subjects that I paint should play a part in recording this fraction of history. I could easily put it to you that by painting these scenes I perform the service of reminding today's generation of the horror and futility of war, but I won't. I would rather you try to understand that my aim is to record

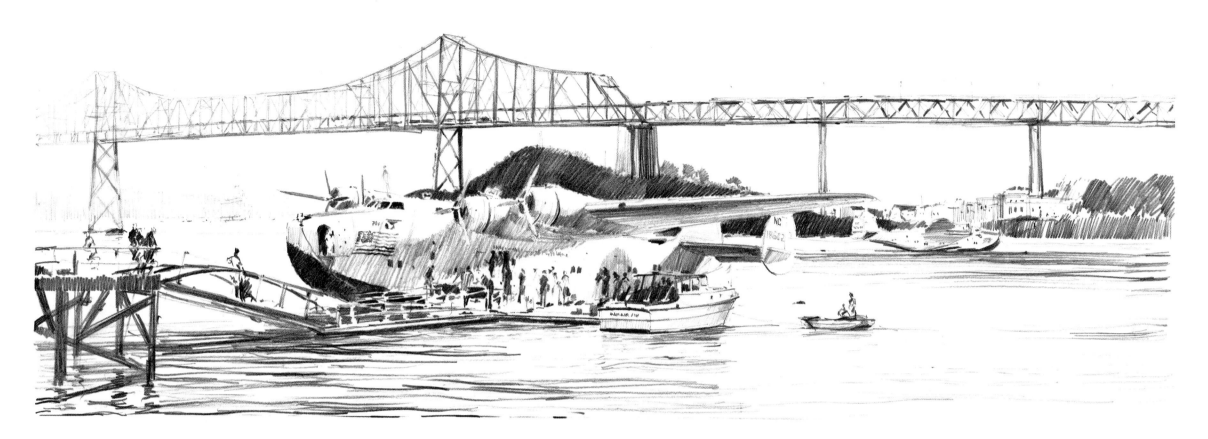

events accurately today so that if any of my paintings should survive for a generation of two, there will be some art available which explains this period in aviation history to future generations. I know I can speak for nearly all other military artists when I say that nothing is further from our minds when painting scenes of war that the glorification of war."

By Robert's mild-mannered standards, this was a strong rebuke. Typically, though, he added, with a friendly smile: 'And you can quote me!'

This is a book of Robert Taylor's combat aircraft paintings. Therefore it contains, by definition, a selection of combat aircraft scenes as recorded by him. Those who know him well and have followed his career as an aviation artist will know that he devotes part of his time to the painting of non-combat aviation subjects which, to him, are equally fascinating, and which he paints with equal enthusiasm and skill.

One of his most famous paintings features the classic Boeing 314 flying boat. This massive canvas, over 6 feet wide, currently hangs in the Smithsonian, and shows a nostalgic scene at Treasure Island, San

Francisco in 1940, a Pan Am Clipper taking on board passengers bound for the Orient. Other fine Taylor paintings of civil aircraft adorn the walls of board-rooms and private homes all around the globe.

As a youngster, it was quite an event for Robert to travel any distance from his native city of Bath. A trip by train to the south-west coastal resort of Weston-super-Mare would provoke excitement a week ahead of the event. Even after he had become a husband and a father, his circumstances did not permit the luxury of much travel and only in his imagination could the aspiring artist visit the exotic ports of the Orient as depicted in Dawson's paintings, or see the exciting cities of the 'New World' of North America as portrayed by Stobart and other artists.

When he became a full-time painter, Robert's horizons started to widen dramatically. It was, of course, important to travel to broaden his knowledge and to gather new material, and for the first time in his life this now became possible – indeed, it was an essential part of his new profession. This new-found freedom released him from the old constraints of his daily obligations at the art gallery, and he soon found

himself visiting and seeing places and meeting people he had hitherto only read about. Today as one might imagine, Robert travels extensively within Britain, Europe, the Mediterranean and, of course, in North America where he has a wide and devoted following.

Robert's international popularity, which was emphasised during his first series of public appearances in Canada and the USA a few years ago, brought home forcibly to him the depth of enthusiasm that exists for his work across the Atlantic. Although he was aware of the demand for his paintings and prints in that part of the world, he had no idea of the genuine admiration that collectors felt for him, and he was amazed by the show of warmth that he found wherever he went.

He recalls a reception at a gallery in Oakville, Canada. His plane had been delayed leaving New York and he arrived an hour late. By the time that he reached the gallery, a queue of people stretched all the way down the street and the gallery was so packed that he could barely squeeze in. 'Obviously I knew that my work was commanding a good deal of interest, but I never expected to get mobbed!'

Robert is, of course, flattered by the attention

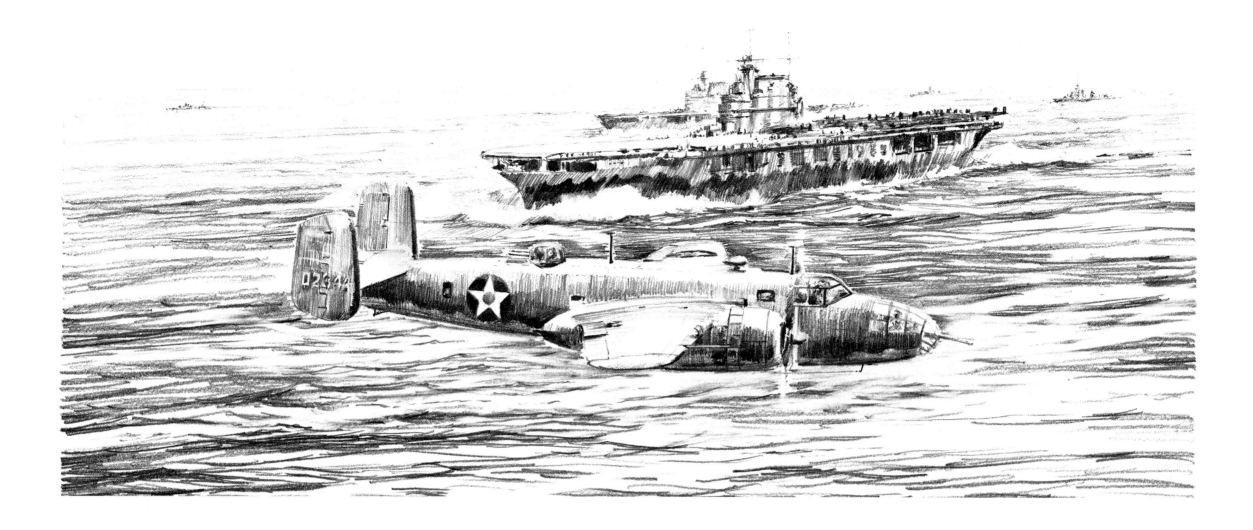

which he receives on his personal appearances, but he neither craves it nor in truth does he need it. He enjoys meeting and talking to those who get such pleasure from his work, and, as he says, 'It helps me when I am in the solitude of my studio wrestling with some difficult aspect of a painting, to think about all those friends I have out there, and their enthusiasm spurs me on.' When he meets his public, without premeditation and in a spontaneous and completely natural way, Robert displays a delightfully good-humoured personality that enables him to communicate across all social barriers as if they do not exist.

But painters like Robert primarily rely upon their art to communicate for them, for that is one of the fundamental reasons for art. A Robert Taylor painting can be appreciated on a variety of levels – for its composition, its brushwork, its clarity and colour – there is something in each one of his canvases for everyone who looks. Through his work he seems able to communicate with the widest possible audience regardless of character, preferences or academic and social background. Perhaps even more importantly, most people appreciate his work for the same reasons.

For all the careful analysis of an artist – his character, his integrity, his motivation, his personality – there is, after all, only one thing that matters and that is the quality of his art. No matter how many exhibitions he gives, no matter how many paintings he paints, no matter how many public appearances he makes, no matter how well an artist's work is packaged and presented by those involved in the commercial world, no artist can achieve lasting recognition without that little touch of inborn genius and skill that comes only by travelling down the long road of experience.

Paintings, and prints from paintings, are not sold, they are bought, and the people who buy art, regardless of their personal level of knowledge of art or sophistication, are always the final judges of an artist's talent. Robert Taylor has achieved, and continues to achieve, enormous success for one basic and very simple reason – people love his paintings. His depth of feeling for his subject and the prodigious skill with which he communicates this through his canvases arouse powerful feelings in those who see his art.

Back from the hustle and bustle of international travel, the radio and television interviews, the public appearances and the hordes of people eager to shake his hand, Robert will sit at his easel in the garden studio to which he loves to retreat. While academics discuss the true merits of his work and dealers and auctioneers spend their days avidly studying world prices, he is most content with palette, paint and canvas, oblivious for the moment of the debates and delights he will once again provoke as this latest work emerges from his studio and enters the public domain.

30

THE PAINTINGS

An appreciation of the Art of Robert Taylor by Colonel Don Lopez, Deputy Director,
The Smithsonian's National Air and Space Museum, Washington DC

In April 1988, the National Air and Space Museum opened what was to be the most popular art exhibition to date, the one-man show of Robert Taylor's work entitled 'Limitless Horizons'. The exhibition featured some forty-five oil paintings together with a large number of pencil drawings, many being the working sketches that were made in preparation for the paintings in the show. The collection comprised mostly aviation subjects but included some fine maritime paintings from his early professional career. Although the exhibition closed well over a year ago we still regularly receive complimentary comments from visitors who were fortunate enough to have seen this excellent exhibition of Robert's work.

Robert's subjects range from the old wooden sailing ships of the Napoleonic period to the carriers of the Falklands, and from the flimsy bi-planes of World War I, through the classic piston engine era, to the modern fast jets of today. The moods of his paintings vary from the serene beauty of the three patrolling SE5As in *Dawn Patrol*, as they climb into a beautiful morning cloudscape, to the exhilaration and urgency of a Spitfire in high altitude combat with an Me109, seen in *Combat Over London*.

Aside from his draughtsmanship and mastery of the palette, two characteristics distinguish Robert's work: first and foremost is his great skill in painting landscapes and seascapes and magnificent skies that provide such wonderful background to his pictures. As a lover of airplanes I hate to admit that I believe that most of his paintings would be judged as outstanding works of art even without the aircraft. Secondly, is the amount of meticulous research and preliminary work that goes into his subjects. He makes a painstaking number of preparatory sketches in order to select a precisely balanced composition, and always manages a viewing angle that best depicts his aircraft or the mission he freezes in time on his canvas. Robert thus allows his viewers to see his aircraft to best advantage, while always maintaining a strong air of reality about his paintings.

Robert's attention to historical detail gives value to his paintings over and above their artistic merit. He records scenes which could never be captured in photographs, bringing them back to life in a realistic and not over-stated manner, thus providing most valuable addenda to the written histories of aviation.

Don Lopez

*Don Lopez flew P-40s in combat with the Flying Tiger Fighter Group in China, becoming an Ace in that theatre.
After the war he served six years as a fighter test pilot and completed a short combat tour in Korea with the 4th
Fighter Group. After retiring from the Air Force he became Deputy Director of the Smithsonian's National Air
and Space Museum in Washington DC, a post he presently holds.*

EAGLES HIGH

I painted Eagles High for the most important art exhibition of my professional career thus far. In 1987 I was invited to hold a one-man exhibition of paintings and drawings at the Smithsonian's National Air and Space Museum in Washington DC. To be asked to show one's art at this prestigious museum is an honour and a privilege afforded to few artists, and I felt immensely flattered when the invitation came.

Pan Am World Airways had generously agreed to sponsor the exhibition and during the twelve months prior to the opening my publisher Pat Barnard and the museum's art curator, Mary Henderson, and her staff worked tirelessly planning and co-ordinating the event, locating and assembling at the museum some sixty paintings and drawings from private collections, galleries and other museums scattered around the world. It was a mammoth task.

The exhibition was a huge thrill for me. It was the first time that I had ever seen so many of my paintings together in one place; some of the paintings I had not seen for ten years or more. When I was welcomed into the gallery for the first private viewing by Colonel Don Lopez, the museum's deputy director, I was quite overcome with emotion.

So many people had devoted so much effort into staging the event and all I seemed to have done was turn up! I felt that my meagre thanks to people like Don, Mary Henderson and Pat Barnard, Thor Johnson and Peter Klaus of Pan Am, Virginia Bader and a host of other people who had shown me such kindness and support, were wholly inadequate.

My wife Mary joined me at the opening ceremony which was a very grand black-tie affair. We circulated among a host of famous aviators and dignatories from the world of aviation, politics and commerce and everybody was gracious and kind to us.

Ken Rees from London's ITV network interviewed me during the events, and my mother phoned me from the UK later that night to say that she had just seen me on the national news programme. I think she was more overcome by surprise than anything else!

One of the many famous aviators who flew with me to Washington for the opening reception was the great fighter Ace, Gunther Rall. He has kindly contributed the following brilliantly written romantic account of his love affair with his beloved Me109 – the main subject of my painting *Eagles High*.

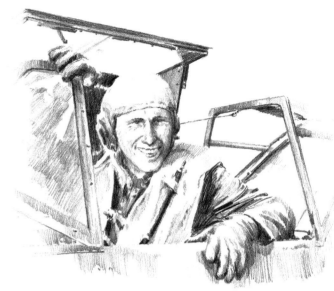

Guenther Rall with III Gruppe JG52 during the Battle of Britain Aug 40

A DIALOGUE WITH THE Me109
By General Gunther Rall

A few years ago some 'old boys' were called to MBB, Manching, where an Me109 had been rebuilt with original parts and a DB 603 engine. We arrived and there she was – the gorgeous little Me109 – proudly standing, nose up, on its high, narrow undercarriage. We briefed the pilots intensively on the difficult take-off procedures: taxiing zig-zag fashion to overcome the lack of forward vision, and immediate application of opposite rudder as soon as the tail comes up to counteract the torque of the propeller. Unfortunately some other unbriefed pilots made a demonstration a couple of weeks later with the unwanted but expected result – a crash!

Standing in front of the old war machine my memories went back 50 years and I started talking to her:
'We were a team, you and I; you – the proud aircraft, and I – the happy pilot. We grew up together in combat over France, England, Rumania, Greece, Crete and Russia; we said farewell to each other over Germany after a five-year love affair.

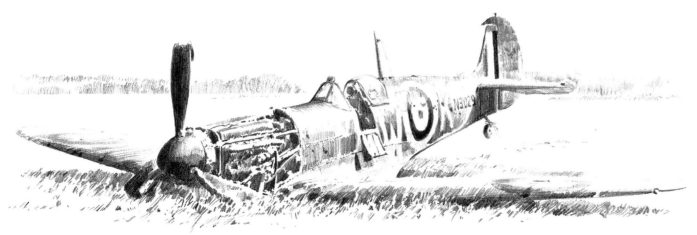

610 Sqn Spitfire crashed landed Graves End, Kent 5ª Sept 1940, went back into service, but was lost on 8ª January 43 while being shipped overseas.

In France, our first encounter, we both felt superior to the Curtis P-36 – you remember how nervous and excited we were – I forced you into tough high-G turns and you responded by extending your slots unequally which caused a stall, but we survived against all the rules. I was happy, but you had many holes and were losing fuel – sorry! Our first victory was a warning but it also built our self-confidence. Over the British Channel you ran into your master – the Spitfire. She could turn so tight in a steep climb and you were unable to follow, but still you did your best, trusting in the skill of your team-member, me, the pilot. We paid our penalty – in part due to the wrong tactics, but you always took me back across the Channel to our little field near Calais – sometimes with injuries and almost always short of fuel.

Then you flew me over Europe down to the Balkans, Rumania, where we were supposed to keep the oil fields safe. Then Greece. At Crete in the hot summer of 1941 I flew you every morning before sunrise, right on the deck of the Mediterranean Sea. We flew ground attacks which you and I did not like. Back to Rumania I got your beautiful streamlined version – the Me109F; by then you had round wing-tips, no struts on your tail section, and a new engine. Against Russia was our game. We felt great against Rata and Mig fighters, IL2, SU2 and DB3 bombers, and our team began to score. But don't you think we were a little over-confident? You got hit in the oil cooler the first time, and the black oil film you threw over your wind-shield made me almost blind. The first belly landing hurt you more than me! Sorry! But after a couple of weeks an even greater challenge for both of us arose: our muddy airfield clogged the coolers under your wings during take-off, and the overheating made us very nervous during combat missions; we should have been concentrating on our opposition rather than on the temperature gauge inside our tiny, narrow and uncomfortable cockpit. In all our dog-fighting the rear visibility was almost nil, your mirror almost useless because of your excited vibration. By the time I could make out an aircraft in the reflection it was almost time to bail out!

And then the winter hit us. You were frozen to stiffness. Sometimes early before dawn we put an open fire underneath you to help get your engine started at temperatures of minus 40 to minus 45. Then you got a device in the cockpit which allowed me to pump fuel for three minutes into your lubrication lines after the last mission of the day. That helped a bit. The unexpected appearance in our area of your German friend and competitor, the Fw190, caused us a mid-air collision with a Lagg 5. The identification came too late. You clipped her right wing off with your propeller and she cut your sleek body – but you brought me back behind our lines, your

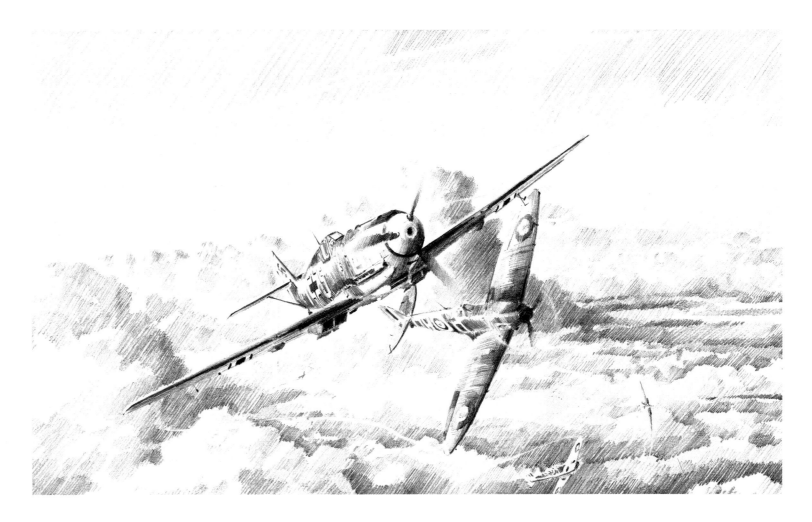

engine vibrating as if it was about to break right off. Down in the Caucasus we ran into Spitfires and P-39s again, but these were different teams from those we had met over the British Channel. These were flown by Russians, and again we felt superior.

I preferred your weapons: your through-propeller 20-millimetre cannon and your two guns above the engine, a qualified set-up but which called for accurate aiming. You relied upon me to use the fixed-image gun site and to place you in position. You always responded willingly. If the rugged Fw190 was a sabre, you were the floret!

After three years of operations from unprepared airfields in Russia, hopping around fighting over snow-covered plains at extreme temperatures, with poor navigation aids inside and outside the cockpit, inevitably we had some belly landings and some crashes. One reduced you to wreckage and put me in hospital for nine months. Reunited, we had our last fight over the Crimean Peninsula where we were bombed almost every 30 minutes. We then flew more than 250 miles over the Black Sea back to Rumania – you almost like a sieve and me, now an experienced pilot with no illusions.

Our final test came over Germany in 1944. Mustangs,

Thunderbolts and Lightnings were our foe, but in your new G-model guise we could match all of them, with our hard-won experience. You could low-speed turn with the P-51 until our opponent's outer wing snapped over. We avoided diving with the P-47 knowing he could withstand 870 miles per hour; you folded your wings at 620 miles per hour. We found the P-38s a good target in a dog-fight but they all had nice new engines. We were losing oil and compression, your engine having to manage up to ninety operating hours. We had just over one hour's endurance – two with external tanks – they flew their fighters another three hours or so. How many of us got killed by them as we made our gear-down final approach to the field, low on fuel and ammunition spent?

And so came the end of our romance – chased by four P-47s, shot and in flames I had to leave you. It was not easy. Hanging on the parachute I saw you disappear into a cloud of debris and smoke. Your narrow undercarriage, your impossible forward vision in taxiing, your breath-taking starting system, particularly in the cold of Russia, the poor visibility from your uncomfortable tiny cockpit (my five year battle station) – all these are forgiven. You were superb. I loved you, my brave little Me109.'

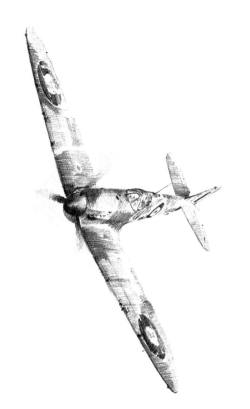

Like a good many of the paintings in this book, *Eagles High* was reproduced as a limited edition print. To commemorate my exhibition at the Smithsonian the edition was signed by a number of RAF and Luftwaffe Aces who had travelled with me to Washington for the opening ceremony. All were friends, but nearly half a century earlier they had flown against each other, so I wanted to be sure that when they sat down together to sign the prints they would feel entirely happy about the picture. I therefore was at pains to ensure that honours were about even between the Me109 and the Spitfire in my painting.

I chose an angle that would show the Me109 at its most awesome and aggressive best. I placed the Spitfire so that its beautiful elliptical wing was clearly demonstrated, and I organised the two in close combat in such a way that there was no obvious outcome to the encounter. I had taken the precaution of consulting with Geoffrey Page at the drawing stage, illustrated on the previous page, and as a result was fairly confident that I wouldn't get too much flak at the signing session. Fortunately I didn't!

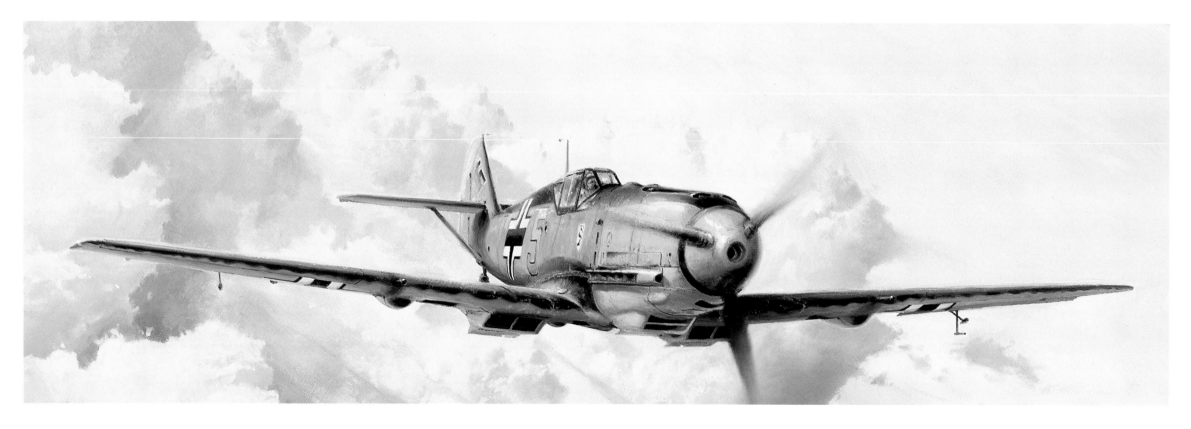

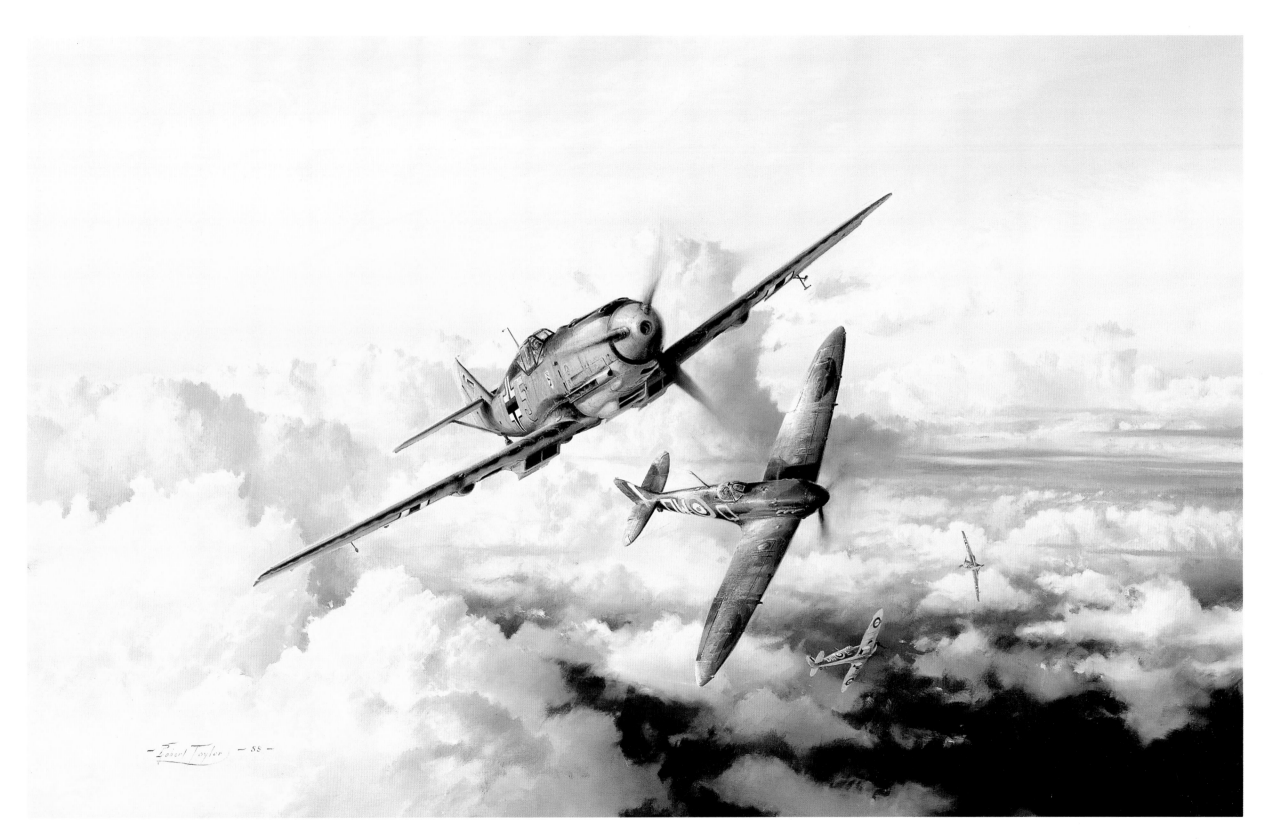

EAGLES HIGH

In the collection of Mr Nick Collias

WELCOME SIGHT

I always make at least one good size model of any aeroplane that I am about to paint. I do this for a number of reasons, not the least important of which is that when making a model one is obliged to examine and handle each individual section of the aircraft during its construction. This helps with familiarisation and often stimulates some piece of further specific research into the configuration of the aircraft in question.

It is not always possible to go and look at a real live World War II aircraft, let alone see one fly. Many types are gone forever. Often the only example of the particular one I want to paint is thousands of miles away and even then it is probably not the right version. Today's scale models, particularly the large ones, are exceptional in their accuracy and detail and are readily available, thus making them a worthy substitute for the real thing.

After constructing the model, I paint it in the colour scheme that will be used in the picture, often to the point of inserting the correct identification markings and other insignia. I then mount the finished model on a wire plinth so that it can be rotated into almost any position. I have this in front of me as I sketch and ultimately while I am painting.

In the case of *Welcome Sight*, in which I had decided to include at least five or six B-24 Liberators, I knew I would need to view the aircraft from five or six slightly different angles, to ensure that each was painted accurately. With the model, this I was able to do.

I don't particularly like using photographs as reference for a painting, much preferring to work from sketches made 'in the field' or, where this is not possible, from sketches made from large accurate models in my studio. I have nothing against the use of a camera as an aid to the artist; indeed, it is an exceptionally useful method of gathering and storing reference material. I use a camera constantly for recording cloud formations and weather patterns, but it is all too easy to be deceived by the lens when accurate shapes, proportions and perspectives are required.

This can easily be explained as follows: if you stand on the ground alongside the wing tip of a stationary aeroplane and take a photograph of the aircraft, what the camera will see is about 90 per cent wing and 10 per cent aeroplane. If you stand back a dozen paces and take another photograph at the same angle the wing area will reduce to about 70 per cent leaving about 30 per cent aircraft, and so on. If a photograph is taken at some distance away – say, 200 yards – using a telephoto lens, the distortion will occur in the opposite way: that is, the wing nearest to the camera will appear disproportionately small. At what precise distance must you take the photograph to avoid any optical distortions? Most photographs of aircraft I have seen are in some way slightly distorted because of the effect of the lens, and it is deceptively easy to fall into the trap of believing that the camera must always be right. It is dangerous therefore to rely upon photographs as the prime source of reference for drawings or paintings.

I made many drawings of the B-24 Liberator for this painting. The sketch featured on the next page I liked very much because it emphasised the link between the B-24 and Ely Cathedral seen in the background. The 900 year old cathedral, towering above the East Anglian flatlands, was a landmark often used as a reference point for disorientated crews returning from gruelling missions over occupied Europe.

After considering the sketch for a while, I decided that there was a little too much emphasis on the cathedral and not enough on the B-24s, so I moved everything up higher and showed a group of six aircraft flying over the town of Ely, with the cathedral clearly visible below. I also moved around further so that I could include the river and dykes on the edge of town, to provide contrasting light reflections which add to the atmosphere.

Painting accurately the engines of the B-24 Liberator is not easy. The air intakes for the superchargers on each side of the radial engines give a slightly asymmetrical impression, and getting the perspective right on all four engines takes a little sorting out.

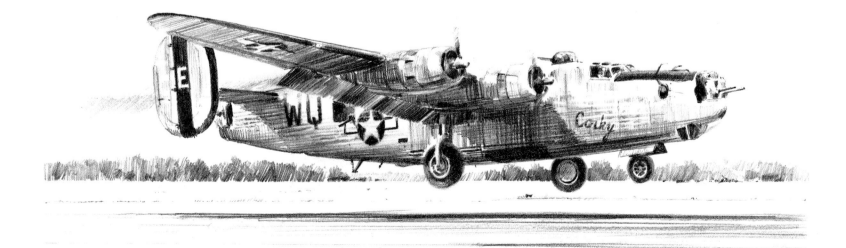

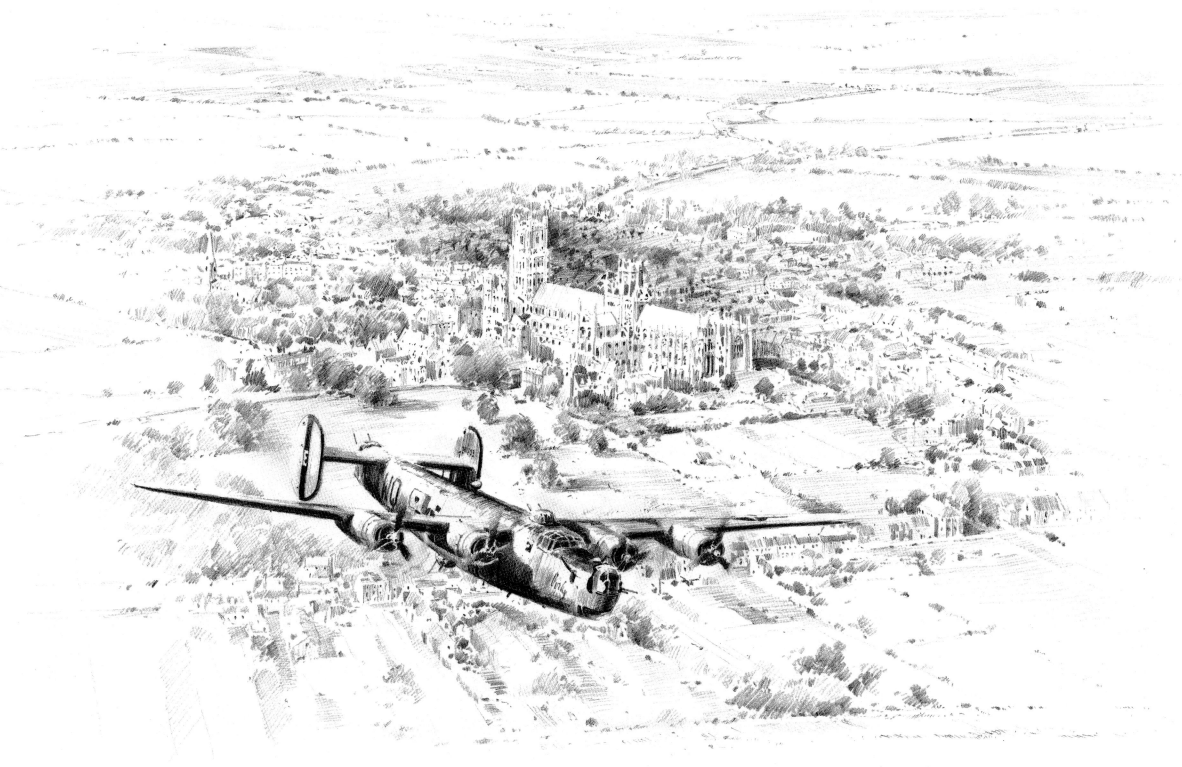

B-24 Liberator of the 44th Bomb Group makes a low pass over Ely Cathedral. Summer 1944.

Most bomber stations during World War II were to be found in the Eastern Counties, being the nearest to their regular targets in Germany. The topography, which is mainly flat, lent itself to the building of airfields, and from 1941 onwards new airfields sprang up all over that area of England. The countryside is beautiful and in good visibility the patchwork of irregular shaped fields, highlighted by shafts of sunlight and patches of cloud shadow, stretches as far into the distance as the eye can see.

In *Straggler Returns*, seen below, a damaged Lancaster limps back to base with parts of its flaps and elevators missing and the port outer engine overheating. To add to the suspense I painted crew members clustered around the pilot – the Lancaster had no co-pilot – indicating that he may be injured and requiring assistance to fly the aircraft home. Below is the familiar East Anglian landscape.

STRAGGLER RETURNS

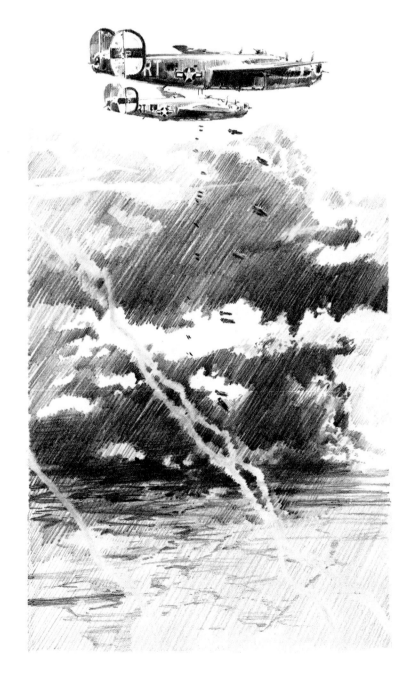

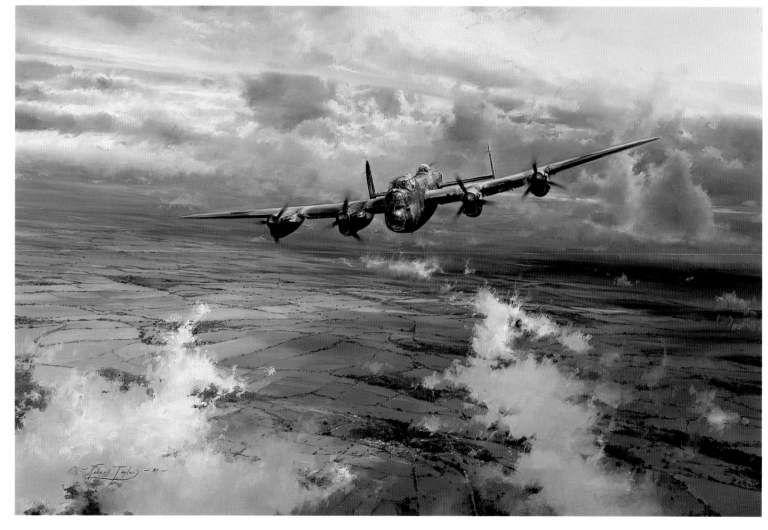

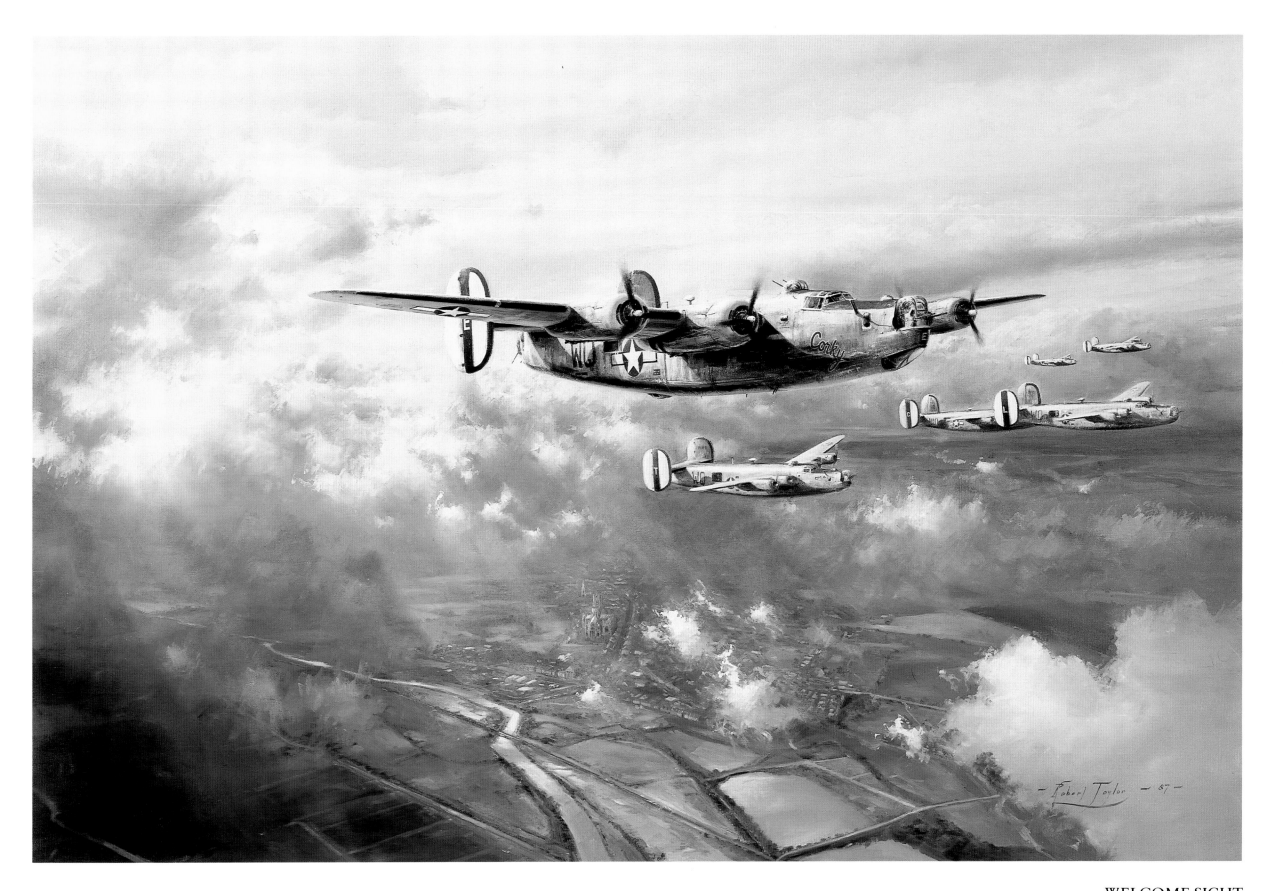

WELCOME SIGHT

In the collection of Robert and Carol Reid

HURRICANE FORCE

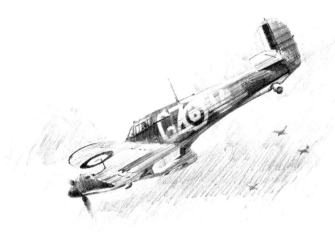

In attempting a trilogy of paintings for prints to commemorate the fiftieth anniversary of the Battle of Britain, my initial task was to think about three separate ideas which, when put together, would provide a broad picture of the great air battles fought in the summer of 1940. I wanted first and foremost to concentrate on the three fighters which for the most part formed the legend of the battle, but to have three quite different compositions which as a trilogy might convey as widely as possible various aspects of the battle so as perhaps to provide an over-view of events.

The central painting, the one I formed first in my mind, featured the Hurricanes as they came diving into great masses of German bombers heading in over London. In some ways this was the easiest to conceive for it is the picture that first comes into most people's minds when they think of the Battle of Britain.

I have known Air Commodore Pete Brothers for some years. Pete flew Hurricanes with 32 Squadron during the French, Belgian and Dunkirk campaigns, and during the first part of the Battle of Britain. He then joined Bob Stanford-Tuck as a flight commander seeing out the rest of the Battle in 257 Squadron, again flying Hurricanes. I knew nobody better qualified to help me with technical advice for this painting, and this he sportingly agreed to do.

In the event, I depicted Pete's Hurricane as the main subject for the painting as seen during a particular air battle on 15 September 1940. I received a letter soon after the prints were published telling me that this particular Hurricane had been shot down on 7 September. Fortunately, Pete's log book confirmed that it hadn't!

The battle was fought ferociously by both sides and at the time wasn't much fun for anybody, even the young pilots who, in the flush of youth, were duelling in the most sophisticated fighter aircraft of the era. The legend that has grown tends to overlook the worst aspects of the war, thankfully, and for my paintings I too prefer, where possible, to concentrate on recording the courage and skill of the pilots and the magnificence of their machines.

Having decided to devote an entire picture to each of the Spitfires and the Hurricanes it seemed important to do the same for the Me109s, being the opposing aircraft which presented the most danger to the RAF pilots. I did this by showing a schwarm – or flight – of four Me109s peeling off to attack British fighters as they in turn were attacking a mass of some fifty German bombers. This painting is illustrated in the next chapter.

Having arrived at three completely differing compositions, each portraying separate aspects of the battle, and knowing that limited edition prints were to be published from the paintings, I realised that there was always a fair chance that they would end up as a set of three hanging on a wall next to each other. It was therefore also important to paint the three pictures with basically contrasting colour predominances. I had fun with this and when all three paintings were completed, was happy with the outcome.

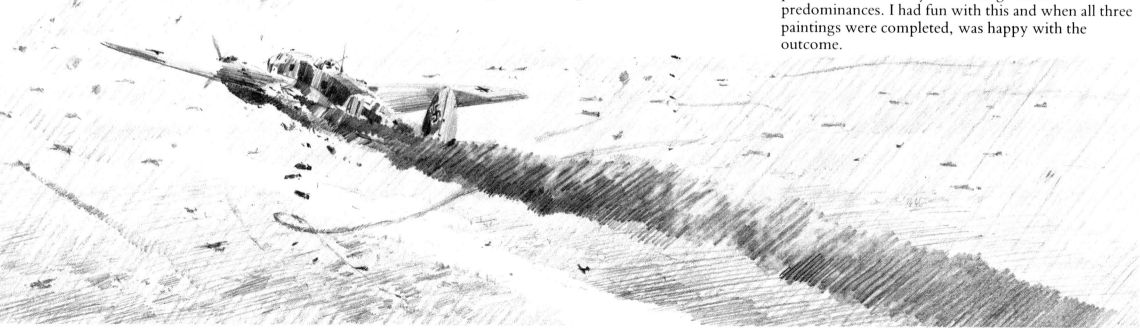

I prepared a couple of preliminary drawings as a basis for discussion with Pete Brothers. I have always found it helps to have something more in front of us than a sheet of white paper when talking to pilots about a subject for a painting.

My first sketch, seen below, was vetoed by Pete on the grounds that most attacks were made in the diving attitude and in any case no Hurricane pilot would have risked pulling up after making an attack on a formation of bombers. I had half expected this comment, but at this stage was looking for a way to paint the Hurricane coming towards me, so thought it was worth a try! The lack of any horizon in this sketch would have made life difficult, too.

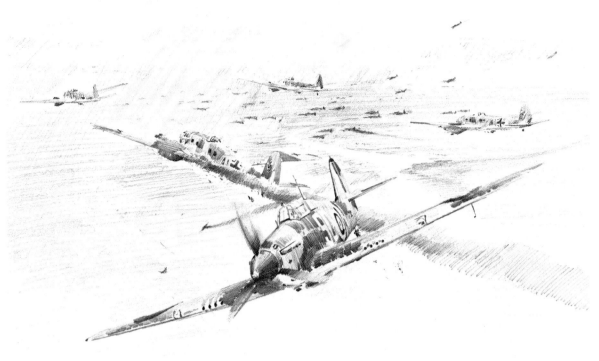

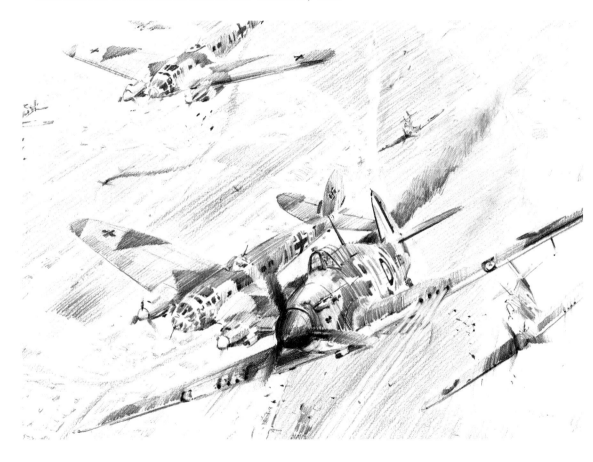

I had in any case already made a second sketch, seen above, introducing a horizon, which I liked the better of the two. The positions of the bombers gave a nice flow to the composition. I had the feeling that the angle of the Hurricane spoiled the flow of the picture, and although Pete like the idea, I knew I had to try again.

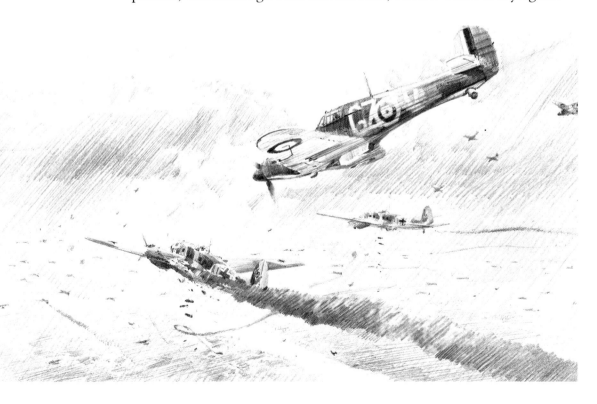

As soon as I had finished my third sketch, seen on the right, I knew I had achieved the composition I was looking for. I had dropped the horizon much further down and turned the Hurricane around so that there was a nice even movement in the picture. Technically everything was now much more authentic, for as Pete had pointed out, the aim of the Hurricane pilot was to make a shallow dive through the bomber formations where possible.

I have said many times how much I love to paint the Hurricane. It was an aircraft of immense character and beauty and it does not surprise me in the least to know that pilots who flew this classic fighter thought the world of it.

Sired by the Hawker Hart, a racy high-powered biplane in service with the RAF in the 1930s, the Hurricane was one of the very first of the new breed of low-winged monoplanes to come into front-line service before the outbreak of war. Although essentially a metal aeroplane, its ailerons, much of the fuselage behind the cockpit, and the entire tail-plane assembly were all covered in fabric. This made the aircraft quite difficult to shoot down, as unless a bullet caught a vital part, it just went straight through, leaving a small neat hole.

Painting a fabric-covered aircraft gives an artist the chance to show how the aeroplane is constructed. When canvas is stretched around an airframe you can almost see the aircraft's heart and soul.

The detail from *Hurricane Force* shown below, reproduced here at about half the size of the original painting, provides a good view of the canvas-covered fuselage and tail section of this wonderful aeroplane.

One point which perhaps doesn't always occur to painters of aircraft is that it is of critical importance to judge the size of the pilot. Paint him too small and the aircraft looks massive; paint him too large and the aircraft looks like a half-scale model!

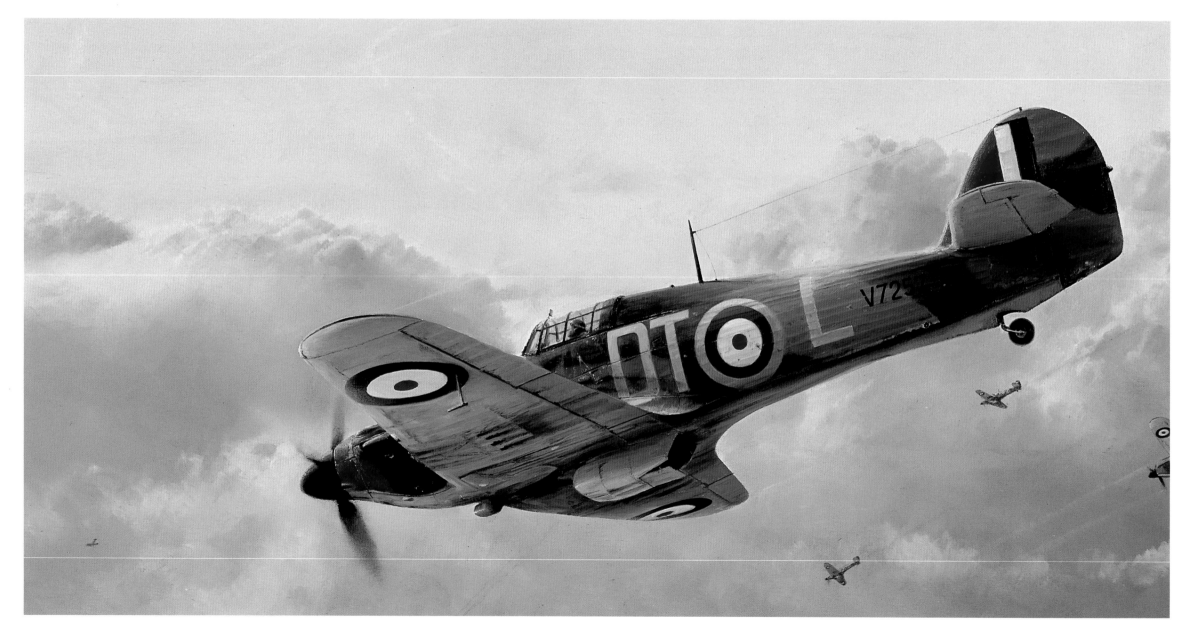

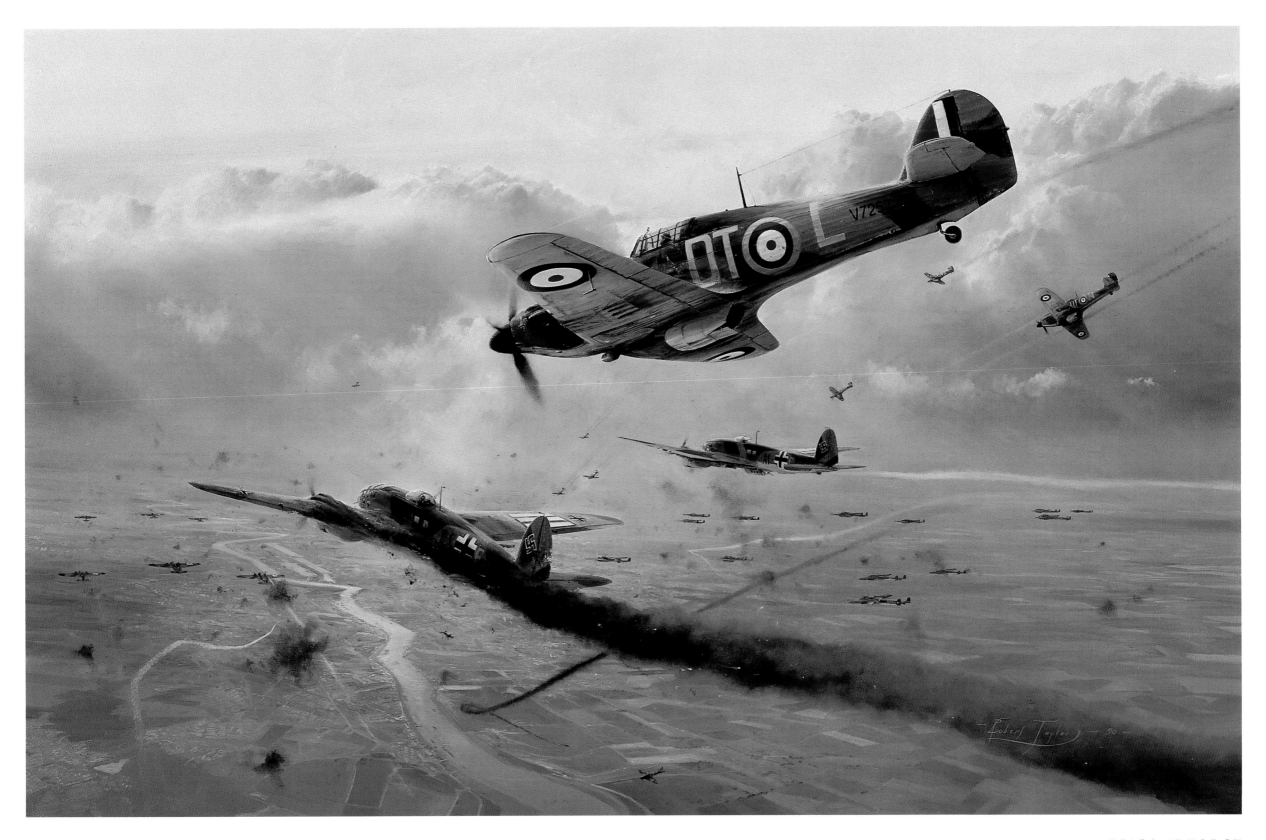

HURRICANE FORCE

In the collection of Mr Nick Maggos

SUMMER VICTORY

Talking one day to Alan Deere, the famous New Zealand fighter Ace, he described to me a particular sortie during the Battle of Britain when he and his squadron pilots had dashed back to their base to refuel, rearm and return immediately to an air battle that was raging over south-east England. As they hedge-hopped their Spitfires a few feet above the countryside, they flew past an Me109 that had crash-landed in a wheat-field – one of their victims in the fight they had just disengaged. Alan's vivid description coincided almost perfectly with a drawing I had already made, and I decided that the concept had all the authentic ingredients I was looking for to paint the Spitfire subject for my Battle of Britain trilogy. I felt that this scene would contrast nicely with my Hurricane combat composition and would convey the essence of those hectic days of that epic summer of 1940.

Many years ago, a famous and respected British artist, Terence Cuneo, whom I also greatly admire, said to me: 'If you want to paint a tree, go and look at a tree – don't make it up as you are painting like so many artists do. A tree painted out of your imagination will never look quite right.' It was a sage piece of advice which I apply to almost everything I paint. It is quite possible for an artist to 'invent' a tree, or indeed a complete landscape, because of the random shapes and sizes, but somehow when a tree or a landscape is painted directly from the imagination the result invariably looks contrived, which often spoils the painting.

After talking to Alan Deere and having pictured in

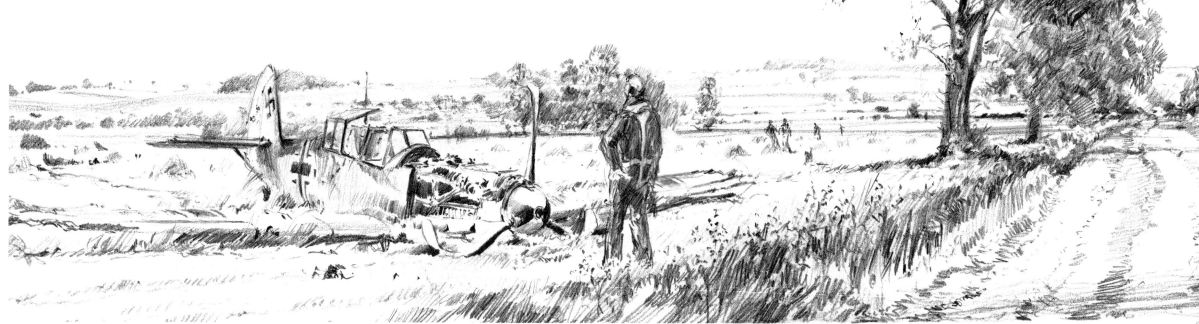

my mind the scene he had so clearly described, I set about looking for a particular piece of landscape which would suit my ideas. I wanted to find it before I started my composition.

In the summer of 1989 I was driving back from RAF Binbrook with Pat Barnard, my publisher, through the beautiful countryside of Lincolnshire, after spending a couple of days as guests of Warner Brothers during the filming of *The Memphis Belle*. Although we were busy talking, I kept one eye on the passing landscape, as I always do when I am travelling. Suddenly I noticed a view which was just perfect for my Spitfire painting and I asked Pat to stop the car.

In the middle of the Lincolnshire countryside, on the side of a near-deserted road, I sat on the roof of Pat's car and made the sketch on the left. I added the Me109 and its hapless pilot when I got back to my studio, but I knew as I sketched the landscape exactly where they would fit in.

The lane on the right is a sealed road today and there were some other small aspects of the view which I changed for the painting in order to date the view, but otherwise the landscape and the trees in it are all authentic. That precise piece of countryside which I had noticed as we sped along in the car was just what I was looking for. It had the exact shape I wanted and I knew it the moment I saw it.

I am sometimes asked if the technique required to paint a landscape differs from that used when painting aircraft. Personally, my basic technique remains the same, irrespective of the subject or composition I am painting. I believe most artists develop their own style and this usually becomes recognisable as their technique develops. When a painter has truly mastered his craft, in the way that Cuneo or Stobart have, his style and technique are as identifiable as his finger prints.

Painting subjects such as aircraft and ships requires a certain eye for detail. The ability to transfer this detail with the aid of paint brushes onto canvas requires that the technique should be fairly tight. But,

having said that, I believe it is important that an oil painter does not attempt to paint in the same tightly detailed way in which illustrators work, or the result may lose its spontaneity and become wooden. Fortunately, working in oil dictates a reasonably free approach, the medium itself making it difficult to overdo the detail whether one likes it or not.

I have painted with oil all my adult life. I even use oil when painting quick rough sketches in colour. I use no acrylics or gouache and personally hate the thought of mixing mediums, although I know it works for some. Oil paint is difficult to mix, slow to dry and is a fairly unforgiving medium – if I am not happy with something I scrape off all the paint and

start again – but I believe that there is no other type of paint which provides such vibrant colours and which gives an artist so much scope.

The majority of aviation enthusiasts, including me, do most of their viewing of aircraft with their feet firmly planted on the ground, and it is therefore easy for most of us to identify with an aviation painting which views the scene from ground level. Most of us enjoy the peace and serenity of the countryside, and it is therefore gratifying when one is able to complete an aviation painting which brings the two subjects together. I hope I am right because I enjoy nothing more than painting a picture like *Summer Victory*.

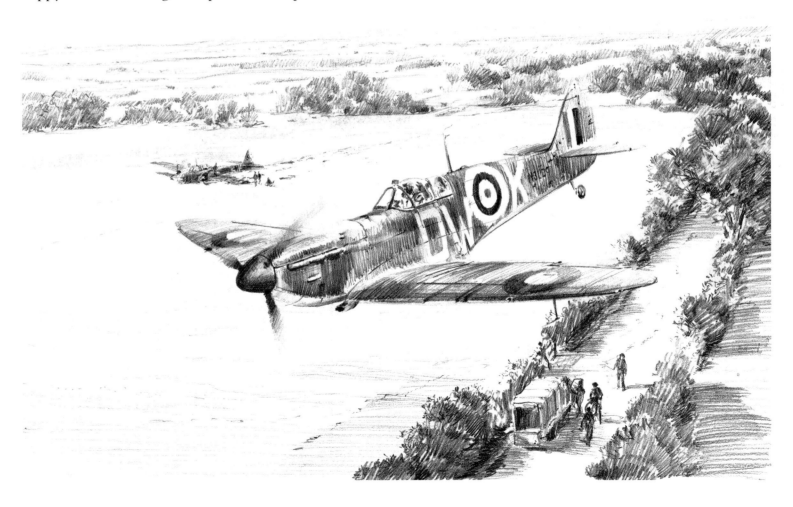

Eagle Attack, the third painting in my Battle of Britain trilogy, is featured below. I have had the good fortune to meet and to become acquainted with many of the pilots who flew the Messerschmitt Me109 in the Battle of Britain – famous Aces like Adolf Galland, Macky Steinhoff, Gunther Rall and Herbert Ihlefeld – and I have found it fascinating to listen to their accounts of the various air battles,

which, when taken with those given by Allied pilots, provide an enlightening perspective of air combat as it was in the 1940s.

There was no doubt in my mind that I should include the Me109 in my Battle of Britain trilogy, for this magnificent fighter played a major role in the contest, and was flown by some of the greatest Aces in history. The Me109 was an archetypal fighter

aircraft of the era. It had all the outstanding qualities of its opponents and was revered by its pilots. Even when the Fw190 appeared later in the war and was generally considered to be a better aircraft, the experienced Me109 pilots preferred to stay with their trusty steeds.

I decided to paint *Eagle Attack* showing a schwarm – or flight – of Me109s with the two nearest aircraft featuring large on the canvas, viewed from the side, just commencing an attacking manoeuvre. I have on previous occasions painted this aircraft viewed from a similar angle, but I was confident that this would not matter for I planned an overall composition which was entirely new.

It is often said that there are only a given number of angles from which one can paint an aircraft. This is, of course, true and during the period of a couple of decades of painting aeroplanes, an artist is bound to paint the same aircraft type, viewed from the same angle, on numerous occasions. In my view the important factor is not the repetition of the angle, but what the artist does with the remainder of his painting that matters. If he does a good job, each painting will be so entirely different that it should never occur to his audience that the aircraft have been painted at the same angle before.

As one painting in the trilogy was set at ground level and the second at about 12,000 feet, I thought it appropriate to have the third up on the edge of the stratosphere. I chose to show a group of high cover Me109s in a peel-off sequence at around 30,000 feet. The light, hence the colours, changes dramatically the higher the altitude, so this concept provided a complete contrast in all respects from the other two paintings in the trilogy. This had been one of my determined objectives from the outset.

All three paintings in the Battle of Britain trilogy were painted on canvases measuring 44 x 28 inches.

EAGLE ATTACK

In the collection of Mr Norio Isogai

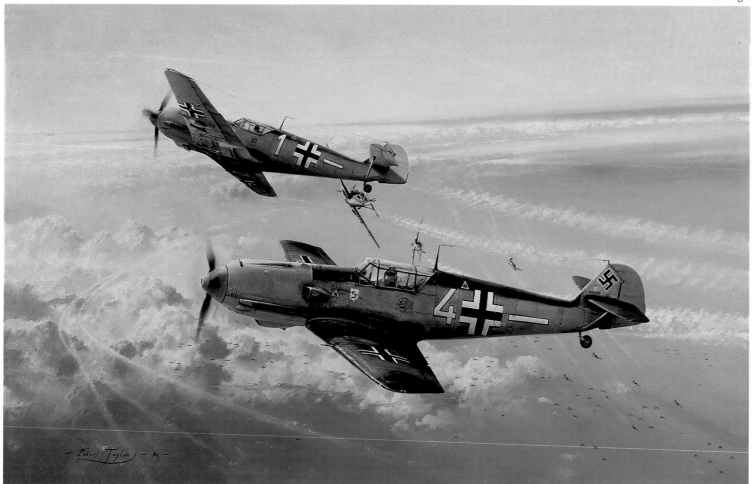

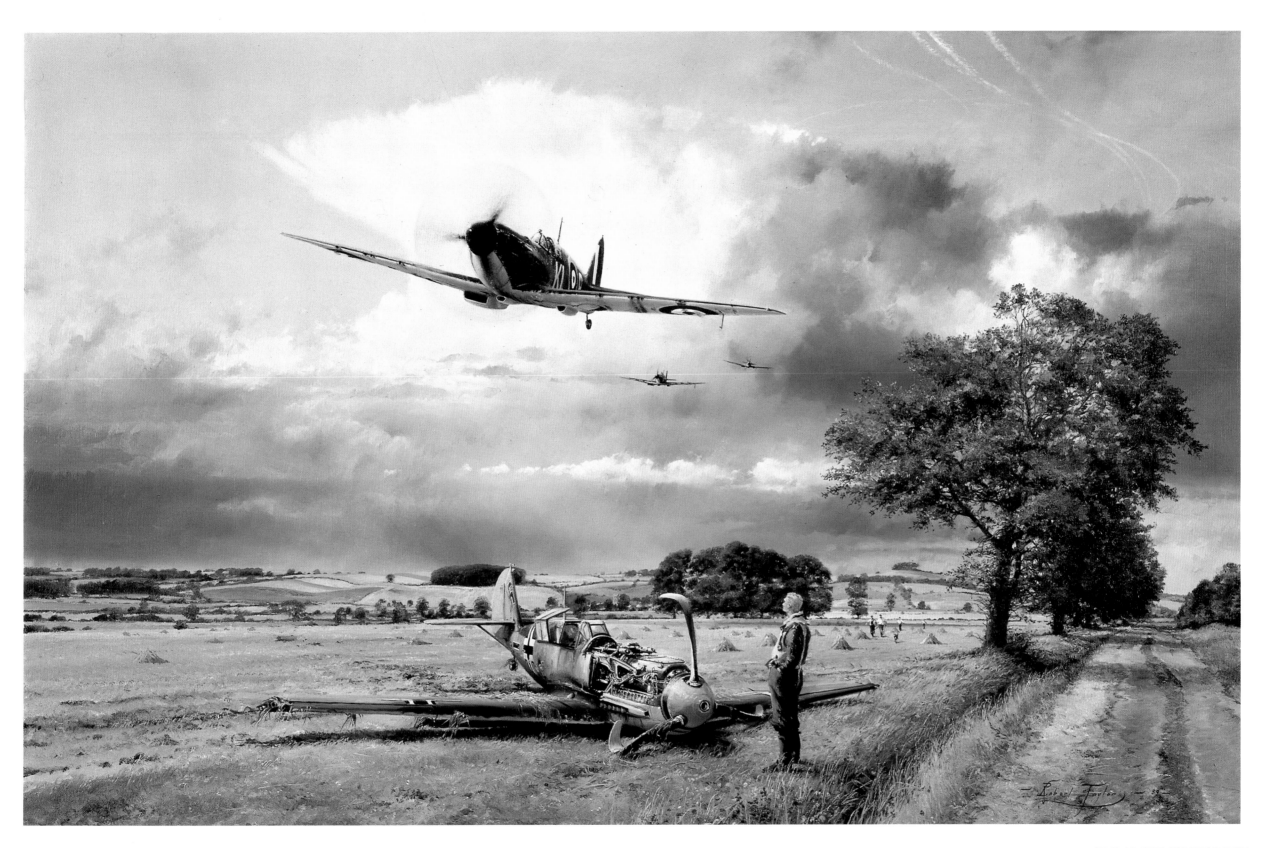

SUMMER VICTORY

In the collection of Mr Norio Isogai

GATHERING STORM

During the period from the late 1930s to the mid-1940s military aircraft were developed in greater numbers than at any time before or since. This may not be too surprising considering the cataclysmic happenings of the time, but, for whatever reasons, these exciting years were undoubtedly the most productive in the history of aircraft design.

Powerful new lightweight aero engines, coming in a variety of configurations, became available for the revolutionary all-metal airframes and monocoques. Designers had to cope with new stress tolerances of hitherto unthinkable levels and sophisticated aerodynamics became of supreme importance in the constant quest for better performance.

The imagination of that generation of aircraft designers was fantastic, and because in those days each aircraft was basically designed by one man – unlike today's aircraft where the computer rules – each was quite different from the next, instantly recognisable by its individual shape, and, indeed, to the enthusiast, by its own unique sound as it flew the skies of that golden era of aviation.

First of the new breed of all-metal low-wing single-seat fighters to taste combat was the Messerschmitt Me109, which cut its teeth in the Spanish Civil War. By the outbreak of World War II this new concept of fighter was in production in various guises in Britain, America and elsewhere,

some rising to greatness and others falling by the wayside into obscurity as further new designs came through.

When the brilliant German designer Kurt Tank launched his brainchild into the turmoil of battle, it caused immediate consternation among the pilots of the RAF. The Focke-Wulf 190 first fired its guns in anger on the Channel Front with II Gruppe, JG-26, in November 1941, quickly announcing its capabilities and intentions by claiming three Spitfires on one of its first combats, thus signalling to the RAF the arrival of something special – and that it was! By the end of the war it had become generally acknowledged as the finest single-seat fighter of the Luftwaffe.

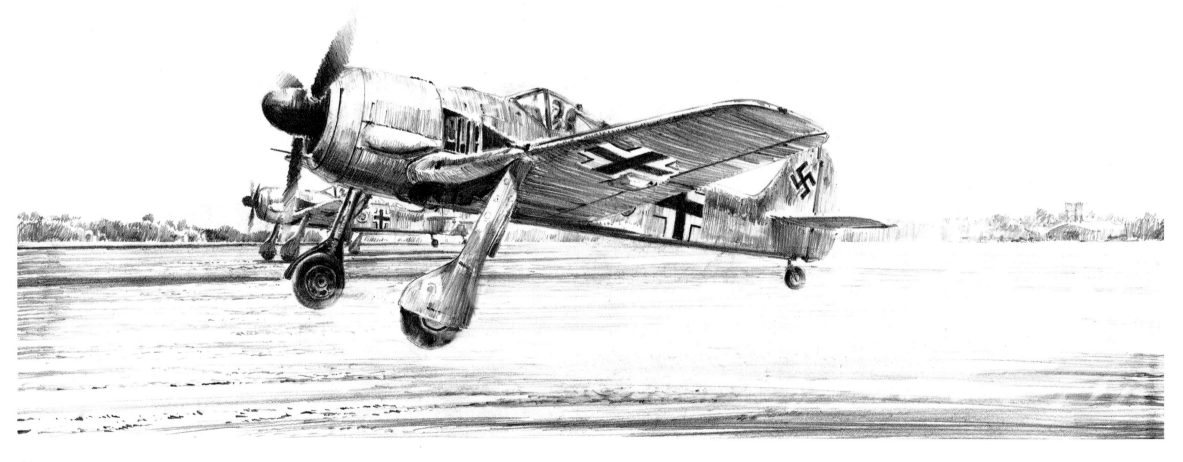

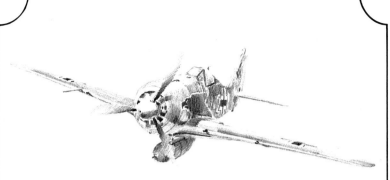

LIMITED EDITION PRINTS

Gathering Storm, like many of the paintings illustrated in this book, has been reproduced as a limited edition print. I am often asked about the history of publishing prints and the significance of the limited edition print.

Print making dates back to the sixteenth century when the process was accomplished entirely by hand. With the introduction of photo-mechanical methods of reproduction in the nineteenth century, the industry advanced, enabling any work of art to be reproduced on paper. During this developing period it became fashionable for an artist to hand-sign prints individually, confirming his approval of the quality of the reproduction.

The numbering of prints was started by artists such as Toulouse-Lautrec, but it was not until the early twentieth century that the public demanded to see not just the individual number of each print, but also the total number in the edition.

Edition sizes have always varied according to the popularity of the artist and the publisher's ability to sell the prints. As the market has grown, edition sizes have risen over the thousand mark particularly where artists' prints are collected on a worldwide market.

Fortunately today, artists are paid royalties by publishers, but in the early days they had to rely on being given a small number of prints, usually about 10 per cent of the edition, to sell themselves. These were known as artist's proofs, and the tradition has remained today.

Remarquing is another traditional practice carried forward to today, in which the artist makes a small original drawing in the print margin, which gives each individual print a degree of originality. An example of one of my remarque drawings is above.

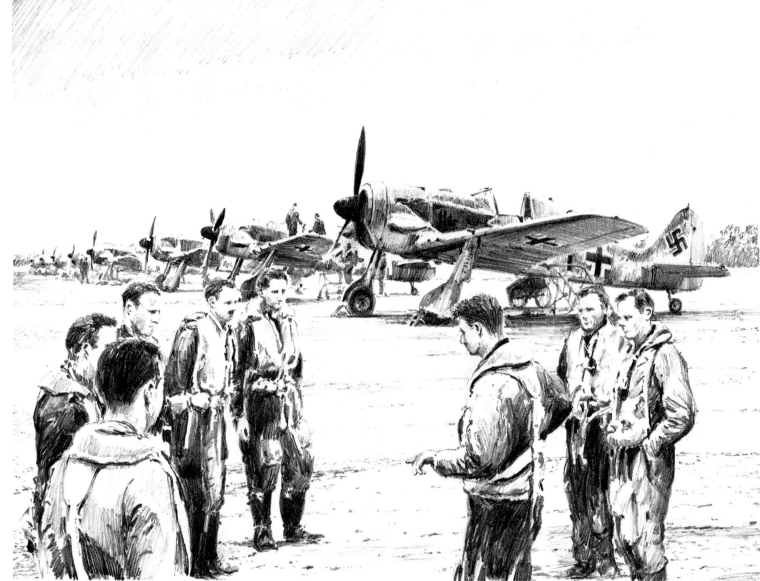

Pilots of JG 2 being briefed before an early morning sortie, Northern France, May 43.

Many of the great Luftwaffe Aces who had learned their trade during the early air battles of the war flying Me109s, have told me that they preferred the 109 to the Fw190, but most have admitted that this was more due to familiarity than to any great performance advantage on the part of the 109. Some pilots, on the other hand, like Heinz Lange who flew both fighters in combat, described the Fw190 as 'superb – for me the first choice of fighter'. Whatever the individual personal preferences were, I am in no doubt that the Fw190 was, in its day, quite superb. One has only to look at the aircraft to know it has class! So it was with enthusiasm that I tackled the painting Gathering Storm.

I decided upon a generic style of painting and made up a model of the aircraft, experimenting with various colour schemes, finally settling upon a Group which had bright yellow identification tail fins and flashes beneath the engine cowling. I carefully planned a very powerful skyscape and was quite pleased with the overall effect, especially with the various views of the Fw190 that the composition of the flight provided. At that stage of the painting I had not included the long-range tanks, and I wasn't completely happy with the aircraft, which I thought looked a trifle benign. After I added the tanks beneath the aircraft it changed the effect of the painting quite dramatically.

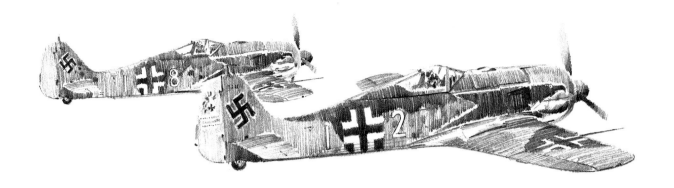

SWANSONG

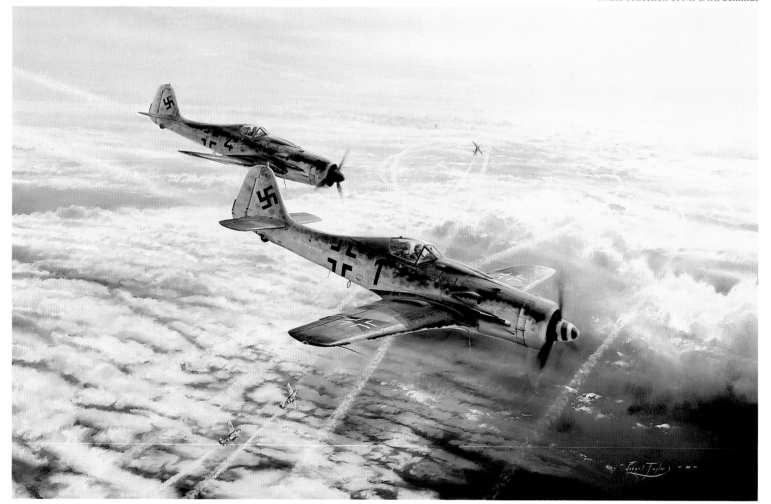

Gunther Rall was and is one of the most remarkable of all fighter pilots. I have known Gunther for some years and have always enjoyed his high spirited, graphic accounts of combat. A natural pilot of immense skill, bravery and good humour, Gunther Rall took part in the Battle of France, the Battle of Britain, and campaigns in Crete and Rumania before he moved to the Russian Front. By 1944 he was back on the Western Front commanding JG-11 and JG-300 Fighter Wings, flying the spectacularly beautiful Focke-Wulf Fw190D.

Gunther flew 800 missions, suffered 3 severe injuries and survived 7 forced landings and a mid-air collision to bring his final tally to an astonishing 275 air victories. He flew against the top Aces of the RAF in the early part of the war, suffered the rigours of the Eastern Front and took on the aggressive fighter pilots of the USAAF after D-Day in the defence of Germany. In spite of a long period of immobility in 1941-42 after crash-landing and breaking his back, he still recorded the third highest number of air victories in history.

The painting on the left, *Swansong*, shows Gunther Rall and his wingman flying the long-nosed Fw190D in a high-altitude combat with P-51 Mustangs over Germany, during the last days of the war. I was pleased when Gunther commented that I had obtained a good likeness of him in the cockpit, even if half his face is obscured by the oxygen mask.

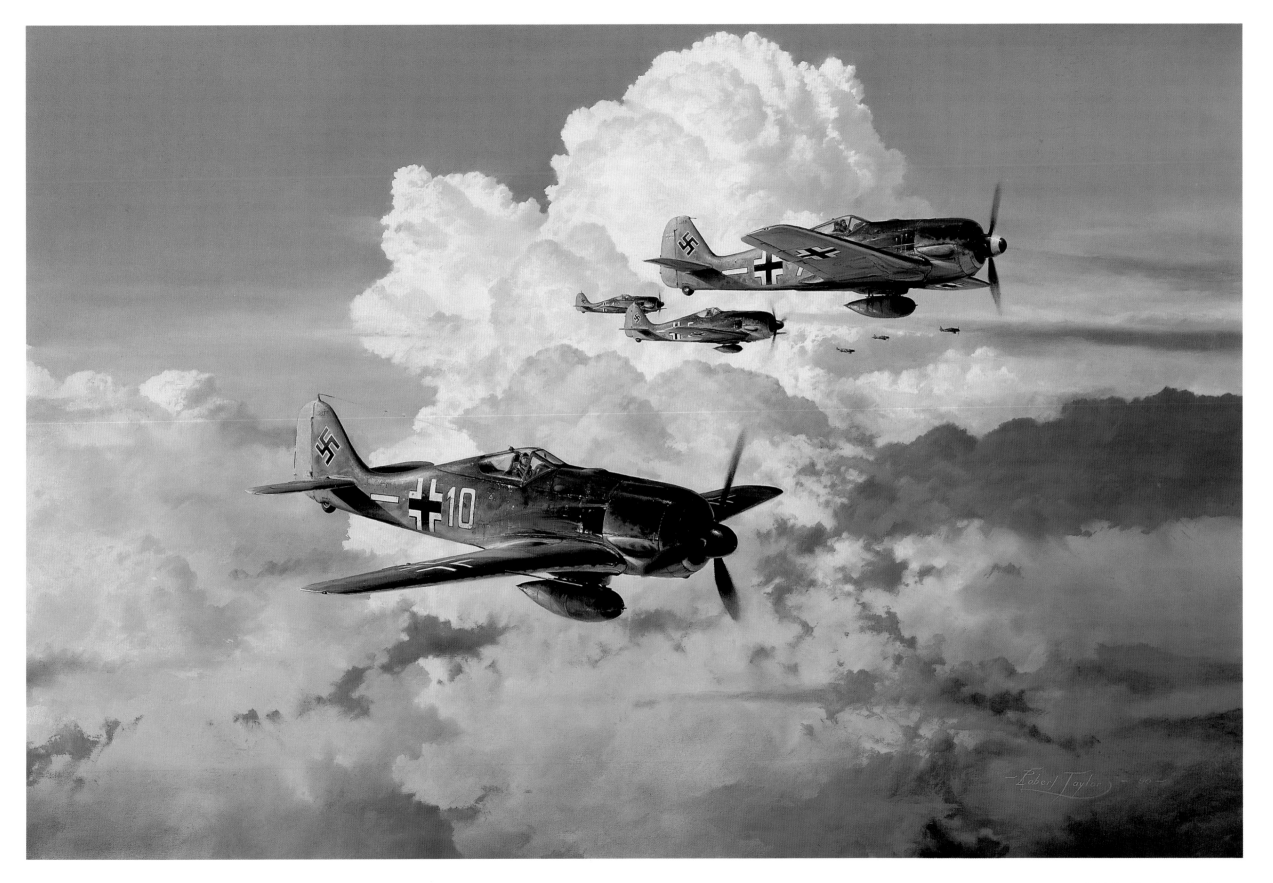

GATHERING STORM

In the collection of Mr Dirk Schmidt

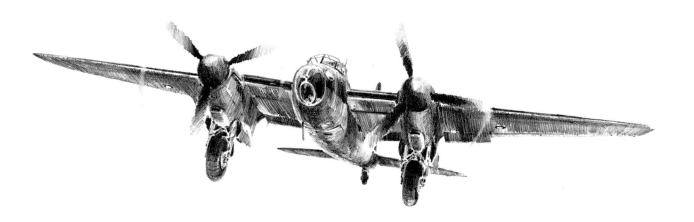

BROKEN SILENCE

When thinking about how I would paint a picture featuring Mosquitos, I was consumed with the thought that this aircraft was made almost entirely of wood. It was manufactured by cabinet makers from the furniture industry and assembled by craftsmen with skills that had been handed down through the centuries; men who had learned to make tables from mahogany, chairs from oak, writing desks from walnut, and all manner of fine things for gentle living, yet here they were in a world that had been turned upside down by war, being asked to make one of the most lethal war planes in history. The thought that one of the fastest, most versatile aircraft of World War II should have its roots in the forests seems utterly incongruous, although it was this fact that gave me the initial thought that my painting of Mosquitos should somehow incorporate a rural flavour.

The Mosquito was an aircraft which had terrific performance. It was extremely fast, having a top speed well above 400 miles per hour, making it a match for almost anything else in the skies, and was incredibly robust, often returning its crew safely home looking like a flying bundle of firewood. It had a performance so versatile that it flew in every role undertaken by the RAF during World War II. It was a beautiful looking aircraft and was adored by its crews. All this I had to try to convey somehow.

My first drawing featured a Mosquito over-flying a hay-making scene, but this put me too far beneath the aircraft and did nothing to emphasise the power and speed I was looking for. After trying a number of other ideas, I selected some East Anglian water meadows and painted the aircraft viewed from ground level. This still left me with the difficult task of portraying the Mosquitos from beneath, so I chose an oblique angle, taking the aircraft across the width of the landscape. This, together with a carefully constructed sky, gave me the effect of movement and speed which I was looking for.

The painting shows Mosquitos as they embark on a low-level precision strike at enemy targets in Holland. As dusk settles over the Norfolk Broads, a working barge moors for the night. The sudden thunder of Rolls Royce Merlin engines shatters the evening silence; wild ducks take flight and a pair of moorhens scuttle for cover in the rushes.

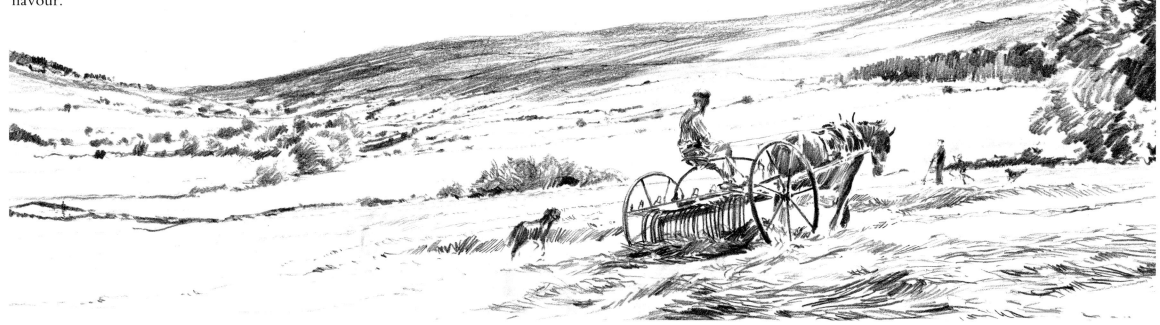

The Mosquito was built almost completely of wood. This in itself may not have been revolutionary, but as a design for a front-line war plane, it was a unique concept in 1940.

The basic structures of all the early flying machines used wood. World War I saw the first moves towards mass production and standardisation of construction methods. Wings basically consisted of two spruce or pine spars with regularly spaced spruce or ply ribs, covered in doped fabric. Fuselages, too, used the wood, wire and fabric formula, and these fragile contraptions were driven skyward by laminated wood propellers.

Before World War I was over, the Germans started to introduce metals into their fighters, the Fokker using welded carbon steel tubes. Later in the 1920s the Royal Air Force decreed that wood should be replaced by metal in all military aircraft. This was in part a strategic decision since the timber used in those days for spars and other parts was not grown in Britain. Although British aircraft moved away from the use of wood, American plane-makers, who were not hampered by the same supply problems, continued to build aircraft using wood components well into the 1940s, the most famous of these being the colossal eight-engined Hughes H-4 Hercules, better known as the 'Spruce Goose'. This enormous wooden flying machine was conceived in 1942, made its one and only flight in 1947, and now resides at Long Beach, California.

At the beginning of World War II a shortage of skilled labour, aluminium and machinery led to a demand for utility aircraft to be constructed of wood. This aimed to take the pressure off metal usage required for front line aircraft and it was this renewed interest in wood designs which brought about the

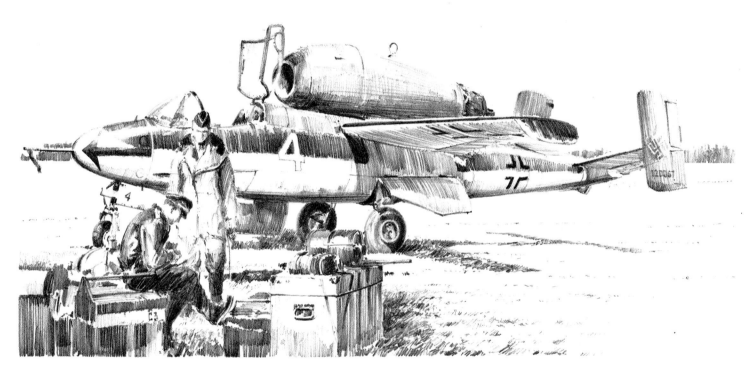

The Heinkel 162 A-2 Volksjäger, designed and built in 69 days, had a one-piece wooden wing and plywood nose.

brilliant concept for the Mosquito. Known as the 'sandwich' construction, the Mosquito was the nearest approach to a true monocoque that had been attempted, its skin being sufficiently rigid to warrant only a light internal framework. Its fuselage was a laminate of ply, balsa and ply, built up over a mould and bonded with Redux synthetic cement. Once assembled it was covered in fabric, doped and sanded to a smooth weather-resistant finish. The wings were a single-piece two-spar torsion box, with a spruce ply skin of diagonally laid strips. All this complex carpentry was completed within a beautiful shark-like aerodynamic design which incorporated two powerful Merlin engines. From its very first flight the Mosquito was a sensation.

I love wood and I love to work with wood. It is a most beautiful substance, available in such a wide variety of forms and can be fashioned in so many ways. Above all, it is a natural substance which, in appearance anyway, never dies. If for no other reason – and there are plenty – the Mosquito is one of my favourite aeroplanes.

53

I enjoy combining the subject of aviation with that of the countryside by placing aircraft and landscapes together. It can be an interesting idea to take a theme and explore how far one can take the concept, to find out where its outer limits lie.

At one end of the scale in aviation art is a painting where the featured aircraft almost totally fills the picture, leaving very little opportunity for the artist to paint anything else. Such a painting does not require much imagination, just a steady hand, and may perhaps be better described as an aeroplane portrait rather than an aviation picture.

At the other end of the scale is a huge landscape or cloudscape, where the aircraft is so small that it becomes almost incidental to the painting, hardly qualifying as aviation art. The idea of painting a landscape which includes only a single very small aeroplane is an interesting one since to make it work successfully as aviation art the painting has to rely almost purely on composition, mood and atmosphere.

I painted *Winter Homecoming* in a way that is intended to test these limits and to make the viewers decide for themselves exactly what the actual circumstances are and to wonder, or even to make them decide, what the outcome will be. Does this qualify as aviation art?

The aircraft, a Lancaster, occupies a tiny portion of the canvas. The picture is essentially a landscape painting, and was planned as such from the start. Knowing that I wanted to put a single aircraft in the landscape I looked for a shape that would accommodate this, but I also wanted to find a composition that would stand up on its own.

If one holds a pencil over the painting in such a position as to block out the small Lancaster, one can assess the painting's merit purely from the landscape standpoint. The big tree in the foreground provides the central interest for the composition and the colours create the atmosphere. Now remove the pencil and look again. Make another assessment as to how it fares as an aviation painting. The same tree in the foreground is used to frame and thus bring attention to the aircraft, small though it appears in the picture.

I completed painting the landscape before I inserted the Lancaster. Although I knew where I wanted the aircraft in the landscape, I was not sure how small I would paint it. In the event, I painted and removed that Lancaster five or six times before I was satisfied.

WINTER HOMECOMING

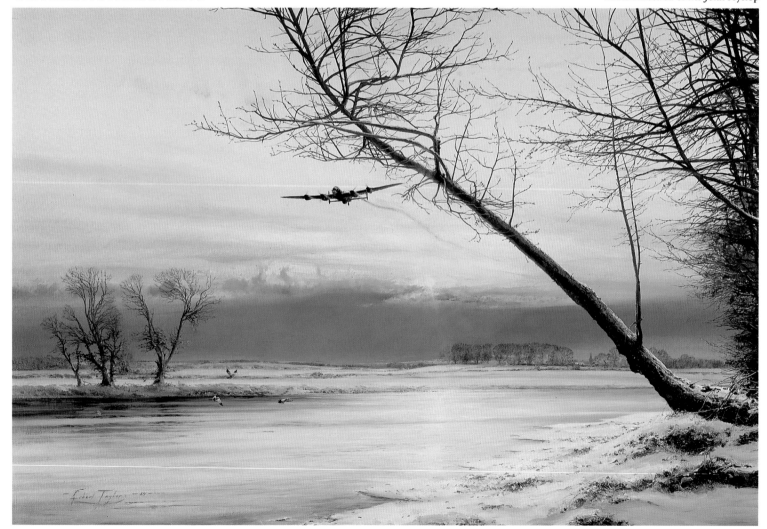

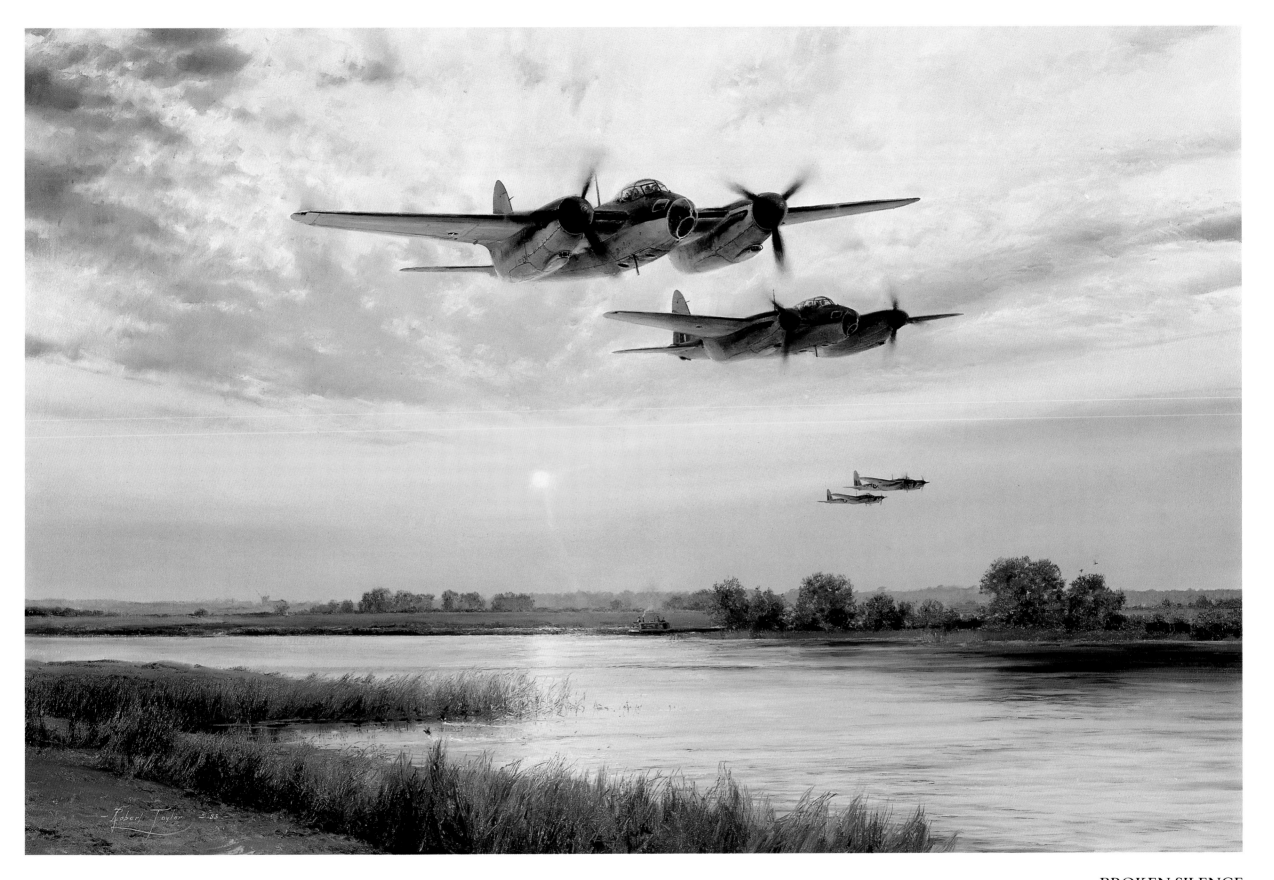

BROKEN SILENCE

In the collection of Brian and Molly Zimmerman

MIDWAY – THE TURNING OF THE TIDE

On the morning of 4 June 1942, about 200 miles north-north-west of Midway Island, a group of US Navy pilots flying SBD Dauntless dive-bombers made what was possibly the single most devastating attack of World War II. In the space of a few minutes they eliminated half of the entire Japanese carrier force, turning the tide of the war in the Pacific and bringing about the beginning of the end of the fortunes of the Rising Sun. It became one of the most famous, most documented, and consequently most painted combat scenes from World War II.

One of the great challenges for a military artist is to interpret the great historic events in a way that has not already been done by other artists. The more famous the battle, usually the more the scenario has been painted, therefore one is obliged to set about clearing one's mind of all the other images before work can commence.

However well I think I know a subject, I always make a point of reading it up before I start to think too seriously about what kind of image I might paint. Next, where possible, I try to talk to eye-witnesses or to people who took part in the event, particularly the air crew in the case of an aviation painting. The more information that is gathered, the more the ideas and images form in the mind. Usually I become influenced by some striking description which has been recounted to me or I have read about, and it is with this in mind that I start making my first sketches.

All military artists are constrained by the facts surrounding the events to be portrayed and it is part of their job to stay within certain established bounds of accuracy in so far as it is dictated by the research conducted, perhaps half a century later.

The most obvious moment of a battle will not necessarily make the best picture. In the case of *Midway*, I did not want to portray the actual attack itself because this had been painted by others so many times before. I wanted to find a new approach. In the event, I attempted to create a scene which would engender a strong degree of anticipation of the forthcoming battle and chose the moment when the SBD pilots had located the Japanese fleet, just visible in the distance in front of the lead aircraft.

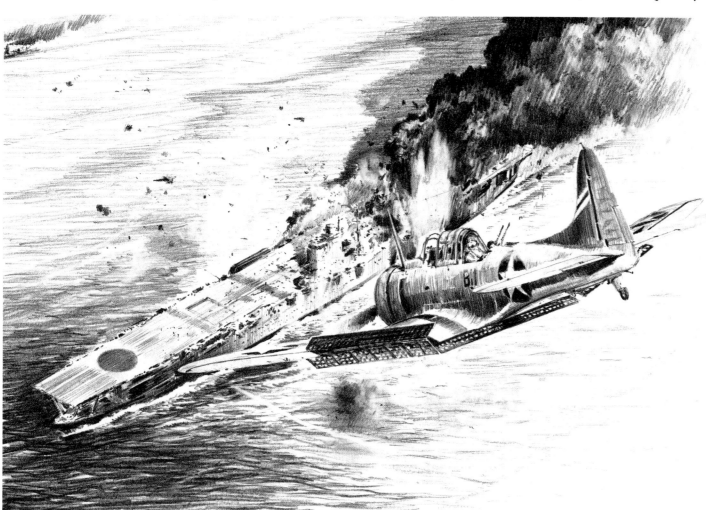

Commander Dick Best, who led one of the SBD squadrons, had helped me during research, and with the aid of his advice and first-hand account I made my final sketch, illustrated below. The drawing measured 12 x 20 inches and I transferred this up on to my canvas, again using pencil, in preparation to the commencement of painting.

I made one or two minor changes at the painting stage to improve the balance of the composition. These included raising the height of the aircraft in the distance on the left, and removing one of the SBDs at the top of the picture. I often find that although I may have been quite happy with my final sketch, when this is actually painted full size on to the much larger area of the canvas, I want to make some small alterations in the interests of the overall composition.

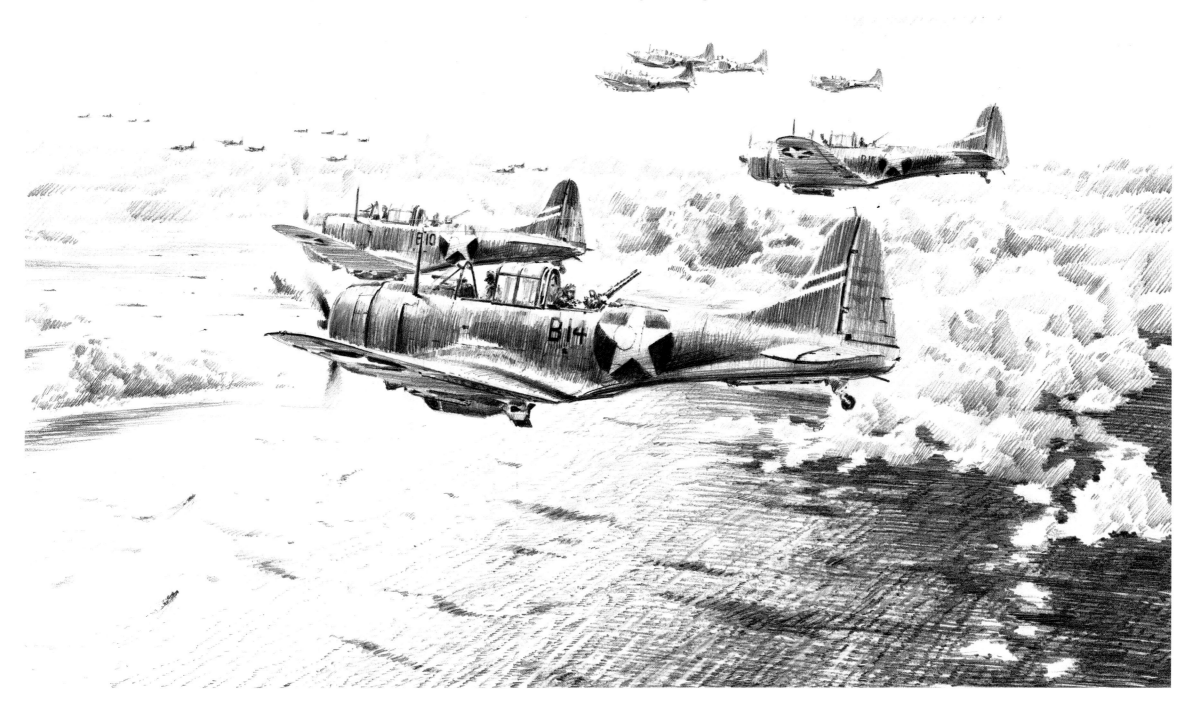

THE DOUGLAS SBD DAUNTLESS
By Commander Dick Best

The US Navy designated their aircraft by the mission and manufacturer. Thus SBD-3 signified Scout-Bomber, Douglas, third modification. Pilots also called it Slow But Deadly. In the later days of the war the Curtiss SB2C finally arrived in production. This was slightly faster and carried a heavier bomb load internally but was a beast on the controls, unlike the SBD which was a joy to fly.

Any pilot who flew the SBD in combat and didn't love and appreciate her was a shoe clerk! Pilots graduating from the BT-1s and SBCs were delighted with the smooth controllable dive, the quick-easy response at pull-out and her stability and responsiveness in all conditions.

In combat the SBD was notable for an ability to soak up damage and keep flying. The self-sealing fuel tanks, the fully armoured pilot's bucket seat, and the wrap around belly armour for the gunner, made a tightly drawn up division of SBDs a daunting target for any enemy fighter. Even alone they survived. At the battle of Midway Lieutenant Commander Wade McClusky, with shrapnel wounds in his arm and shoulder, brought back his plane with three 20 millimetre holes and over fifty smaller calibre holes in his aircraft.

An attack in a dive-bombing squadron started with a straight ahead push-over from 20,000 feet – not the half wing-over later employed when pilots wearied of finding their stomachs in their mouths. A vertical or near vertical dive at a point of aim 50-100 feet short of the target, down to 3,500 feet when the telescope gun/bomb sight was brought on to the target; then 50 feet over to allow for bomb trail and a release at 2,000 feet. The flaps were slapped shut and a high G pull-out was followed by a quick look over the shoulder to observe the fall of the bomb. By that time everyone below was shooting, necessitating a twisting jinking retirement.

The most frequent cause of loss of planes was from running out of fuel. The torpedo planes at Midway were in general shot out of the air by fighter or surface fire, but the dive bombers, with minimal vulnerability to the anti-aircraft fire because of the angle of approach, were usually in and out before a fighter pilot could intercept. And after lumbering along with a thousand pound bomb slung underneath, the SBD responded like a fighter when the load was released. She was the thoroughbred workhorse of the United States Navy, and an outstanding aeroplane in combat.

MIDWAY – THE TURNING OF THE TIDE

In the collection of Mr Dirk Schmidt

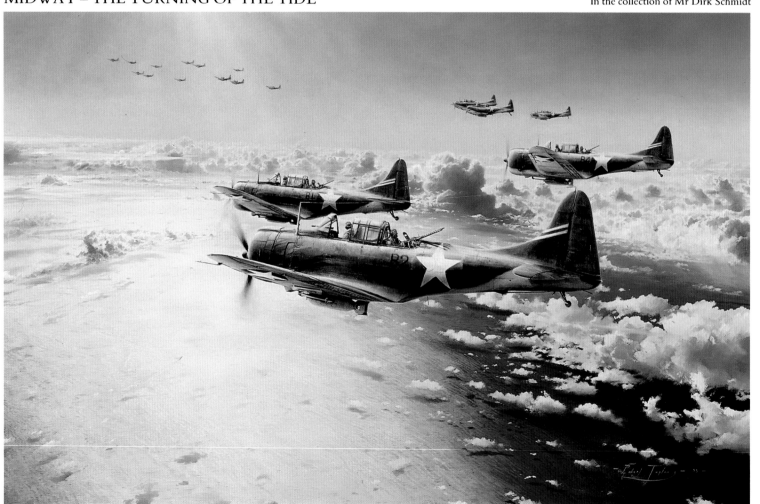

On the facing page is a detail from *Midway – The Turning of the Tide*. To the left is the complete painting. The SBD Dauntless was the brain-child of one of the greatest of all aircraft designers, Ed Heinemann. For me it personifies the American combat aircraft of the era and is without doubt one of my all-time favourite American aircraft. It oozes character; it has a wonderfully balanced shape and the most gorgeous cockpit area in which the crew can be clearly viewed. It is an aviation artist's dream aircraft.

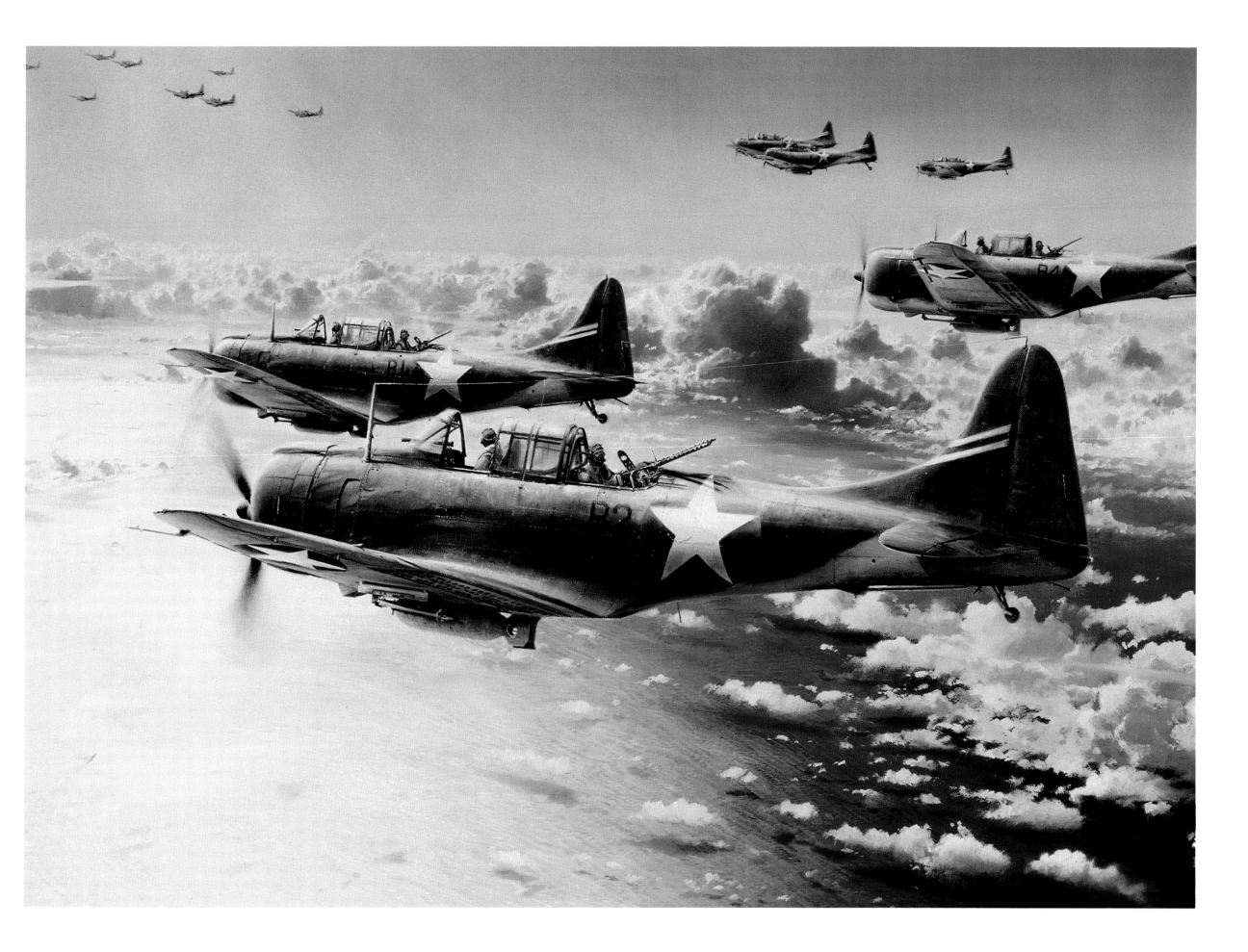

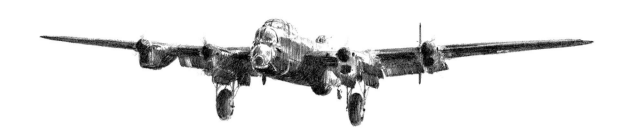

EARLY MORNING ARRIVAL

The sketch below was made as I sat on an old Cotswold dry stone wall, overlooking the beautiful Wiltshire countryside near where I live. The lane winds down the hill to a farm and ends there. It is surely one of the most peaceful places in the whole of England.

It was a different story in 1944. Half a mile away from where I sat used to be the busy RAF airfield of Colerne, one of the large Air Force stations built in the 1930s and operational throughout the war. It is still there today, no longer operative in service, but always a constant reminder to the local population, bringing back memories of the past.

On the morning of 6 June 1944 as the Allies were making their first landings on the beaches of Normandy, a four engined Lancaster of RAF Bomber Command made its way back to Colerne after an early morning bombing raid. It was a brand new aircraft, and was returning from its very first mission. Aboard was a Canadian crew, with an average age of 21.

Lancaster V-RA had a short but distinguished career. At first light on D-Day, her young crew had made a low-level strike, bombing the heavy coastal gun emplacements at Arromanches in northern France from just 1,500 feet – a spectacular and exceptionally dangerous introduction to the hazardous business of aerial bombardment.

The next night they took out a bridge at Coutances in West Normandy from 1,200 feet and on the third night they raided the Achere marshalling yards on the outskirts of Paris. Their final mission against the Cambrai marshalling yards on the night of 12 June ended in heroism and disaster.

Attacked by a Ju88 night-fighter and set on fire, the Lancaster was doomed. The captain ordered his crew to bale out, but at the rear of the aircraft the tail gun-turret was jammed, its gunner trapped. Pilot Officer Andrew Mynarski went back to help, but with fire all around him could do nothing to assist his tail gunner. His own parachute by this time was burned and the fire was so intense he was forced to jump, bidding

goodbye to his trapped friend with a salute. His efforts to save his comrade cost him his life – the charred remains of his parachute bearing testimony to a hero.

The pilot had trimmed the burning Lancaster into level flight before jumping and obligingly V-RA pancaked into the flatlands below, the tail gunner miraculously surviving the crash. Andrew Mynarski, who could have saved himself, was awarded posthumously the Victoria Cross for his conspicuous act of bravery.

Forty-four years later, on 28 September 1988, a Lancaster, lovingly restored by enthusiasts at the Canadian Warplane Heritage Museum, took to the air from Mount Hope Airport, near Hamilton in Ontario. She flew in the colours and markings of V-RA in tribute to Andrew Mynarski. It is a moving story and when I was commissioned to paint the return of V-RA on that eventful and historic morning forty-four years earlier, I took on the task with great enthusiasm.

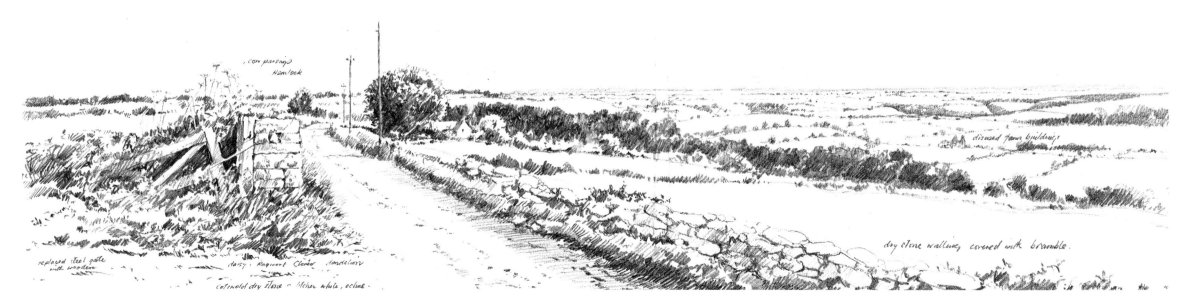

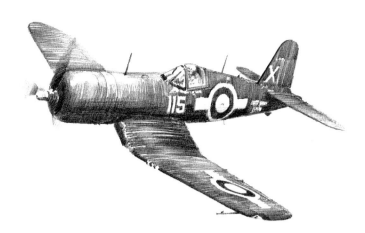

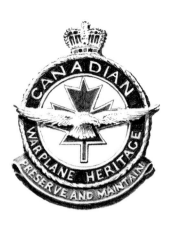

CANADA'S FLYING MUSEUM

I visited the Canadian Warplane Heritage Museum at Mount Hope's Hamilton Airport in May 1990 to see the Lancaster which had been dedicated to the memory of Andrew Mynarski, now generally known as 'Mynarski's Lanc'. The most famous British bomber of World War II, the Lancaster took part in some of the most spectacular raids of the war, including the sinking of the *Tirpitz* and the breaching of the Mohne and Eder Dams. Thousands of Canadian air crew and personnel served with RCAF and RAF squadrons and played a vital part in the ultimate success of the Lancaster bomber forces.

The Canadian Warplane Heritage Museum, CWH for short, is made up from a large group of volunteer enthusiasts, and its aims are to preserve in flying condition a complete collection of military aircraft which were flown by Canadians during World War II and the Korean conflict. On my visit I was given a fascinating guided tour by CWH's General Manager, Roy Walker, which culminated in a visit to the flight deck of the Mynarski Lanc, one of only two Lancasters that are still flying today.

Like all aviation museums, CWH is staffed by aviation enthusiasts, many of whom devote most of their time to the efforts of the museum. These dedicated people restore and preserve these wonderful aircraft for future generations and I have untold admiration for these devoted enthusiasts. The Canadian Warplane Heritage Museum is a wonderful example of what can be achieved by people who simply love aircraft.

The drawing below shows two aircraft which are currently in the CWPH's flying collection, the Avro Anson and the Cessna Crane. Both were designed before the war as passenger aircraft, and pressed into service in Canada to train bomber pilots. The Anson was the RAF's first monoplane and flew with Coastal Command in the general reconnaissance role at the outbreak of war.

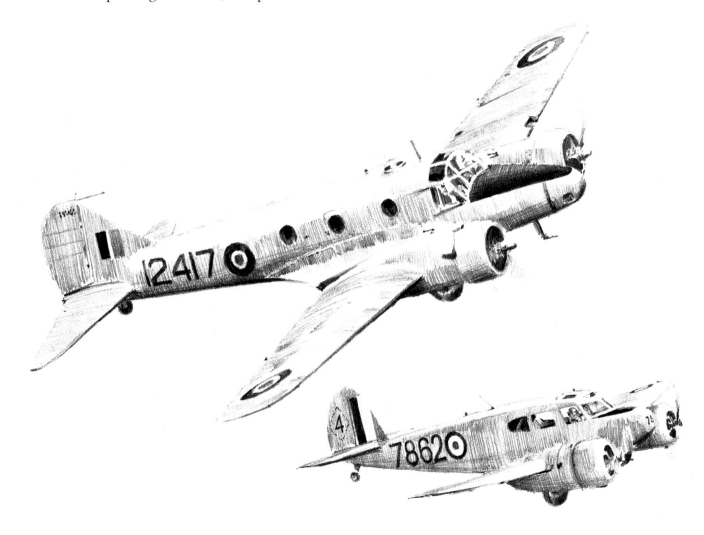

Avro Anson V and Cessna Crane of the Canadian Warplane Heritage Museum.

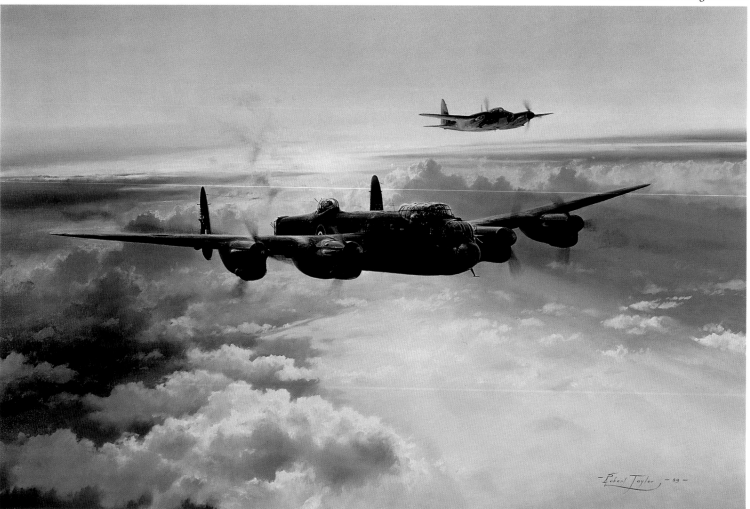

There are two fundamental types of aviation art. There is the painting which recreates a specific event, in which all the facts stated in the painting must be carefully researched and included in the most authentic way possible. Then there is the generic type of painting, which sets out to portray a certain type of aircraft, or a kind of operation in which specific types of aircraft participated, but which does not necessarily illustrate an actual event which took place. Both present a different kind of challenge to the artist and both require a great deal of creative thinking before work can commence.

Where a painting portrays a specific event the artist is, of course, constrained by all the facts which surrounded the event, the most crucial of which to the aviation artist are the precise aircraft involved, their colour schemes and identification markings, and so forth. Next the artist needs to study the location and the secondary reference that must be included in the painting in order to set the scene. Last, but not least, he needs to know the prevailing weather conditions at the time.

Often the artist is hampered by bad weather conditions, grey skies perhaps and the resulting

sombre colours. This may be aggravated by uninteresting colour schemes of the participating aircraft, and all this can be further complicated by having to position the aircraft in a way that unbalances the painting in the cause of authenticity.

True, one is permitted some artistic licence, but if the painting is to have any real significance the event must be recreated as accurately as possible. In such cases the artist must use his creativity to find the most interesting aspect to light the painting so as to make his aircraft look exciting and to find ways to cope with the bad weather which may otherwise destroy the whole effect if it is allowed to. An example which comes to mind, is featured in my previous book *Combat Paintings*, Volume 1. The picture, entitled *Canadian Wing*, shows Spitfires over the Normandy beaches. Over the Channel on 6 June 1944 the sky was an overcast grey, consequently the sea below was grey, and in 1944 Spitfires' camouflage schemes were predominantly also grey. The historic facts presented quite a challenge!

A good example of the generic type of painting is *Cloud Companions*, featured left. Such a painting allows the artist a considerable amount of freedom, but nevertheless demands careful thought and planning if the result is to be pleasing. *Cloud Companions* takes an emotive theme – a solitary Lancaster being escorted home by a friendly Mosquito, an event which sometimes occurred, particularly as the two types were often based at the same airfield – but the painting does not relate to a specific event. Here I was unencumbered by any weather or time of day limitations, and was able to choose my mark of aircraft and place them in a setting that suited me.

Conversely, with *Early Morning Arrival* I had to be specific about the aircraft and to paint an accurate landscape as it was back in 1944. The weather cleared from the west on the morning of 6 June and the huge bank of cloud in the painting is the tail end of the weather front that was moving eastwards. The painting is therefore viewed looking almost due east.

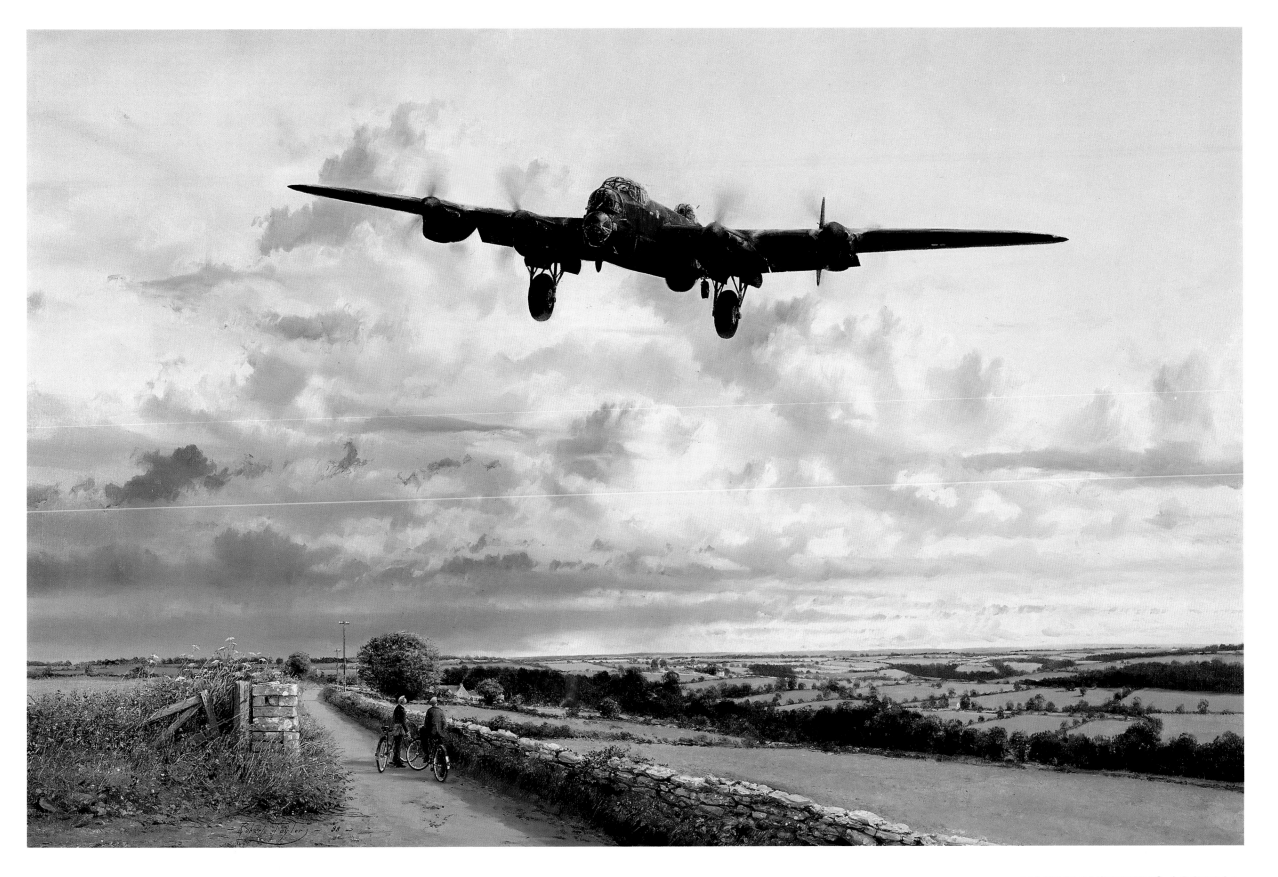

EARLY MORNING ARRIVAL
In the collection of Mr and Mrs D. Haddow

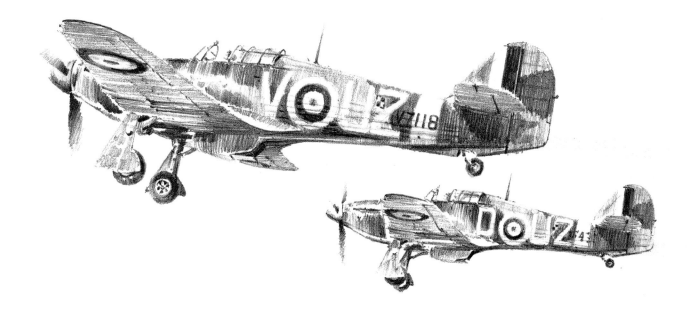

HURRICANE SCRAMBLE

Certain events in life leave a permanent mark on the memory. Most people can remember exactly where they were and what they were doing when they hear some earth-shattering news. In much the same way, a pilot always remembers every last little detail about his first solo flight, and, irrespective of how many other exotic aircraft he later flies, the events of that first solitary adventure into the sky remain vividly in his memory for ever. Talking to pilots who have experienced combat, it seems that the same everlasting impressions remain in the mind concerning the aeroplane that first took them into battle, the allegiance to the type staying with them for ever.

During the early part of World War II, the RAF had vastly more Hurricanes than Spitfires and therefore many of the young fighter pilots started

their combat careers flying this redoubtable classic fighter. I have never met a pilot who flew the Hurricane in combat who has a bad word to say about it, and most love it with a deep affection, often convinced that the aircraft was the reason for their success and indeed survival.

Group Captain Peter Townsend, who commanded 85 Squadron's Hurricanes during the Battle of Britain, once described the Hurricane to me as 'that most lovable and dependable of all fighters'. Wing Commander Geoffrey Page, who suffered the most fearsome burns when his Hurricane was hit and exploded in flames, recalls the aircraft with great affection in spite of his terrible ordeal.

Ginger Lacey, one of the RAF's top-scoring Battle of Britain Hurricane Aces, visited my studio not long before he died and talked to me at length about the

merits of this good-looking fighter, its stability as an aerial gun-platform and its resilience under fire. He loved the Hurricane.

It has been said many times that the Hurricane never received the credit that was its due. True, it may not have had the sleek thoroughbred lines or the nimble aerobatic performance of Mitchell's Spitfire, but there is no question that the Hurricane did its stuff when it mattered most. Its sturdy shape said 'You can rely on me' and its character saw to it that its pilots could. The tales of its exploits are legend and it will for all time be remembered as the fighter that won the Battle of Britain.

When I was commissioned to paint a picture featuring a squadron of Hurricanes as they scrambled from a 1940 Battle of Britain airfield, I looked for a way to show the aircraft as near to head-on as I could. Painting aircraft from a head-on position doesn't provide much of a view to work with, but the effect can be quite dramatic.

After some experimentation, I decided to offset the angle of the approaching aircraft just a little in order to see more fuselage and to get a view of the pilots' faces in the leading aircraft. Starting with the Squadron Commander's Hurricane in the forefront, I arranged the aircraft in a gentle arc, taking the eye back to the Hurricane on the right. This one I painted coming directly head-on. The wheel tracks in the grass in the foreground are all structured to take the eye across the airfield to the activity in the area of the dispersal huts and the landscape beyond in an effort to give depth to the painting. The cloud formations are devised to help highlight the aircraft and they add a nice blend of colour to the overall composition. These Hurricanes are probably taking off for the fifth or sixth combat sortie of the day and have probably done the same every day for the past few weeks, so I have endeavoured to make them look as if they have been flown hard and furiously.

I never start a painting without first making a series of sketches. Drawings start only after I have completed most of my research and the first ones are more like scribbles than anything else. Initially I try to work out at the 'scribble' stage the overall composition, what direction the light will come from, how bright it will be, and I also start to think about colours. These thumbnail sketches are usually small. For an implement I use a pencil or sometimes a drawing pen. I usually draw on cartridge paper because I always have piles of it about, but I also draw on board and sometimes even produce temporary sketches on the formica surface of my drawing-board.

Sketching outdoors is invariably done quickly using a pencil and these become fairly well covered with hand-written notes made at the time to remind me of colours, light, shadow and sometimes a point of detail which I will need when I paint. Sketches made quickly on location are totally uninhibited and as a result are often quite inspirational. I have sometimes tried later in my studio to reproduce in more detail one of my 'field' drawings only to find that I cannot recapture the spontaneity of that first quickly sketched image.

Like all tasks in life, some go smoothly and some do not. I sometimes think people believe that artists simply walk up to the canvas and start to paint, each time without fail able to produce a satisfactory work of art. I wish it were so. Before I can start to paint I have to convert my scribbles to more serious drawings, often producing two or three of these to a fairly finished standard. My finished drawings usually measure around 23 x 15 inches.

When I am happy with everything I transfer my final drawing on to the canvas. For years I used the laborious method of drawing out a grid on the canvas, but today I prepare a transparency from my final drawing and project this on to the canvas. I then sketch in a rough outline in hard pencil. This provides greater flexibility and is a much cleaner process.

I paint only in oil on canvas. I prefer a fine tooth canvas, and this I place on stretchers which I make myself, before applying two priming coats. Some artists like to prime their canvas with a soft, fairly neutral colour, but I prefer to paint directly on to a nice clean white base.

I am often asked by aspiring amateur artists how best they can get started into painting. I always reply: 'With a pencil!'. In my mind, nobody can master the art of painting, certainly in the school of representational art, unless they have first mastered the technique of perspective and the art of drawing. Drawing is quick, very effective, great fun and very inexpensive. You can't say that about too many things today.

In the same way that black and white photography often can be more artistic than colour, a drawing, which places great importance on tonal values, can sometimes be just as effective as a painting. I know some artists who have mastered the art of drawing so well and enjoy it so much that they have never bothered to progress to using paint.

I have sketched since I was old enough to hold a pencil and enjoy it as much today as I ever did. When preparing final sketches, I use the pencil to establish areas of light and shadow, and the general tonal values which I will subsequently use when applying paint. This is achieved by the method known as 'hatching' – a series of freely drawn, roughly parallel lines, applied in varying strengths, often using pencils of varying density, or softness.

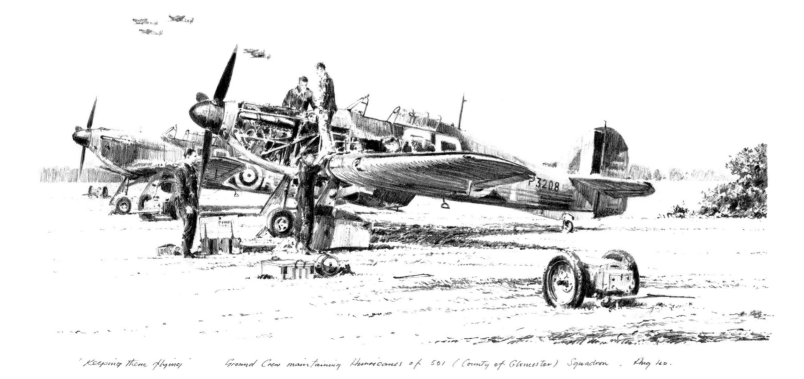

'Keeping them flying' Ground Crew maintaining Hurricanes of 501 (County of Gloucester) Squadron. Aug 40.

I seldom start a painting until I have gathered all my research. I like to know exactly what I am going to paint, how I am going to paint it, and to have thought about the colours I intend to use. I very rarely work on more than one painting at a time. Many artists who work in oil have two or three canvases on the go at any one time, allowing areas of paint to dry or 'go off' before proceeding with the next stage. I find I work best if I can thoroughly prepare myself prior to starting and then devote all my attention to one painting, thoroughly immersing myself in the job both physically and mentally until it is completed. During the time I am actually painting – and sometimes a picture can take up to six weeks to complete – I like not to be disturbed so that I can complete the work without having to take my mind away to other matters. It might seem very anti-social, particularly as I enjoy meeting people at other times, but it really breaks my concentration to be interrupted at my studio while I am in the middle of a painting.

Most of my paintings are quite large, a common size canvas measuring 42 x 28 inches, with even larger canvases where the subject warrants it. Oil sketches are of course made to smaller sizes, but generally speaking I like to work with a good expanse of canvas.

The painting on the left is one of my smaller ones, the original measuring 30 x 20 inches. It shows an unusual event which occurred at Speke airfield, near Liverpool, during the Battle of Britain. A Junkers 88 intruded the area and Denis Gillam scrambled his Hurricane just as the enemy aircraft prepared to bomb the airfield. Still accelerating and with wheels still in the process of retracting, Gillam shot the Ju88 down with a single burst, completed his circuit of the airfield and landed. It is believed that it was the quickest air victory ever recorded – he was airborne for only six minutes.

FASTEST VICTORY

Private collection

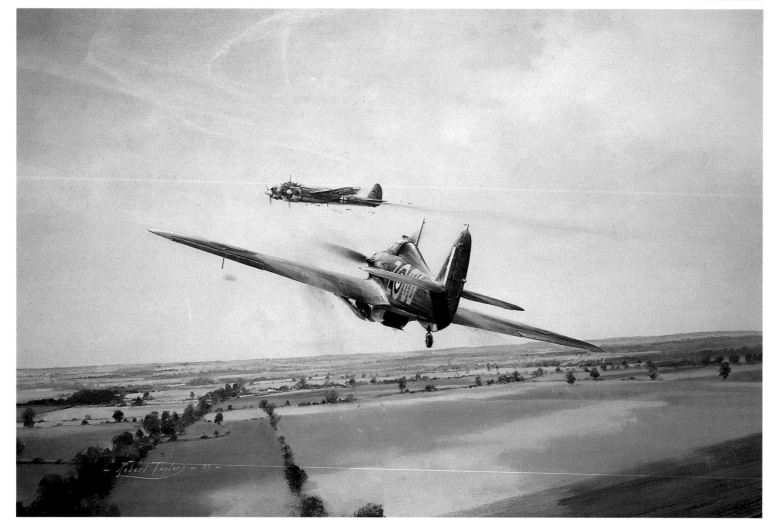

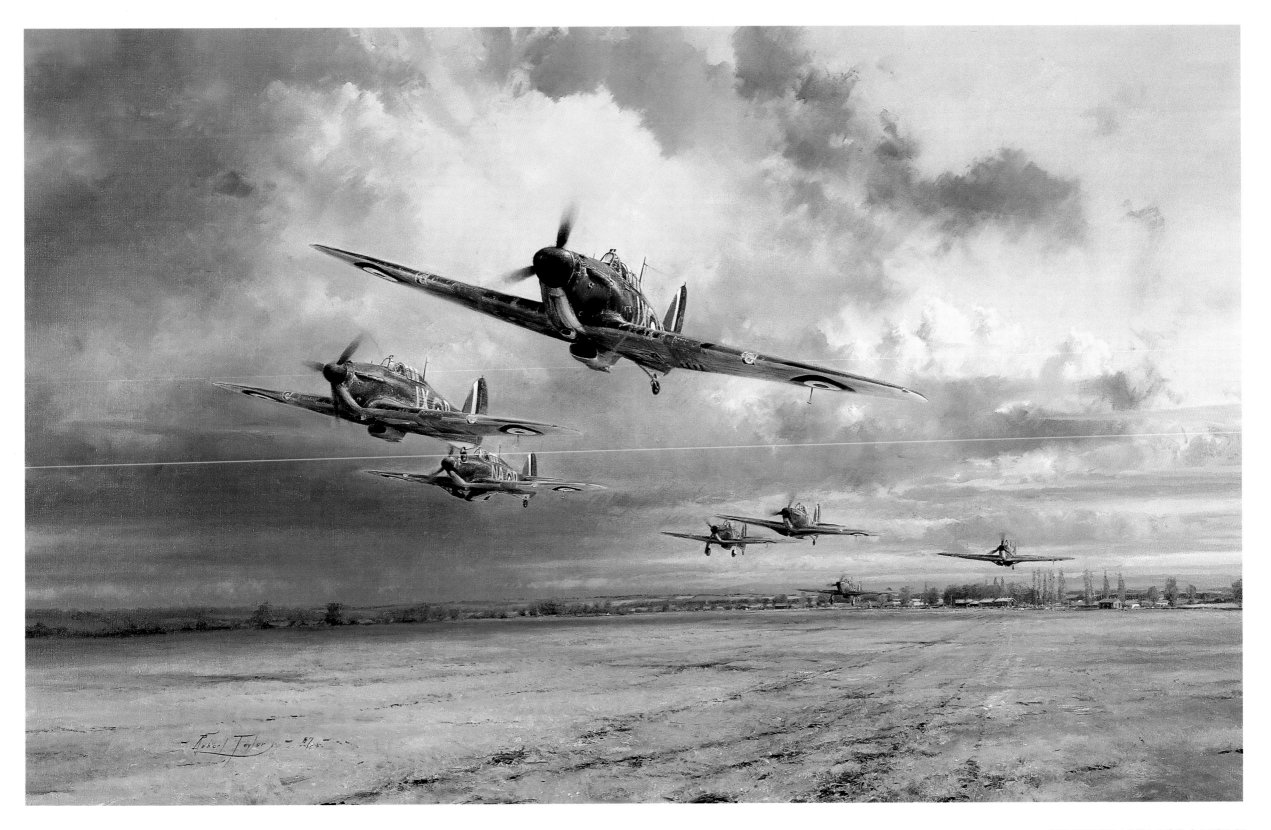

HURRICANE SCRAMBLE

In the collection of Penn Mutual Life Assurance Company

ZERO ENCOUNTER

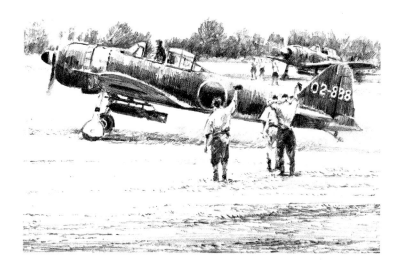

When the first US aircraft landed at the captured airstrip on the island of Guadalcanal on 12 August 1942, there was still heavy ground fighting within 3,000 yards of the airfield. A few days later it was named Henderson Field, after Major Lofton R. Henderson who led the Marine dive-bombers at Midway. The name of this small airfield is synonymous with the war in the South Pacific and it became home to some of the greatest Marine pilots who took part in the air fighting in that theatre.

When I was asked to complete a painting to commemorate the Cactus Airforce – the Marine Air Force at Guadalcanal – as part of a project for the Nimitz Museum in Texas, it seemed that with all the many choices of composition available, the most obvious should be that which included the airfield itself. Knowing that two famous US Marine pilots and two famous Japanese Zero pilots were to be involved in the project, I looked for a suitable way to incorporate all this together. A dog-fight over Henderson Field seemed the logical answer.

The main task of the F4F Wildcat pilots at Guadalcanal was to attack the Japanese bombers whose target was to obliterate the airfield. The usual F4F tactic involved a direct overhead or high-side pass on the bombers, avoiding their tail gunners, followed by a quick burst at the ever-attending Zeros and a dive out of the immediate area. Like all aerial combat, things didn't always work out to plan and many dog-fights between F4Fs and Zeros developed.

The highly manoeuvrable Zero could always out-turn the Wildcat, and because a one-on-one combat usually went in favour of the Zero, the Wildcat pilots, when possible, always fought in pairs. The painting shows such a one-on-one dog fight above Henderson Field with a Wildcat locked in combat with a tight-turning Zero. The outcome of this particular duel will depend entirely on the skill and experience of the competing pilots; at the precise moment depicted in the painting seen overleaf, honours are about even.

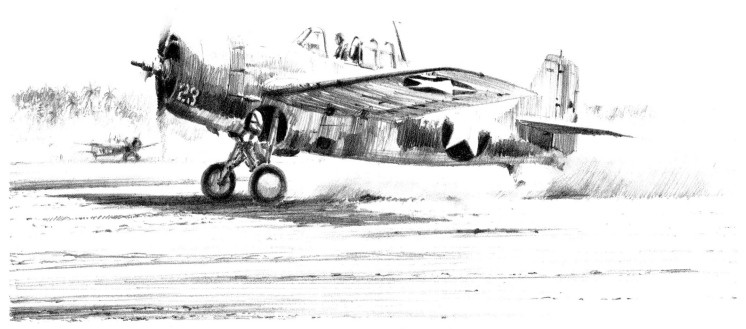

A Marine F4F-4 of VMF-223 beginning its run. Henderson Field. Guadalcanal during the Summer 43.

In the never-ending search for accuracy in aviation paintings I have come to appreciate the enormous task that faces the dedicated historian. Like most people, if I want to learn about a particular historical event, I simply open a history book, never giving thought to its accuracy or to the tremendous research that must have gone into it. However, over the past few years I have come to think of the historian as something of a kindred spirit. It did not take too long in my career as an aviation artist to realise the inadequacy of relying solely on the written word. I do not now consider my research as complete until I have consulted the leading authorities, checked log books, weather reports, photographs, etc, and where possible, talked to those who were there – the latter being a privilege not open to most historians. Even then it is interesting and sometimes amusing to spend a few days with three or four pilots who were all present at the same event and to hear three or four different perceptions of it. How much more difficult it must be for the historian trying to get at the truth of events many hundreds of years ago.

With most of the events I portray, such as with *Zero Encounter*, there are often numerous people alive today who either have first-hand knowledge of the event or who are very knowledgeable about the activity of the period even though they were not actually present. I have learnt that it is better to hear from these people before I start to paint, not after! Of course, all this groundwork takes considerable time. A question I am often asked is how long it takes me to paint a picture, and I feel I haven't given a proper answer unless I also discuss the period *before* I put paint on canvas. This latter part, by the way, usually takes between three and six weeks' working time at the easel, depending on the complexity of the painting.

Research is the life blood of the military artist. In my constant quest for information, I have made many friends and have come to rely on a number of people without whom my work would be almost impossible. To all those people I would like to extend my special thanks.

Having said all that I have about research and accuracy, I believe that there is also a danger that an artist can become obsessive about detail. Painting is a

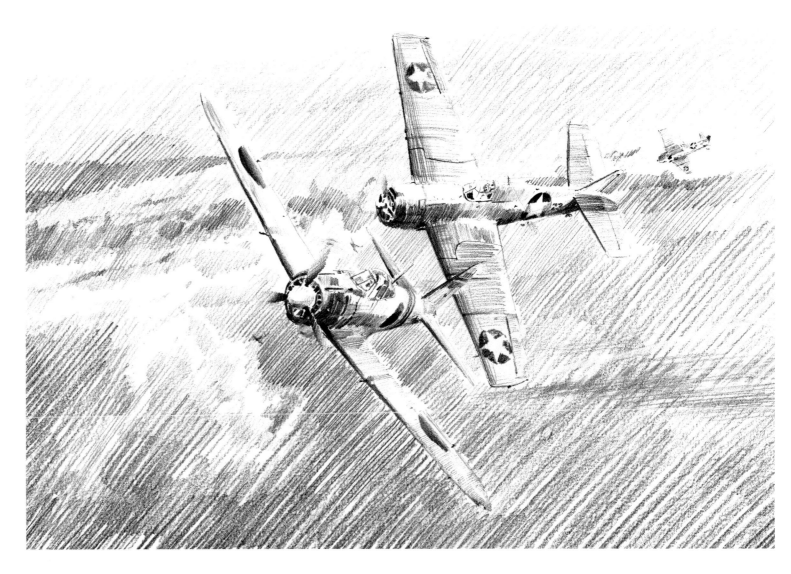

creative occupation and if an artist becomes overwhelmed by his obsession for accuracy and detail, all the inspiration goes out of his paintings. There has to be room for the artist to inject some of his own personality and ideas into his pictures, to dream a little as he works, to add some colour that perhaps was never there and to put his own interpretation upon events using all the imagination that he can muster. Only in this way can an artist breathe life into his paintings.

I had a letter not long ago from a very technically minded artist in which he went to great lengths to show me how I had some aircraft wrongly positioned in a particular painting. He included a series of

tracings showing perspective lines going in all directions, numerous carefully measured geometric angles, tangents and a lot of technical calculations. To add weight to his point he included a page from an old navy pilot's handbook showing by diagram exactly how my formation of aircraft should have appeared. Well, maybe he was right, but I did my best to explain to him that, as a fine art painter rather than a technical illustrator, I constantly look for ways to bring my aircraft to life so as to create an atmosphere of reality and this precluded any thought of painting in a format to coincide with government regulation! We had some friendly correspondence, but I think we were on different wave-lengths.

Not long after the US Navy and Marine Corps pilots had concluded their part in the successful Guadalcanal offensive, their Grumman F4F Wildcats were supplemented with the arrival of what many refer to as the finest carrier-based fighter of World War II – the Vought F4U Corsair. Named after a famous band of eighteenth-century pirates, the arrival of the F4U brought a new generation of ship-board fighters to the Pacific theatre and by the end of the war the Corsair achieved an incredible eleven-to-one victory ratio against the Japanese pilots. The oil sketch below shows this worthy fighter which, from the time it first flew in 1940 to the end of its production, saw over 10,000 aircraft constructed.

F–4U CORSAIR

In the collection of Mr and Mrs Jim Kettlety

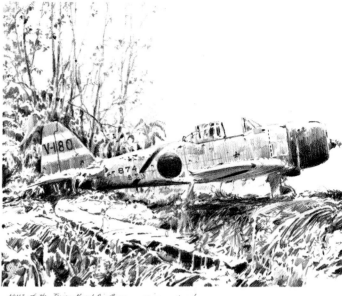

A6M2 of the Tainan Naval Air Group · going nowhere!

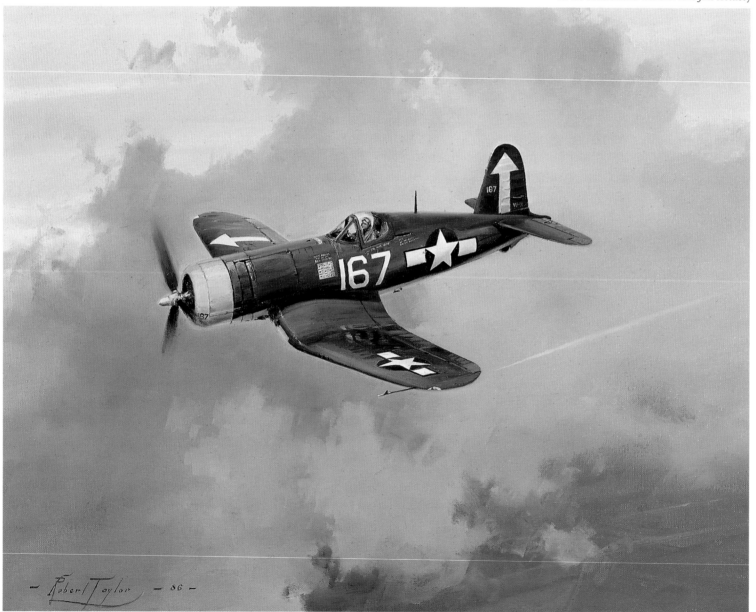

Robert Taylor – 86 –

I obtained plenty of good reference for Henderson Field from various ever-helpful museums, but none of the photographs showed the airstrip at the angle I wanted, so before starting the painting I spent much time redrawing the field and surrounding landscape to show the angle I needed.

When working with old photographs and maps, it is best to use these simply as a guide. Although it can be laborious, it usually pays dividends to reconstruct the subject by redrawing it from a different angle. Simply to copy a photograph is to fall into a trap: when looking at two-dimensional photographs, one sees a great deal less than the whole. With the aid of a number of supporting photographs, the preparation of a new drawing, especially when it is made from a different angle, ensures that the subject is more fully understood. The exercise alone forces a thorough investigation into the subject and sharpens the practice of perspective drawing.

In the case of Henderson Field, I changed the angle of the runway only about 10° from that in the main photograph used for reference, but this was enough to ensure that every other item in the picture had to be viewed at the same 10° change of angle. It took ages to complete the drawing to my satisfaction, but by the time I finished I knew that airfield inside-out.

Many of the dog-fights over Guadalcanal started at 20,000 feet or higher. Most aerial contests descend quite rapidly as they progress and in my painting the combatants are down to around 8,000 feet and probably close to running out of ammunition, indicating that we have a battle of pros on our hands.

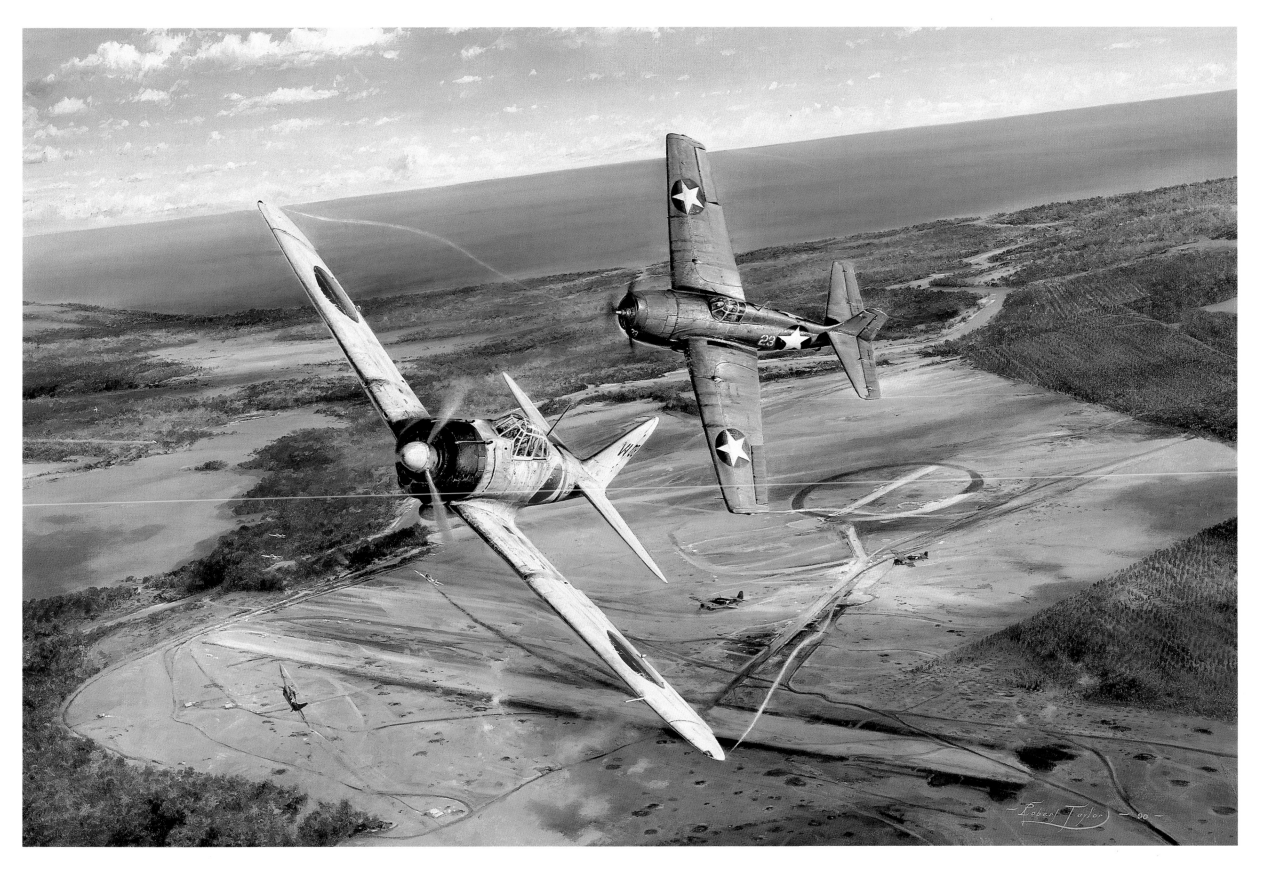

ZERO ENCOUNTER

In the collection of The Military Gallery

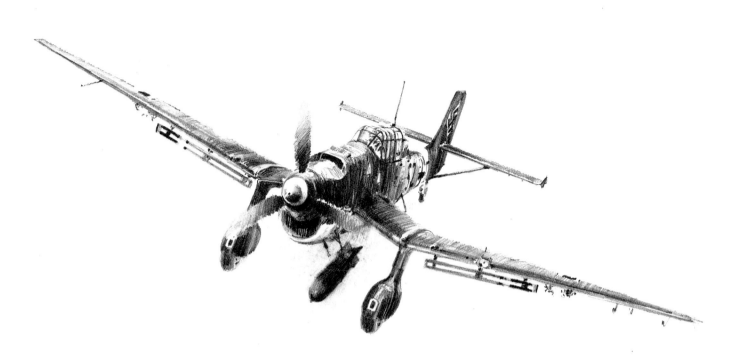

STUKA!

I don't often paint clean, neat and tidy aeroplanes. I like battle-weary, dirty, cordite-stained, mud-splattered, paint-chipped, well worn machines that look as if, although properly maintained, they are the oldest ones on the squadron. If they have got slots and flaps, struts and masts, fairings and trim tabs, oleos, ducts, cooling louvres and great big air scoops, I like them even better. If I can find an excuse to put a hole or two through an aileron or an elevator and still keep the beast flying, I'll do it. And I like big greenhouse-like glass canopies, of the sort I can slide open and get a good look at the colour of the pilot's eyes. The more bulges and bumps, conflicting angles and shapes, bits there are protruding and things hanging down, the more individual the aircraft becomes in my eyes, the more it reveals to me its own personality and the more I become attracted to it. We are talking about the Stuka!

Beauty is in the eye of the beholder. Talk to any aviation enthusiast and you will soon realise that there isn't an aeroplane built that somebody doesn't find beautiful. Certainly most of those which ever made their mark in aviation history seem to have been endowed with a certain charm, although I am sure there will be those who don't agree with me. 'What about the Stuka?' I hear some of you ask. A good question!

While the Spitfire, Mustang and Me109 are competing for the title of World War II's most beautiful aircraft, the Stuka is busy qualifying high on the list for the title at the other end of the scale. But wait a moment – does it?

Agreed, the Stuka was an extraordinary looking aeroplane, evil-looking perhaps, its cranked wings and spatted undercarriage giving it the appearance of some monstrous bird of prey, but the aircraft had an unmistakable and unique individualism that deserves some further evaluation. I ask you to consider its unusual qualifications and to make an artist-view appraisal with me. Let us start at the front and work towards the tail.

The nose area of the Stuka is quite magnificent. It has a gorgeously huge spinner which flares beautifully into the engine cowling, out of the side of which protrude a lovely line of exhaust ejector stubs and below these hangs a great big air scoop complete with an array of adjustable flaps at the rear. On top of the cowl is another air scoop, this one for the oil cooler, and just behind is an intriguing extractor flap.

A pair of huge talon-like wheel spats are suspended beneath the bird-like wings which have a collection of air-brakes, flaps and ailerons dangling off the trailing edges. (To add to these wing appendages, as if there weren't enough already, I have fitted 300-litre drop-tanks.)

Now let us study the truly magnificent cockpit area. It is massive, affording us a splendid view of what is going on inside. With the hood slid back we can see the pilot almost down to his waist, his armoured seat-back, a big anti-crash hoop, and behind that we get a good look at his radio operator/gunner crouching at the ready.

The tail section is classic, with lovely large control surfaces, bracing struts and faired mass balances on the tops of the elevators. Below hangs a nice big tail wheel.

And there we have it. Magnificently beautiful in its unaerodynamic ugliness; a true individual down to its last rivet. What more could an artist ask for?

The drawing below shows pilots of I/StG3 conferring after returning to their Sicilian airfield after a sortie against a convoy heading for Valletta, Malta, in 1941. During these attacks the Ju87 was usually assigned to pin-point specific targets, while the He111s and Ju88s saturated the area with larger bombs. The maximum range of the 'R' Stuka was rated at 779 miles at 13,124 feet, and it was these types which were used extensively against British shipping in the Mediterranean.

Supplies to the beleaguered island of Malta had reached a critical stage when on 23 March a convoy successfully reached Valletta harbour; however, even before unloading began, thirty Ju87s, escorted by Me109s, arrived overhead. In the ensuing battle two merchantmen were hit, though RAF Hurricanes and the ever-effective anti-aircraft gunners brought down eight of the Luftwaffe's force.

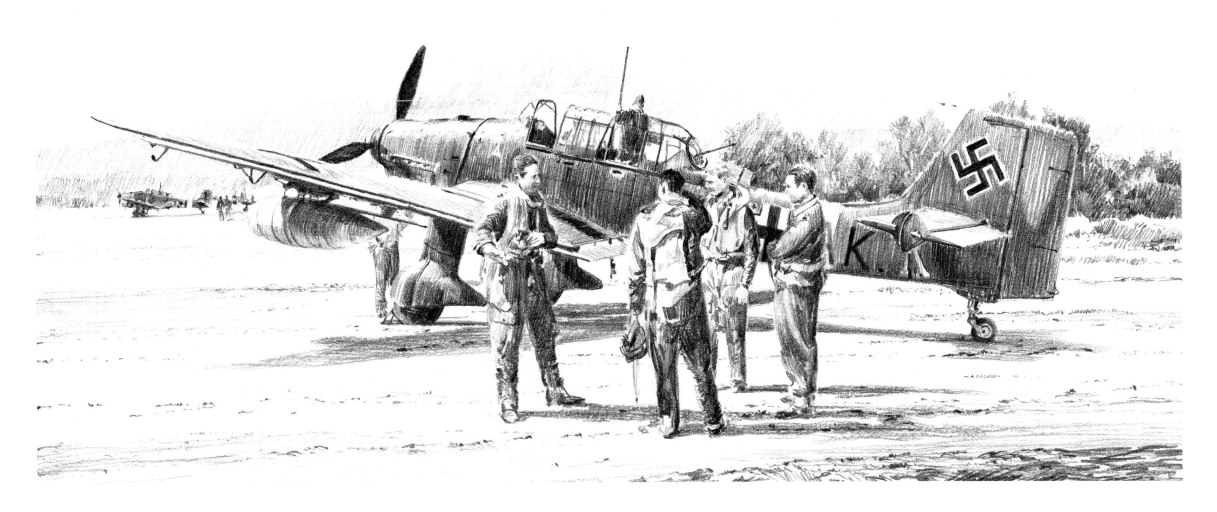

The detail from the painting below shows the three uppermost Stuka aircraft; they are reproduced here about the same size as I painted them on the original canvas. Close scrutiny will reveal that the brush-work on the aircraft is not nearly so sharply defined as it is on the nearest aircraft. This is not because of any difficulty I may have had in applying detailed work; quite the contrary. I have deliberately worked with a reasonably large brush so as to *avoid* painting in too defined a way, in order to create the illusion of distance in the picture.

In reality, the further one moves away from a subject the less sharply one is able to observe its detail as the subject disappears into the distance. To paint a high degree of detail therefore on these three Stukas would have been incorrect. The deliberate looseness of the brush-work, together with a softening of the colours, helps to place the aircraft at the right distance away from the nearest aircraft. The technique which helps to create the illusion of distance is carried through to the mountains in the background, where there is almost no clear definition visible.

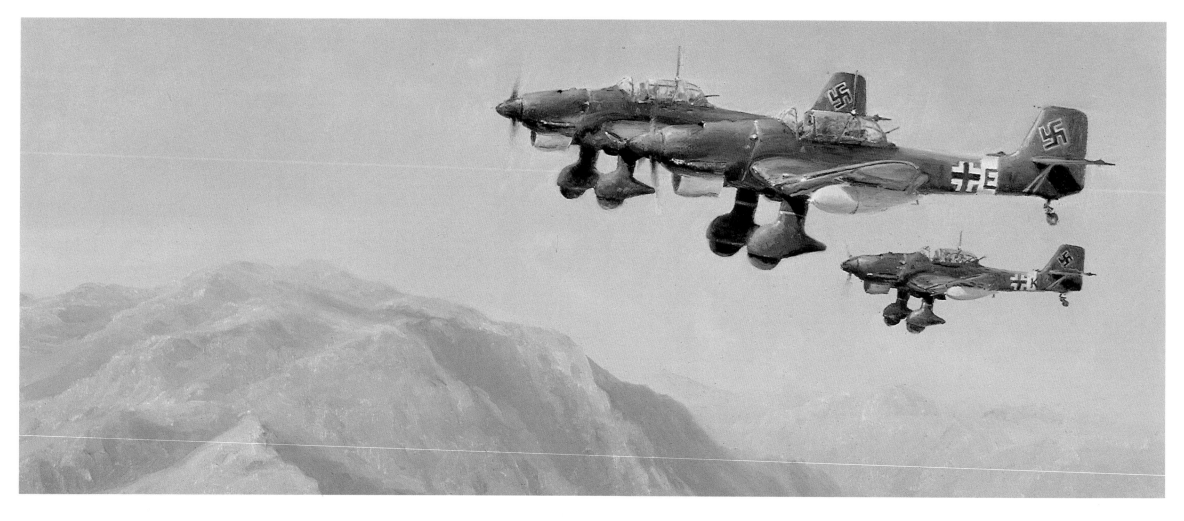

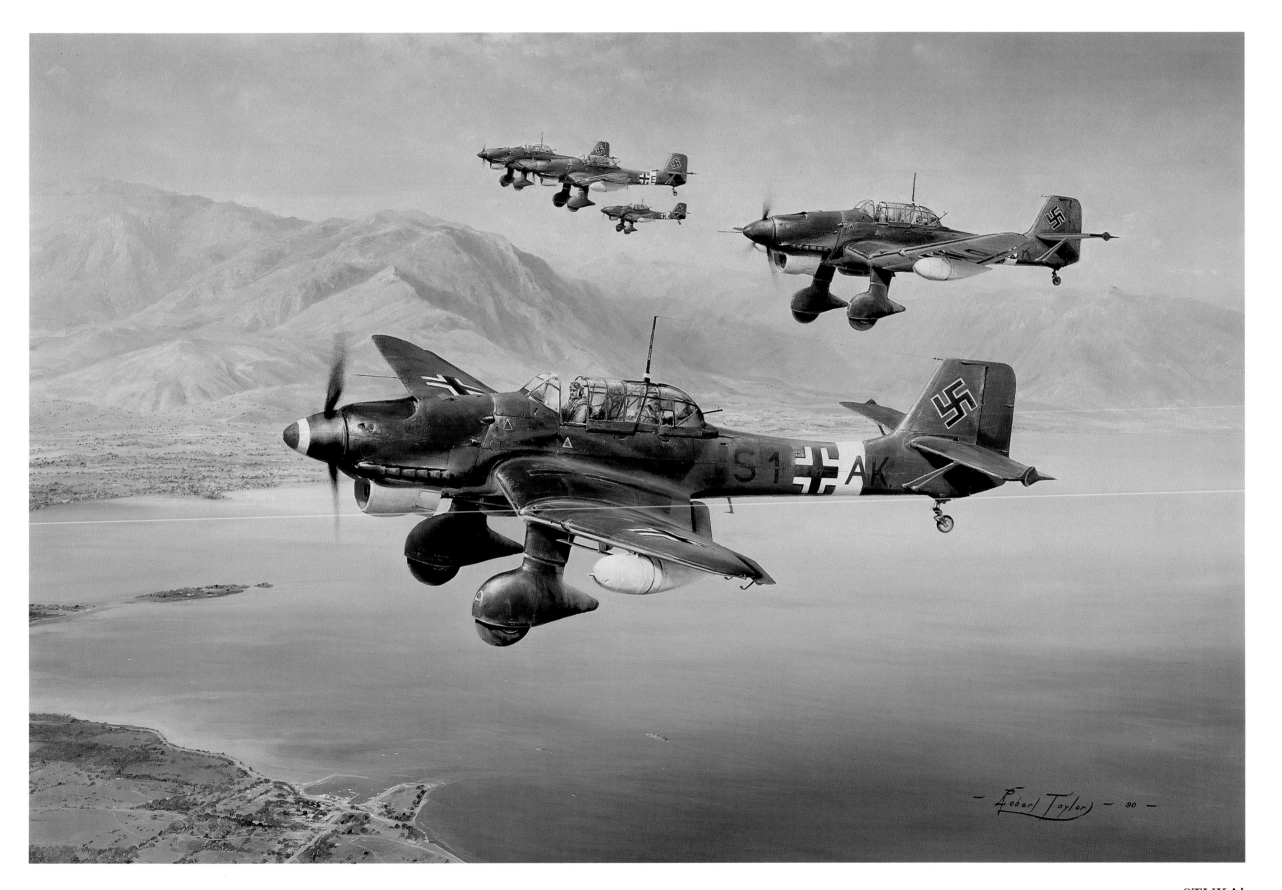

STUKA!

In the collection of Mr Wolfgang Rohm

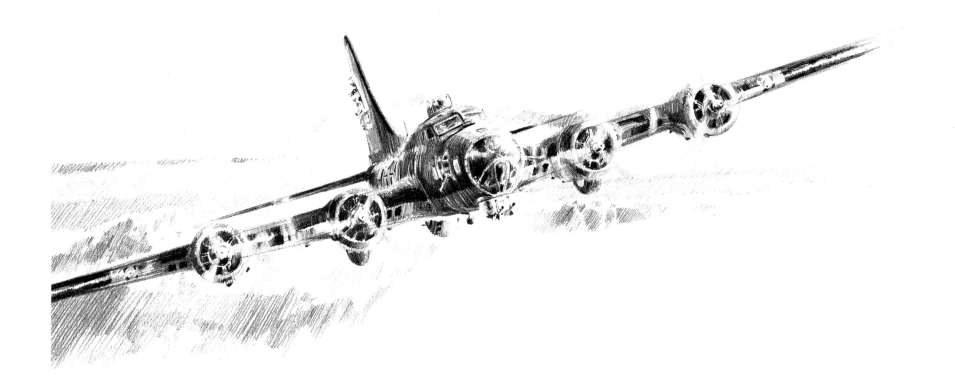

MISSION COMPLETED

76

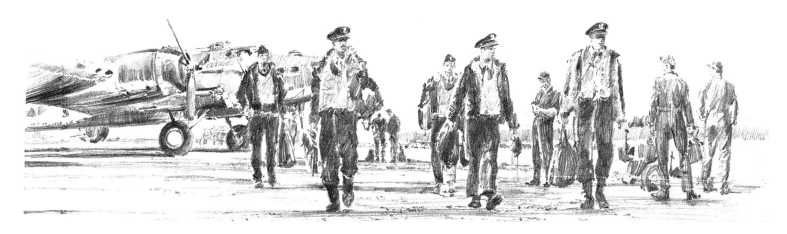

Between 1942 and 1945 the English landscape became as familiar to many USAAF aircrews as it was to locals who lived there. To the crews of the American 8th Airforce, for a vital period in their lives, England was home. The rolling green pastures and golden harvest fields were, to the returning battle-weary air crews, a sight that became everlastingly dear to their hearts. I have spoken to scores of men who flew the great warbirds from airfields deep in the English countryside, and know the affection they have for this 'green and pleasant land'. I approached

the painting of *Mission Completed* with this very much in my mind, the aim being to portray the final moments of a mission: a battle-torn B-17 Flying Fortress makes its final approach, safely home from the ravages of war, descends into a scene of peace and tranquillity, a haven of respite for its crew – at least until tomorrow.

I had previously painted some aviation pictures viewed from ground level, taking in complete landscapes, and they had seemed to work quite well. There are some composition problems with this type

of painting, not the least being that it is necessary to view the aircraft from beneath in order to ensure that a realistic perspective is maintained. Looking up under an aeroplane does not always produce the most aesthetically pleasing aspect. This problem is only partially overcome where an aircraft is shown making an approach. Careful choice of the viewing angle is of great importance, and the precise positioning of the aircraft in relation to the ground is critical if the painting is going to work.

Having already decided that I wanted to paint the last moments of a B-17 combat mission, my first task was to select a suitable landscape, and to construct this so as to help the composition once the aircraft were positioned. I wanted also to paint a powerful sky and in order to allow myself enough room to do this, leaving plenty of space for the main B-17 in the picture, I elected to position the horizon at about one third of the height of the canvas. The towering, ever-changing cumulus clouds which build up during the afternoons and roll across the English summer sky are an endless fascination for me, and this painting gave me the opportunity to indulge myself.

I suppose most artists harbour the dream that their paintings will stand the test of time, and hope that at least a few of their works might last long enough to give some future generations an insight into the past.

Simply to paint a picture of a classic aircraft from its most beautiful angle is not enough to convey atmosphere from the period, and I believe that to make the extra effort to research and then paint all the ancillary subjects that are necessary to convey this atmosphere is of some considerable importance if a painting is to have any merit.

One way to date a painting is to paint a landscape. The landscape is ever-changing and in rural England, for example, it is for the most part quite changed today from how it was fifty years ago. Many of the old hedgerows have gone, to make way for larger fields to accommodate modern farm machinery. Trees, too, in some areas have made way to progress and in the case of the majestic elm, which John Constable painted into immortality, have disappeared because of disease.

Grain was harvested differently fifty years ago, the binder being the modern agricultural machine of the 1930s and 40s. These contraptions, the early ones being horse-drawn, cut the straws and bundled them into sheaves that were tied with a single twine. Collected by farm workers, they were placed, usually six at a time, into stooks and left to stand for a few days in the summer sun to dry, before being collected and placed into corn ricks to await the threshing team later in the year.

The binders always cut the fields by moving from the outside towards the centre, so each row was shorter than the previous one. This meant that, as the farm workers gathered the sheaves, the resulting pattern of stooks became irregular, exacerbated by the irregular shape most fields had to start with.

All this might sound a little irrelevant to an aviation artist, but if one is to paint a B-17 coming in over a wheat-field in 1940, he had better know what a wheat-field looked like in 1940. Interestingly, it is not difficult to see today exactly how it used to be, because there are a few farms in the depths of rural England where they still harvest 1940 style – binder, stooks and all! In order to paint *Mission Completed* it was not only important to know all this, but fascinating and great fun to research into this golden era of our history.

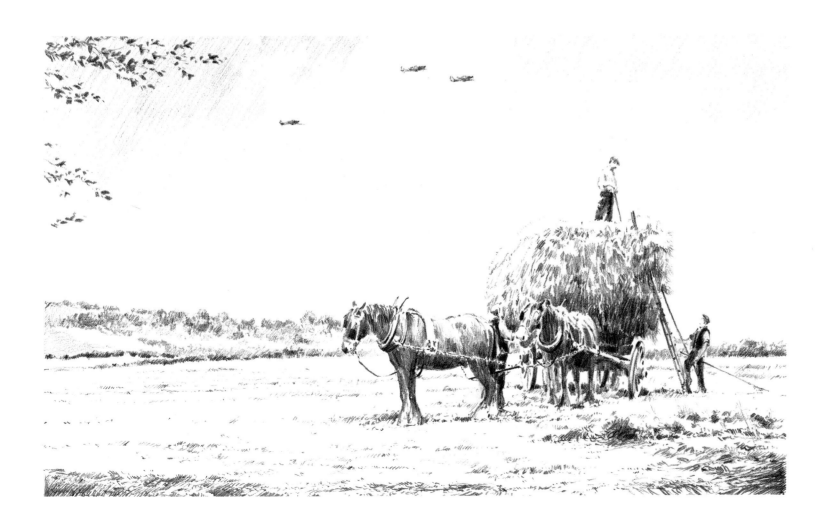

Boeing named their B-17 bomber aptly when they called it the Flying Fortress. No other aircraft that I can recall ever had so much armament, the fuselage fairly bristling with machine-guns from nose to tail.

P-51 OIL SKETCH

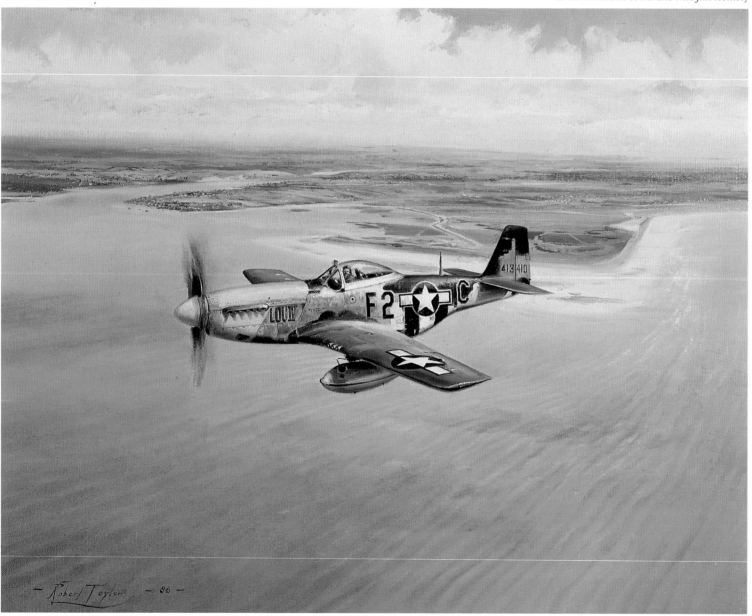

It was just as well, for the task the Army Air Force had in mind for this formidable aeroplane meant that it would need all the self-protection it could get.

The Royal Air Force had abandoned daylight bombing as far too hazardous well before the B-17s and their crews arrived in England. Fighters were not available with the range capable of escorting bombers across Europe and home again, so the British bomber crews plied their trade under cover of darkness. The introduction of the heavily defended B-17 changed all that, but this new challenge was met in earnest by the crack fighter squadron of the Luftwaffe based on the Western Front.

In theory, the combined fire-power of a group of B-17 Fortresses would devastate any opposing fighters, enabling all but the odd unlucky bomber to sail majestically on to the target and home again. Like so many theories, sound as they may look on paper, the reality is often quite a different story; and so it was when the B-17s went to war.

The aggressive German fighters quickly found ways of making successful attacks – one popular manoeuvre being to come in from the beam at high speed and, streaming cannon and machine-gun fire, flip on to his back, making an inverted pass beneath the lumbering bomber. The pilot then pulled the stick into his stomach and dived out of the immediate vicinity to prepare for another attack. From start to finish the hapless gunners aboard the B-17s had but a few brief seconds to sight their target and squeeze off a few rounds. Brave as they were, the crews of the B-17s were unable to keep the enemy fighters at bay and their losses were appalling until the advent of the long range fighter escort later in the war.

I have talked to many fighter pilots from both sides who flew missions both in escort to, and in offence of, the bomber crews of the USAAF and RAF, and, not surprisingly, without exception they have an enduring respect for the courage and fortitude of bomber aircrews.

The oil sketch on this page shows a P-51D Mustang of the 361st Fighter Group. The same aircraft appears again in my painting *Home Run*. The P-51 was the ultimate bomber-escort fighter aircraft of World War II.

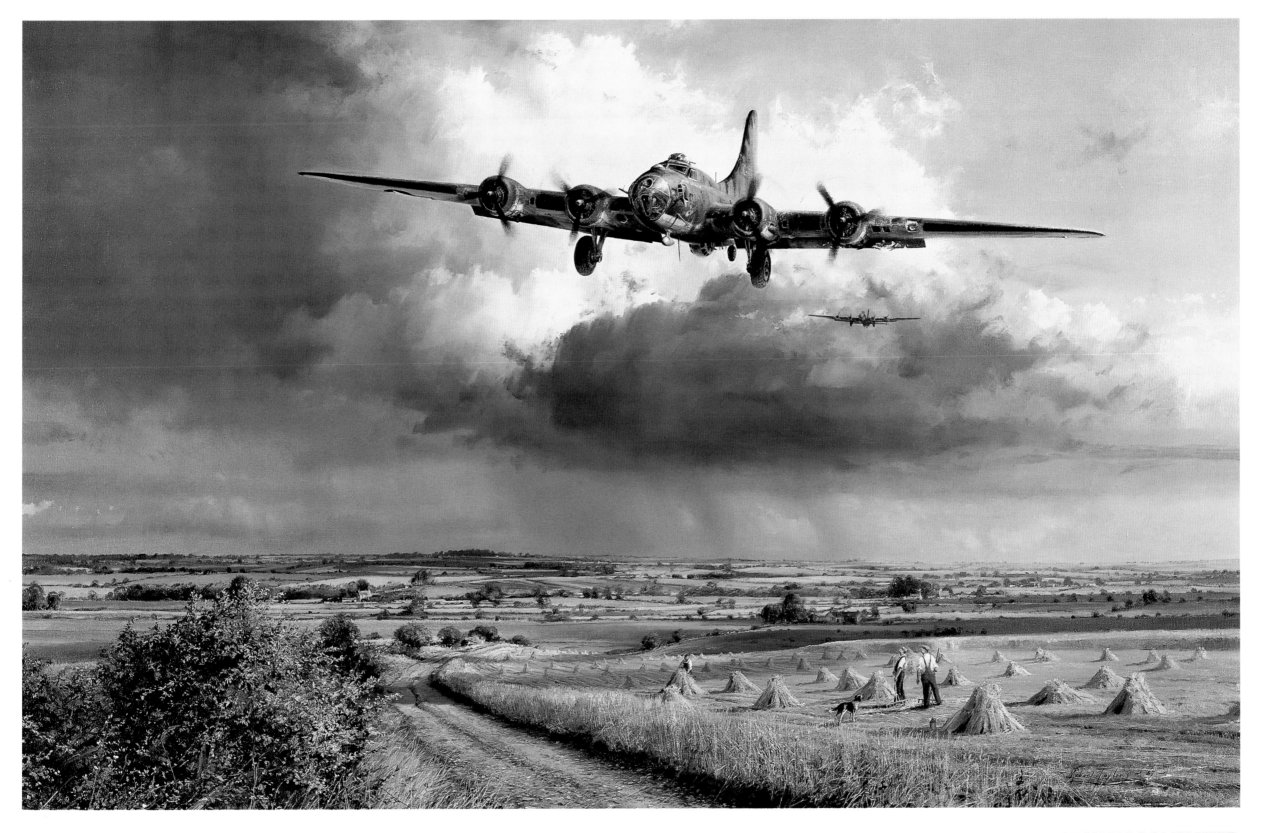

MISSION COMPLETED
In the collection of Virginia Bader

LIGHTNING STRIKE

There were very few successful aircraft with the radical twin tail-boom design. Certainly, the only one to have had any significant combat history was the Lockheed P-38 Lightning, and, having such a unique configuration, it provides the artist with some very interesting shapes to work with. This strange-looking flying device first appeared as early as 1938. It always seemed to me as if its designer, in a quest to achieve more speed, had the idea of bolting two aircraft together and, forgetting at the time that he needed a pilot to fly the device, added a little cabin in the middle as an afterthought; there he sat the pilot in isolated splendour, apparently having little to do with all the important parts of the aeroplane. In fact, of course, this unique flying device proved its worth in combat; indeed it was the first USAAF aircraft to shoot down a Luftwaffe plane and went on to see action in North Africa, the Mediterranean and the Pacific, as well as Europe.

Because of its unique configuration, the P-38 is a fascinating aircraft for an artist to portray: two huge engines, each flared into its own sleek fuselage with great bulging waist-radiators half-way back; strange-looking exhaust outlets above the engines which left a trail of burnt paint and carbon deposits down the length of the bodywork all the way to the tail. The cockpit capsule is gorgeously streamlined, the pilot seated high in a huge bubble canopy that provided a view over his engines to left and right. At the back is what must have been the biggest tail-plane and elevator assembly of World War II. (I was told by a P-38 pilot that, on his first operational mission, looking into his rear view mirror, he mistook the upper and lower mass balances on the elevator for an enemy aircraft on his tail. He went into the most violent and spectacular series of evasive manoeuvres and only when he saw that his 'assailant' was still positioned on his tail in exactly the same place did he realise that he had been trying to evade part of his own aeroplane.) With all its unique features, the P-38 is a really enjoyable aircraft to paint, but I have found that it is quite difficult to get good movement into a painting showing this aircraft. Maybe this is because of its unusual shape. Viewed from the side it is very sleek, but the special character of the P-38 Lightning is provided by its twin boom configuration and I feel that this feature should always be emphasised when painting the P-38. It would be taking the easy way out to paint a side view, so one simply has to find a way around the problem.

Looking for ways to emphasise movement in a painting is not always easy. Where the picture depicts aircraft in flight one is not always seeking to get the effect of great speed, but always trying to obtain a feeling of movement. Simply to paint an aircraft in the sky is not enough to achieve a feeling that the machine is actually moving. In fact, unless one consciously sets out to achieve movement in a painting, the aircraft will end up looking entirely static, as if it is suspended in thin air and going nowhere.

If one looks at the beautifully air-brushed technical illustrations of aeroplanes found in books – and some are quite superb – the static effect of these illustrations is the aim of the artist. In my case, armed only with brushes and tubes of paint, my prime task is to try to make my aircraft actually 'fly' on the canvas.

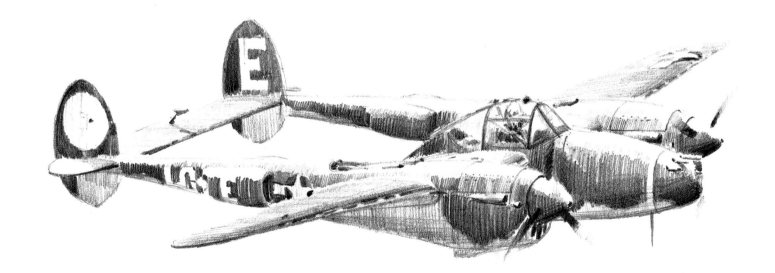

In reality, if an aircraft ceases to move forward, it drops out of the sky like a stone. I have seen some paintings where the aircraft look as if that is exactly what is about to happen. I don't wish to seem unkind about other paintings – that is not the purpose of the remark – but simply to illustrate the point and emphasise the difficulty all aviation artists have in achieving this effect, and to reiterate the importance of addressing the problem with each painting we do.

I think about movement all the time. Almost every part of every painting I do that features aircraft in flight is painted in some way with the thought of making my aircraft appear to move on the canvas. In the case of *Lightning Strike* and the P-38s, I found it particularly challenging.

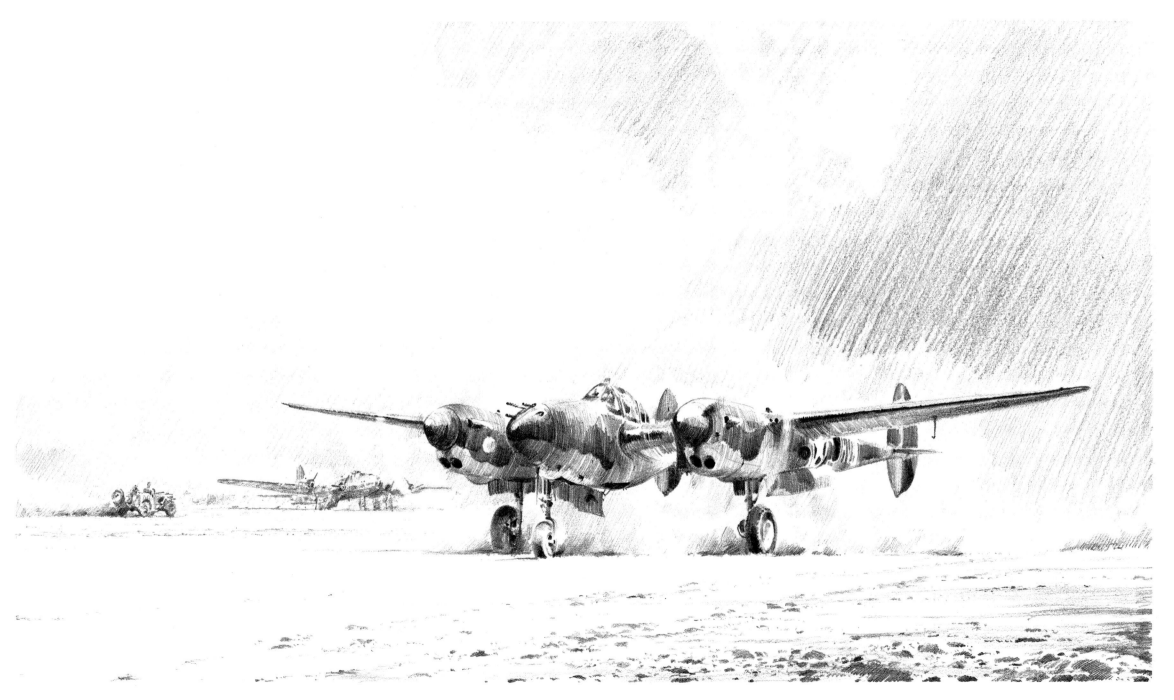

Dubbed by the Germans 'Der Gabelschwarz Teufel' – the Fork-Tailed Devil – the distinctive P-38 Lightning saw combat in Europe, North Africa and Pacific theatres. After an inauspicious start to its combat career, the Lightning was developed into an outstanding long-range fighter bomber. Its endurance of 1,100 miles was instrumental to that historic occasion when, some 550 miles away from their Pacific island base, P-38 pilots intercepted and shot down the aircraft that was carrying the Japanese Commander Admiral Yamamoto. In Europe its great range enabled it to escort the B-17s from the UK to Germany and back, helping to reduce the losses on the daylight raids by some 75 per cent. The P-38 looked fast, and it was, having a top speed in excess of 400 miles per hour which made it one of the quickest aircraft of World War II.

In the detail below, which shows a battle-hardened P-38 in the European theatre, many of the features of the aircraft that are discussed on the previous pages may be seen, including the elevator mass balances which my friend thought was an enemy aircraft on his tail!

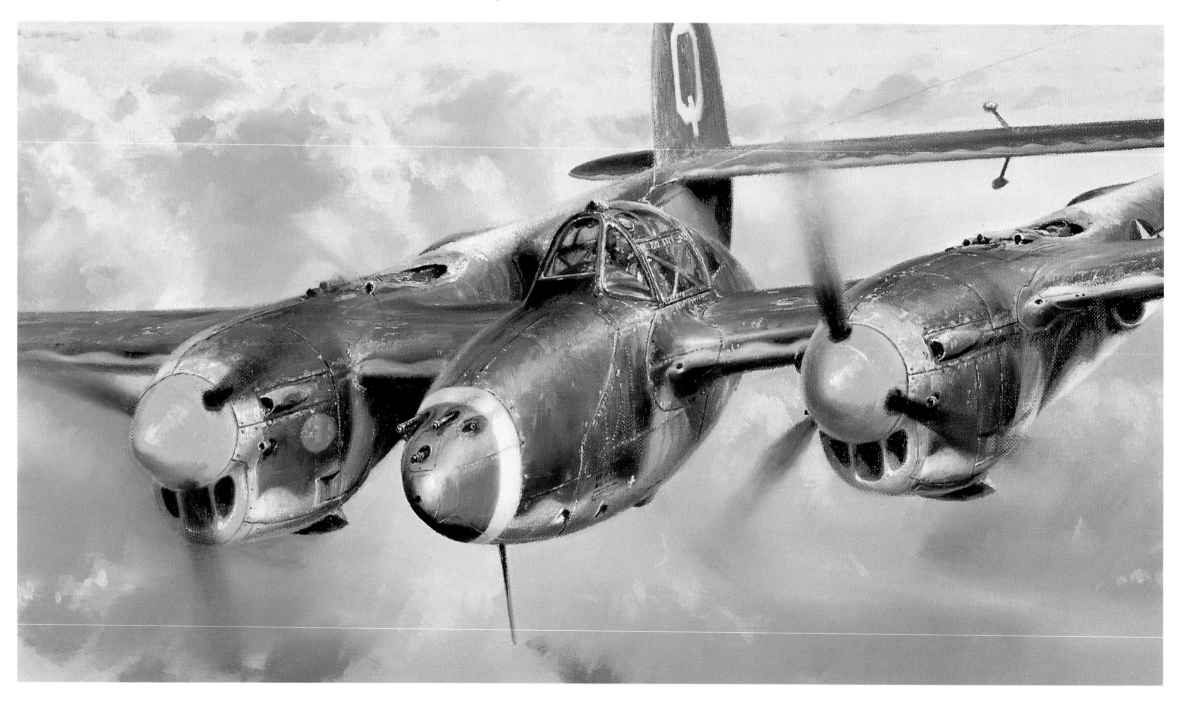

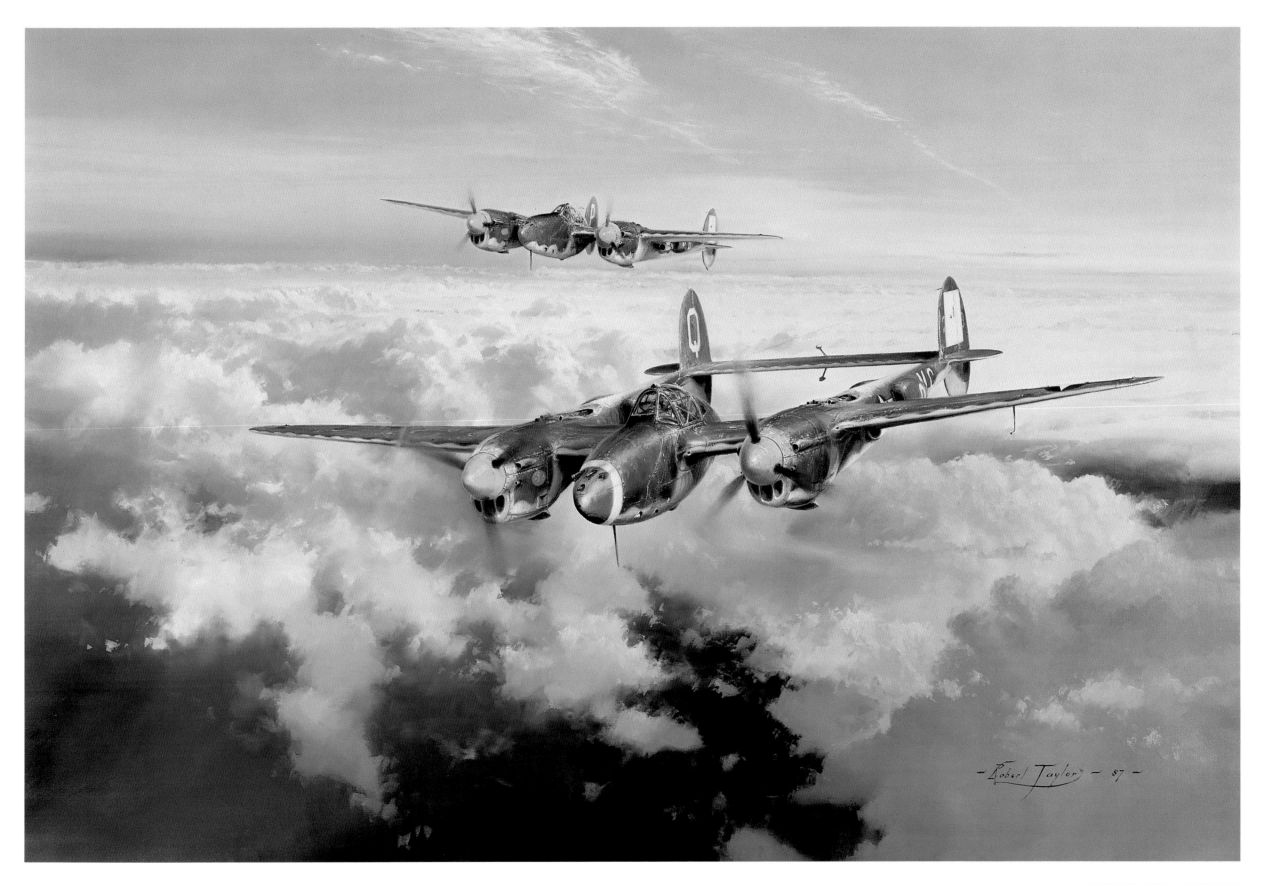

LIGHTNING STRIKE

In the collection of Dr Richard V. Erkenbeck

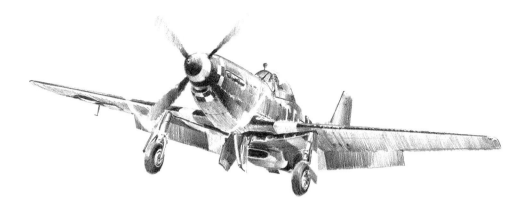

HOME RUN

I am often asked by aviation enthusiasts if there is one aeroplane that I enjoy painting more than any other. Actually there isn't. In truth, I usually feel that the aeroplane I enjoy painting most is the one I am working on at the time. Some are more difficult than others and therefore present a greater challenge; some, to my way of thinking, have more character or personality than others and in this respect perhaps are more enjoyable, but the fact is that I enjoy painting aeroplanes so much that I never give much thought to favourites.

Certainly, some aircraft impress me greatly and a few, to my artist's eye, approach perfection. The North American P-51 Mustang is one of these. 'If it looks right it will fly right'; never was this adage more appropriate than when it is applied to this lovely fighter, and it is without doubt an aeroplane that I shall never tire of portraying.

The remarkable P-51 was originally developed to a British specification in the dark days of 1940 before the United States had joined the war. Looking for a new fighter aircraft which could be built in numbers at factories out of reach of the ever-attendant Luftwaffe, the RAF contracted with North American to build the P-51. Within four months of the ink drying on the signatures, on the 26 October 1940, the first prototype took to the air and by 1941 production models were in service with the RAF.

So much has been written about this outstanding fighter that it is difficult for me to say anything new; however, there are a few things about its development which I find fascinating. Initially the P-51 was powered by an unsupercharged Allison engine which was unable to do justice to the wonderful aerodynamic airframe. However, even with that disadvantage, all the pilots who flew the early models loved the handling characteristics – a sure sign that an aircraft has a future. Its performance above 15,000 feet, where the air started to thin, was disappointing, but at low altitudes the early P-51s acquitted themselves well against the low-level hit-and-run tactics of the Fw190s, and also in the ground attack role making strikes against enemy installations across the Channel.

When in 1942 the two-stage supercharged Merlin engine was fitted, the P-51 Mustang came into its own, and as the aircraft was modified, improved and developed, finally culminating in the P-51D model, it not only became the best all-round single-seat fighter of the war, but also contended strongly with the Spitfire for the mantle of being the most beautiful.

The year 1990 saw the fiftieth anniversary of the P-51 Mustang and I was delighted to be commissioned to paint this lovely little fighter to commemorate the occasion.

We don't see too many P-51s flying in Europe, but I did get the chance to watch a beautiful Mustang during the making of the film *The Memphis Belle*. While David Puttnam and company were busy filming Matthew Modine and others climbing in and out of static aircraft, I walked away from the five B-17s on the set to view the scene from a distance. Suddenly, behind me a P-51 roared down the runway, taking off a few feet away, and immediately snapped into a steep climbing turn. I don't know if he was trying to impress anybody, but he certainly did me! I spent a happy couple of hours sketching this beautiful P-51 after he returned to earth, and these drawings were of great use to me when I came to paint *Home Run*.

During the early stages of the preparation I talked a good deal to an old friend, Colonel James Goodson. Jim was one of the early Eagle Squadron pilots, subsequently a Fourth Fighter Group Ace and a great P-51 exponent. It was at this time that he kindly agreed to write some notes for my book about flying the P-51 in combat.

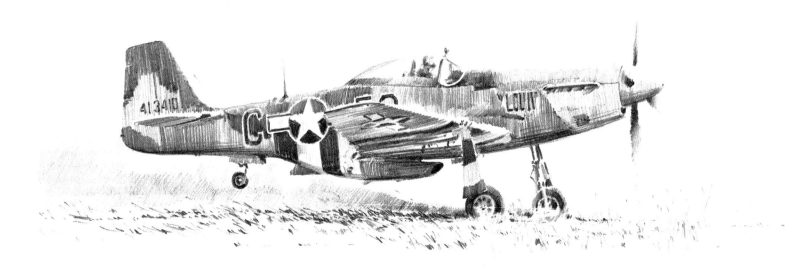

FLYING THE P-51 MUSTANG IN COMBAT

By Colonel James Goodson

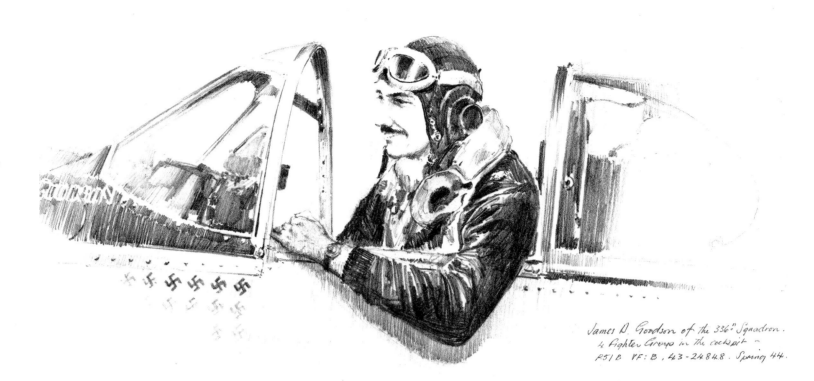

James D. Goodson of the 336th Squadron. 4 Fighter Group in the cockpit – P51D, YF:B, 43-24848. Spring 44.

When we transferred from the RAF Eagle Squadrons to the 4th Fighter Group of the US Air Force, we had confidently expected to be equipped with the P-51 Mustangs. Instead, we got P-47 Thunderbolts. When the first ones arrived, we stared up in disbelief at the massive 7-ton machine. After our little Spitfires it looked like a Stirling bomber!

On one of our first missions flying Thunderbolts, Don Blakeslee shot down an Fw190 and a little later, he and I and my Wingman, Bob Wehrman, dived down on a swarm of Fw190s that were coming up from their base at St Omer. In the ensuing mêlée we accounted for about five of them. We realised that the Germans could no longer get away by out-diving us. But as Blakeslee said, 'It damn well ought to be able to dive – it sure as hell can't climb!'

Perhaps he had reason to be a little irritated. We had had to nurse him back over the Channel to Manston, where we counted 64 cannon shots in his oil-covered P-47.

We had to admit that the 'Thunderjug' could take a lot of punishment and, considering its size, it was surprisingly manoeuvrable, but we still begged our Generals to get us the P-51.

We were lucky with our Generals in the 8th Air Force. They gave us our P-51s and although some of us had previously flown only a few hours in the Mustang, she was such a lady that we had no problems converting to her. And it was thanks to the P-51 that we were able to escort the bombers to any target, even including a shuttle raid from Debden in Essex to Poltava in Russia, to Foggia in Italy and back to Debden.

It was also the P-51 that enabled us to escort the first raids over Berlin. Someone once asked Goering when he knew that Germany had lost the war. His answer was: 'When I first saw those red-nosed Mustangs over Berlin.'

I was soon given an opportunity to test the Mustang against an Fw190 in manoeuvrability at altitude and in the dive. We were escorting B-17s over Magdeburg at about 30,000 feet when I saw two Fw190s coming in on a diving attack on the bombers. I had a slight height advantage and was soon closing on them when the number two suddenly broke off his attack and went into a vertical dive. The number one continued his attack until I was almost within range of him, then, at just the right moment, broke into my

attack so violently that it was all I could do to follow him.

I whipped into a tight turn as fast as I could and pulled so hard that I was blacking out. The plane was close to stalling, but still I couldn't gain on him; as I looked over my shoulder I saw that he, in fact, was gaining on me. I could see him easily, the grey fuselage, the black crosses on the wings and, above all, the sinister nose, not yet pointing far enough ahead of me to give enough deflection, but steadily creeping forward.

I was using every ounce of my strength, sweating, gasping, choking, my oxygen mask slipping down on my nose and mouth, and my body was crumpled by the force of the turn. I knew I had only one hope. I let my right hand drop to feel for the flap lever. I found it and let down about 5 degrees of flap.

It worked. I began to out-turn him and was able to pull the turn tighter and to start to gain on him. But just as I was able to get enough deflection on him and my thumb closed on the trigger, he saw his danger. He slammed his stick into the forward corner and dived for the deck.

I should have caught him then, but the flaps that had just saved my life now saved his. By the time I got the flaps in again, he was getting away from me, but still only for a few seconds, before I started to gain on him in a vertical dive. I didn't dare open fire before I had him well in my sights. I had already been mixing it with other German fighters and knew I must be low on ammunition. What's more, glancing

at my watch, I saw that I should have turned for home ten minutes earlier.

The 190 had now flattened out on the deck. I was still gaining on him, but he was heading east, taking me further from home. Just in range, I squinted into my gun-sight and gave him a long burst. I thought I saw hits and fired again. Nothing happened. I had to turn for home. It later transpired that the pilot flying that Fw190 was none other than General Adolf Galland, the famous German Fighter Ace and General of the Luftwaffe Fighter Command.

The Mustang was not only equal to a 109 or 190 in the turn, it was superior in speed, both straight and level, and in climb and dive, provided it was not carrying its enormous full load of fuel.

There have been tales of Mustangs crashing on take-off. The fact that it could take off at all with two 108 gallon droppable tanks suspended under the wings, in addition to every available internal inch being used for fuel tanks, was remarkable! But, inevitably, if one did not take off in a straight line, the fuel sloshing around was likely to cause problems.

Once the external tanks were dropped, however, the plane handled beautifully and had no vices. That it had such superior performance miles from base and could escort the daylight bombers wherever they went was, in my opinion, one of the most important factors in our victory – an opinion shared by my friend, Adolf Galland.

I have painted the P-51 Mustang a number of times and in the preparation for *Home Run* I was looking for an angle which would be different from anything I had done previously.

One of my earlier paintings, *Fourth Fighter Patrol*, illustrated below, became quite well known after Jim Goodson and I were interviewed by an American nationwide TV channel – I can't remember which one – while we discussed the painting during the opening of my exhibition at the National Air and Space Museum. Jim, who has lived in England for a number of years, had flown to Washington DC to attend the opening ceremony and the American press took the opportunity to grab him while he was visiting his native country. His best-selling book *Tumult In The Clouds* had just been published and as one of the USAAF's top-scoring Aces, he is a popular personality. Jim Goodson was kind enough to say at the time that *Fourth Fighter Patrol* was his favourite painting featuring his favourite aircraft.

FOURTH FIGHTER PATROL

In the collection of Mr Nick Maggos

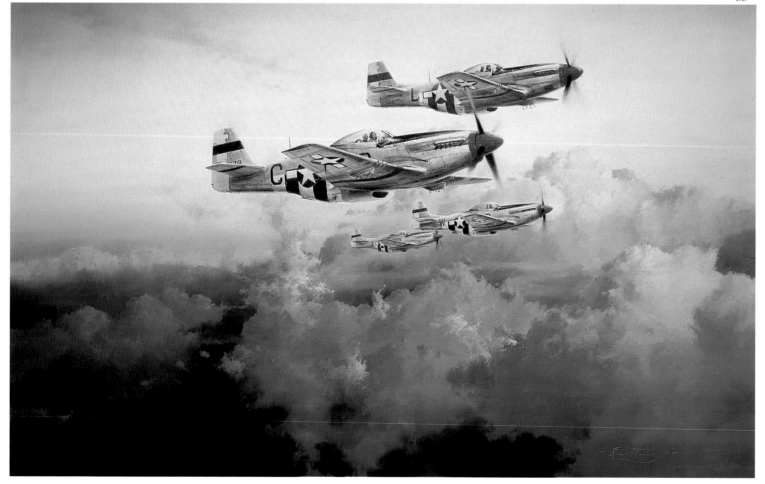

I had previously painted the P-51 in all sorts of attitudes, at all sorts of altitudes, but never at low-level, so I decided that to celebrate its fiftieth anniversary I would paint a happy scene with P-51s playfully charging through the Rhineland on their way back from a combat mission. In fact the attitude of the aircraft was inspired by some film footage I had seen showing P-51s air racing at Reno in Nevada. The particular clip showed a group of P-51s dicing with each other as they banked steeply around a pylon coming towards the camera. I thought this looked so dramatic that I would sketch a small group of aircraft in a similar attitude and find a suitable piece of landscape to fit the composition.

At any given time, I have references on file in my studio showing landscapes which I have been attracted to on my various travels. Some are sketches and some are photographs that I have taken. The particular landscape I used for *Home Run* is one I had wanted to use for a number of previous paintings, but on each occasion the shapes had not quite fitted my requirement. It was, however, perfect for the landscape I wanted behind my P-51s. The shape of the river was ideal, allowing the low-level speeding P-51s to bank around the bend, following the flow of the river as they look for 'targets of opportunity'.

I felt it appropriate to portray the 'D' model for this celebratory painting, for that was the ultimate development of this supreme fighter, but I also wanted to include at least one P-51B. These earlier models continued to fly to the end of the war, and although they were not perhaps quite so glamorous to look at as their later versions, they were nevertheless almost as good an aircraft. I checked with Jim Goodson to make sure that they would have flown together in 1945: 'Hell yes, Robert, we flew anything and everything that would fly during the Battle of the Rhine.' The P-51B is the middle one.

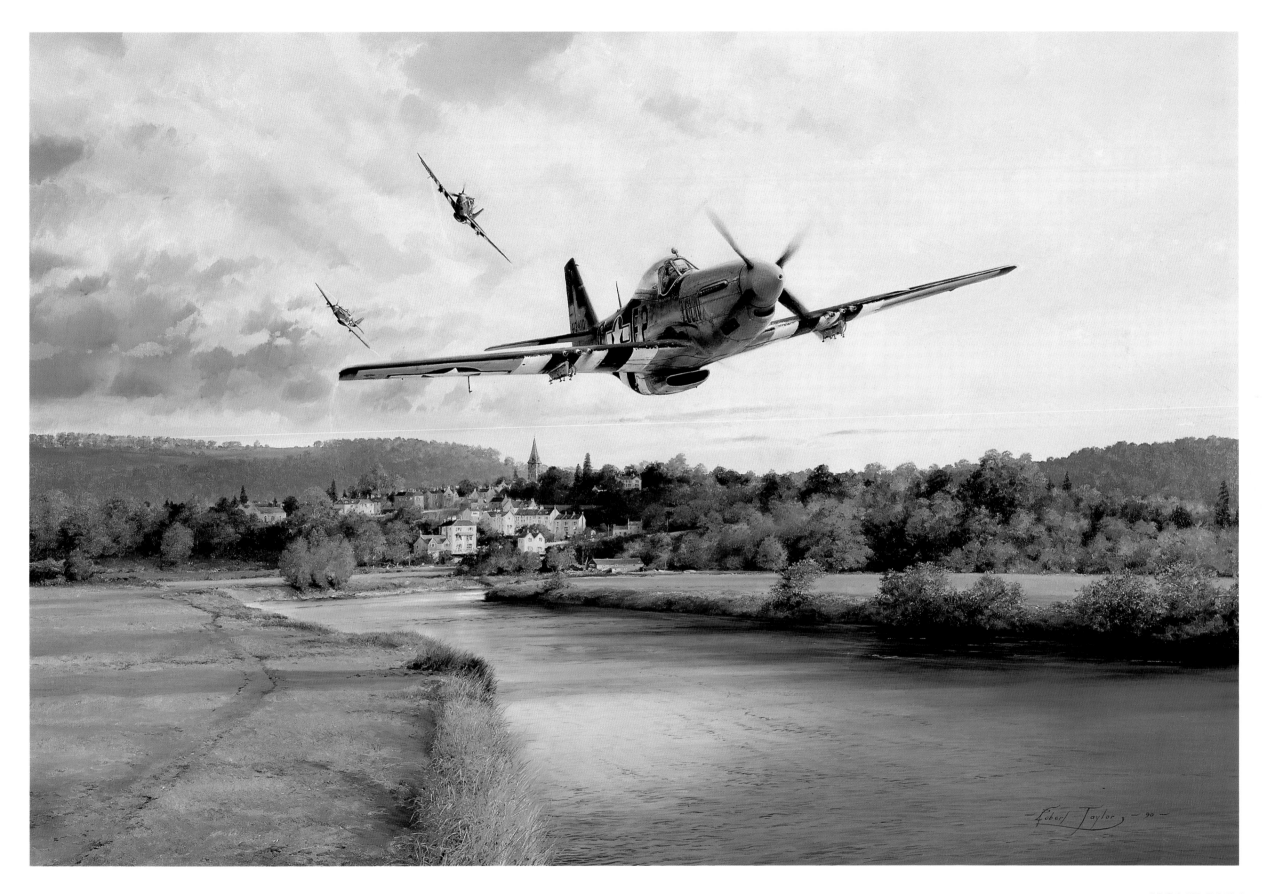

HOME RUN

In the collection of Dr and Mrs Jeffrey Walker

RETURN FROM SCHWEINFURT

One day during conversation with Air Vice Marshal Johnnie Johnson I asked him if, of all his operational missions in World War II, there was a single combat which remained foremost in his mind. In talking to one of the all-time great fighter pilots, I expected to hear about some epic duel with an Me109 or Fw190 high over the Channel or Northern France. His reply was immediate. He needed no time to think about it and what he told me came as quite a surprise: 'For me, 17 August 1943 was a day I shall never forget.' He went on to describe the events.

On that day Johnnie Johnson had led his Canadian Spitfire Wing off from Kenley, flown to Bradwell Bay to refuel and made rendezvous with two combat wings of B-17s en route to attack the Messerschmitt factory at Regensburg and ball-bearing factories at Schweinfurt. The Regensburg force, led by the legendary 35 year old Commander of the 30th Group, Curtis LeMay, would make their attack and fly on to North Africa, while the Schweinfurt bombers would return to England.

Johnnie's Wing picked up the Fortress formations over the North Sea, took up their escort positions a few thousand feet higher and down-sun over the bombers, and flew with them to the Dutch border. Then, because of the Spitfire's limited range, they had to return to base, leaving them escorted only by a few squadrons of P-47s who, after a few minutes, also had to return to England to refuel. The B-17s were left to make the four hour flight to Schweinfurt and back alone against the flak and the crack fighter squadrons of the Luftwaffe.

After refuelling at Bradwell, the Wing took off again and over Belgium, four hours after they had left the Fortresses, they could see them coming from a distance of 20 miles or more. It was a sight which left an indelible impression upon the Allied Air Force's top-scoring fighter pilot. 'Heading into the setting sun, which at their height of 23,000 feet was still well above the horizon, the B-17s, their windscreens glittering in the cold clear air, thundered westward. It was like the return of the cavalry!'

About ten miles separated the two Combat Wings as they made their way home. For four hours they had been pounded by flak and had fought a running battle with fighters who had pressed home wave after wave of attacks. At the rendezvous between Liège and Antwerp the enemy fighter attacks had intensified as the depleted bomber formations fought their way home. Above the bombers, Me109s and Fw190s made white contrails which disappeared as they hurtled down into the warmer air. Heavy flak burst stained the sky; stragglers, miles behind their parent formations, were being picked off. Hub Zemke's 56th Fighter Group P-47s fought valiantly over the rear combat wing, but at the limit of their endurance and as the Spitfires arrived, they had to withdraw. The battle moved across the map at 180 miles per hour, its course plotted by flame, smoke, parachutes and debris from disintegrating aircraft. 'Yet they still came on – these ragged yet somehow majestic formations, closing the gap between us until they were almost beneath my Wing and I was able, at long last, to lead my Canadians into the arena.'

Such a moving account of what was one of the epic raids of World War II, made me desperately want to paint the scene which Johnnie had described so graphically. I chose the moment when Johnnie Johnson took his Wing into the fray, the contrails behind his Spitfires seen in the top right-hand part of the painting. The 56th Fighter Group's P-47s, now low on fuel and ammunition, are contrailing away from the scene, to the left.

The damaged B-17 in the foreground, the main subject of the painting, I hope conveys the majesty of this great aircraft and is a reminder of the courage and determination of its valiant crews, as it thunders on, bloodied but unbowed.

On a visit to General Le May's home he kindly told me that he was greatly impressed with my painting. I am sure he was being polite, but nevertheless it was a nice compliment from somebody who was well qualified to comment.

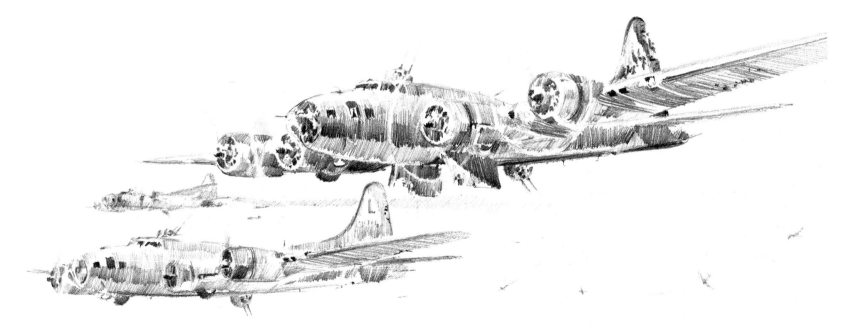

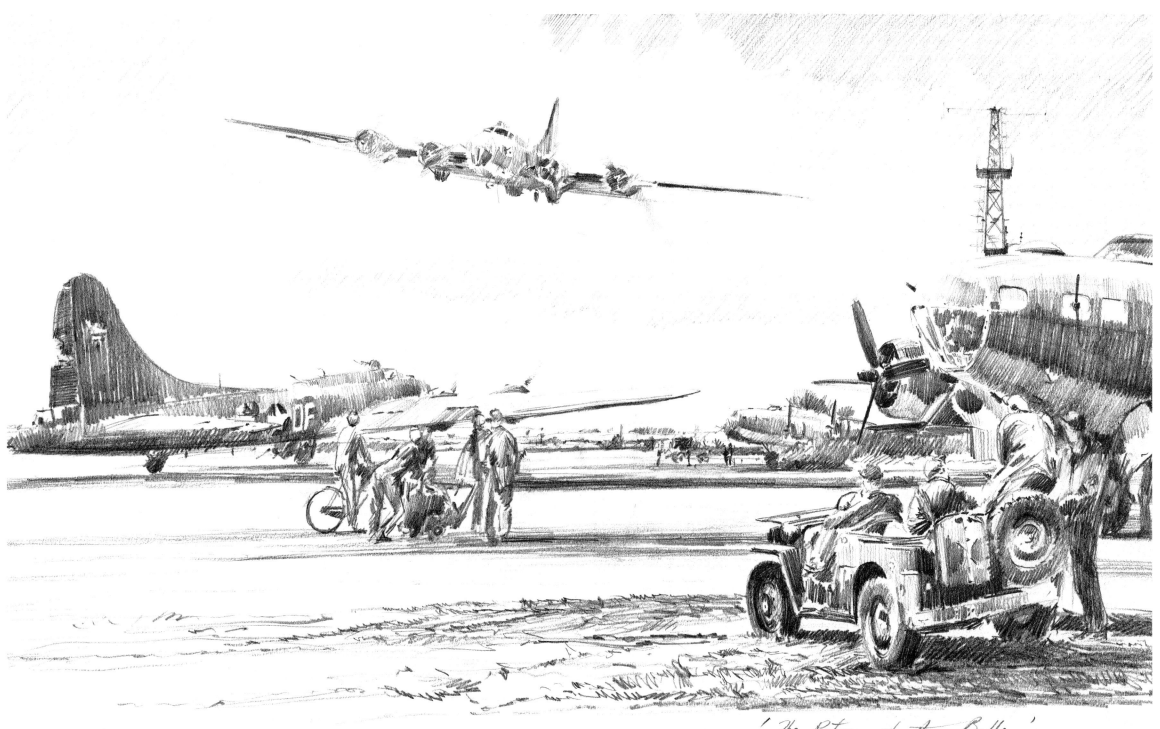

' The Return of the Belle. '

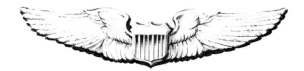

Below is a detail from another painting of the great B-17 Flying Fortress. It shows a damaged aircraft struggling to make it home after a raid, down on power and speed, having lost touch with the formation and alone in a hostile sky. To give the painting a somewhat romantic story, I have brought in a lone P-51 Mustang, himself probably low on fuel and ammunition and weary from combat. He has assessed the B-17's desperate plight, and closed in to escort his big friend on the long journey home.

To add to the atmosphere I have set the scene late in the day, the sun having already set on the ground below. The dark area in the foreground was designed to create a foreboding reminder that this drama is, as yet, unresolved.

HELPING HAND

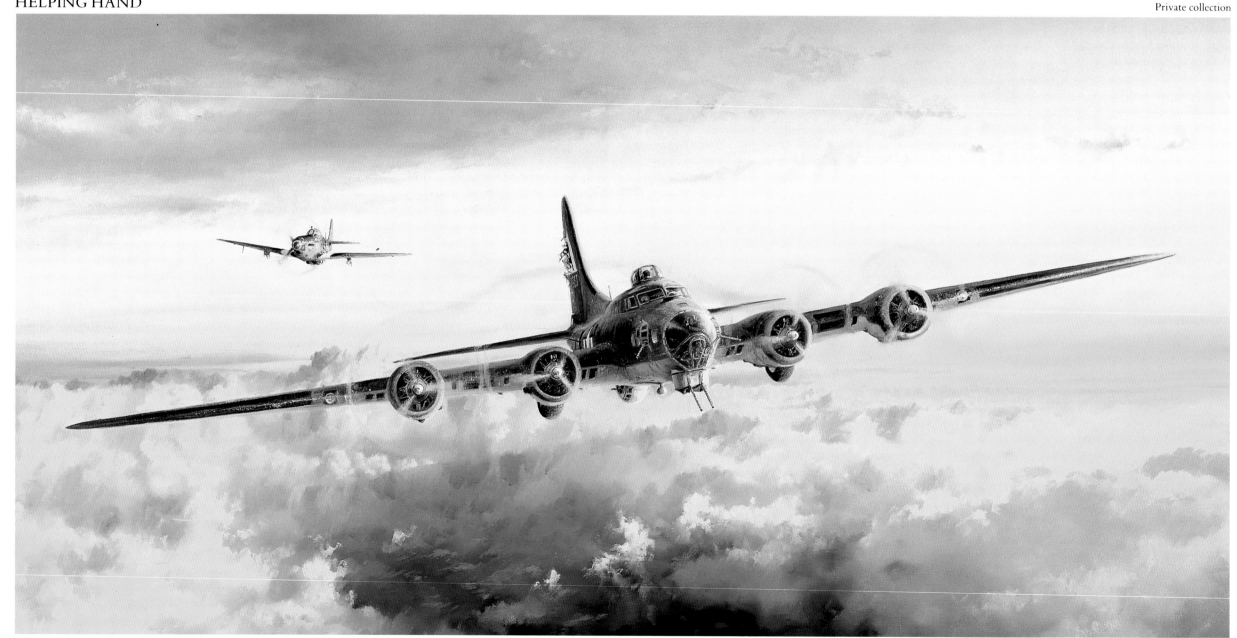

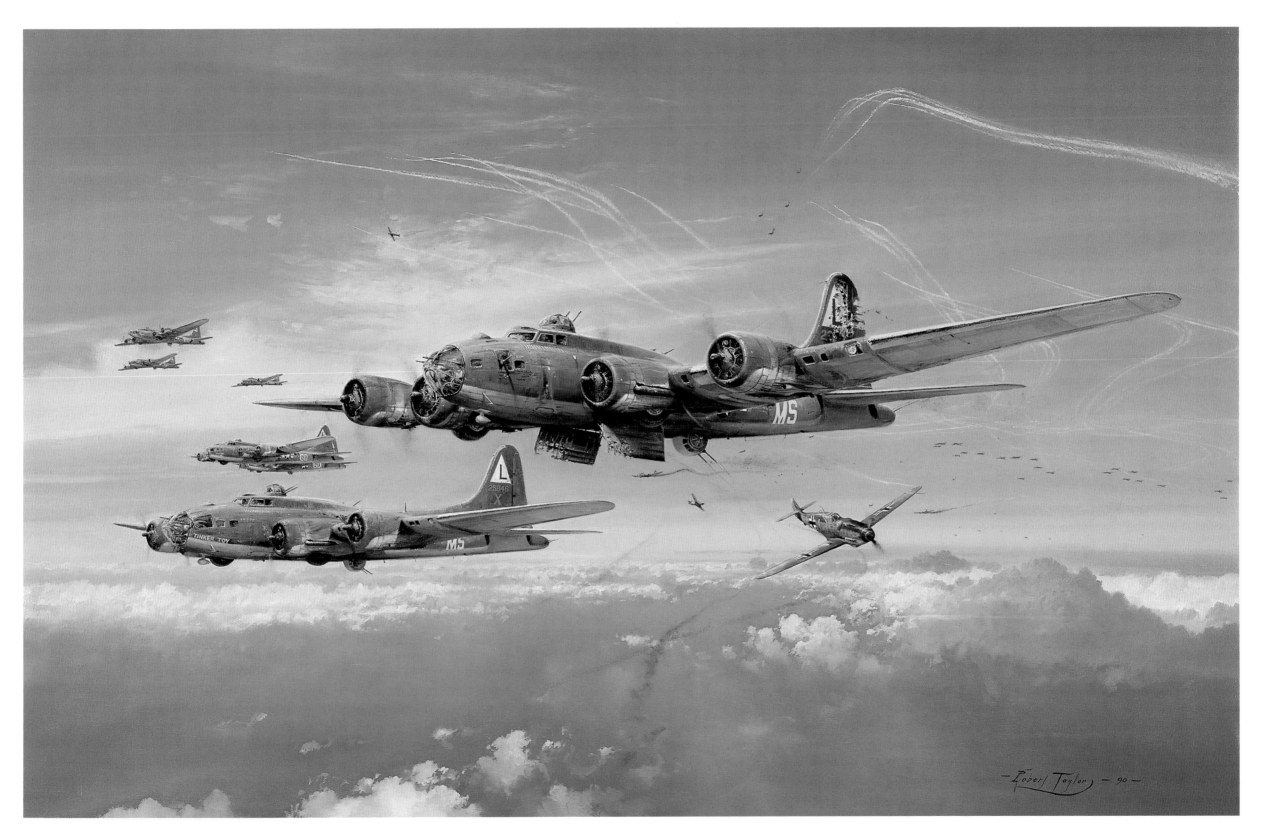

RETURN FROM SCHWEINFURT

In the collection of AVM Johnnie Johnson

ST CROIX-SUR-MER

Summerfield 'Tracking' was a kind of wire mesh matting which could be laid quickly by rolling it out on roughly prepared ground to form a temporary airstrip. It was used extensively throughout World War II where advance airfields needed to be hastily constructed, and was highly effective. I don't know how easy it was to lay but I can say with great authority that it is a nightmare to paint – for an artist, that is.

St Croix-Sur-Mer is a quaint little village in Normandy, northern France, and on 10 June 1944 its name went into the history books for it hosted the first RAF fighters to touch down on French soil

following the fall of France four long years earlier. Converted from virgin farmland into a serviceable airstrip by Service Commandos in just three days, the RAF's first airfield across the Channel became operational four days after the 6 June landings at Normandy. The distinction of being the first pilots to land went to Johnnie Johnson's Number 144 Canadian Wing, and I was commissioned to record the event.

When researching the painting, I was helped considerably by Johnnie Johnson who provided some excellent photographs and maps showing the locale of the airfield, and naturally I was able easily to get all

the details I needed to paint the aircraft; Johnnie's photos did not show, however, the Summerfield Tracking clearly at all, so I had to delve into my library to get some accurate information. I found several illuminating photographs from the period showing troops actually laying the tracking, and from these I was able to gauge the width of each roll, and therefore estimate the width of the strip. It took me days to paint this part of the picture.

When Johnnie saw the finished painting he said: 'You've got the strip too wide, Robert. As I remember it, we had only just enough room to fly Spitfires off two abreast.'

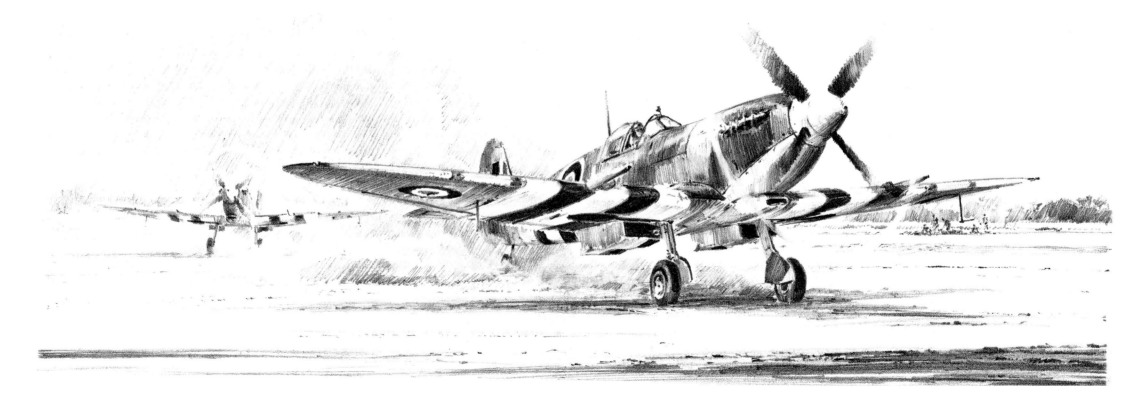

Johnnie had no idea how long it had taken me to construct the airstrip on my canvas, and I was aghast at the thought of all the hours I had spent tediously painting areas of Summerfield Tracking that were never actually there. 'We can sort it out in a jiffy old boy,' said Johnnie, and within a few moments he was on the phone to one of his old friends Peter Scott, now a director with Sir Robert McAlpine, the international construction group. In 1944, as an 18 year old Corporal with the 64th Road Construction Company, Royal Engineers, Peter Scott had been one of the invasion force troops who had laid the Summerfield Tracking at St Croix-Sur-Mer. It transpired that I had got the width of the individual strips right, but I had painted too many strips, so out they had to come.

It occurred to me later that Wing Commander Johnnie Johnson, leading No 144 Canadian Wing on 10 June 1944, must have had more important things on his mind than recalling the exact width of a roll of Summerfield Tracking, yet forty-six years after the event he was able to spot my error in an instant.

When Johnnie and his Canadians landed at St Croix-Sur-Mer, they were refuelled, rearmed and ready for take-off within twenty minutes, a fine testimony to the ingenuity of the highly trained Service Commandos. The painting shows Johnnie Johnson leading the take-off for the first fighter sweep to emanate from French soil after the fall of France. Later, in Oakville, Toronto, in Canada, I met the other three pilots whose Spitfires appear in the painting, at a lively gallery reception hosted by another Johnson – Mike – who is my publisher's distributor in Canada. He is Johnnie Johnson's eldest son!

When originally commissioned to paint this picture, and after talking to Johnnie Johnson, my first thought had been to paint the Canadian Wing Spitfires coming in to land on the hastily constructed airfield at St Croix. The drawing below shows how I first visualised the scene, but, as I often do, I changed my mind from the first idea, the reason in this case being that I decided that it was important to show some of the ground troops in the painting. It was, after all, quite a feat of engineering, completed under hazardous conditions of war in an amazingly short time, and if for no other reason the troops deserved a place in the picture. To accommodate all this I went to the other end of the airfield and painted the Spitfires taking off.

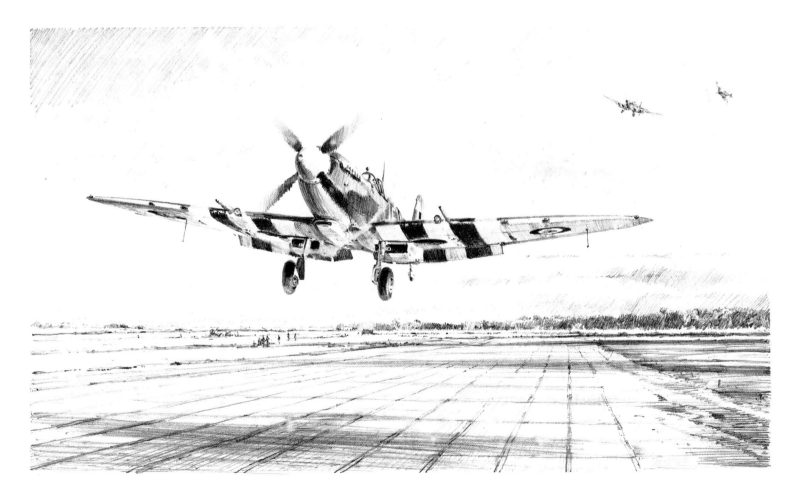

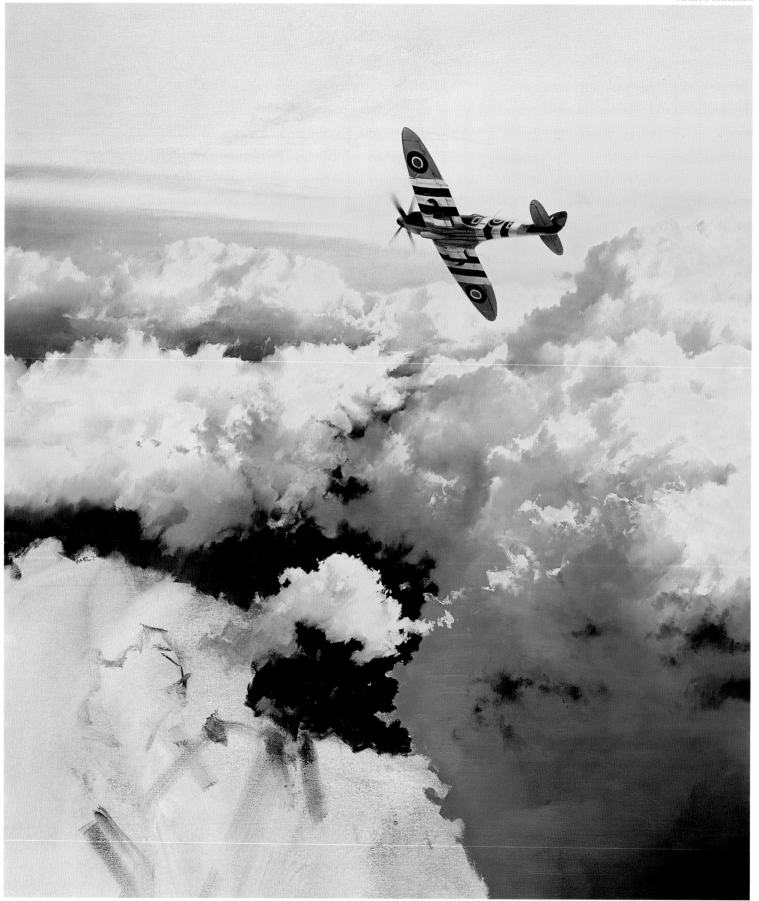

The painting on the left isn't quite finished yet!

A few years ago a TV company wanted to film me actually working on a canvas, the idea being that I would be interviewed as I painted. I had been interviewed live on TV a few times before, which I always found somewhat unnerving, but I was sure that this would be no problem. I was mistaken!

The director asked if I could 'do something with lots of clouds in it, as this seems to be your trade-mark'. I wasn't sure that I liked the accolade much, but agreed. I thought that I had better go a bit overboard with emphasis on the clouds if that was what he wanted; but in the event I think I took him too literally because he said afterwards that if I had painted the Spitfire a bit bigger he would have bought the painting!

The camera crew came to my studio and set up all their lighting and camera equipment, and a bit later the director and interviewer, Derek Robinson, arrived. They started filming with Derek asking me a few questions and we moved over to the easel. It was all going quite smoothly until I started painting. I have not found too many problems talking in front of the camera, and I don't seem to have too many problems painting, but at this interview I discovered that I am not very good at being interviewed and painting at the same time. A good half of the film they shot ended up on the cutting-room floor!

This reminds me of signing sessions when I have sat down with groups of pilots to sign limited edition prints. Inevitably there is much boisterous chatter and I have noticed that many people, when talking and writing their name at the same time, will occasionally lapse into writing down a word they have just spoken instead of their signature. This always causes great hilarity and leg-pulling amongst the pilots, but after my experience in front of the cameras with brush in my hand, I can entirely appreciate the problem.

Derek Robinson, the TV interviewer that day, seemed very well informed about aircraft, and asked me some extremely knowledgeable questions, which surprised me at the time. It was not until after we had finished filming that I discovered that this was indeed the same Derek Robinson who wrote the book *Piece of Cake,* which was later made into an extremely successful, though controversial, television film.

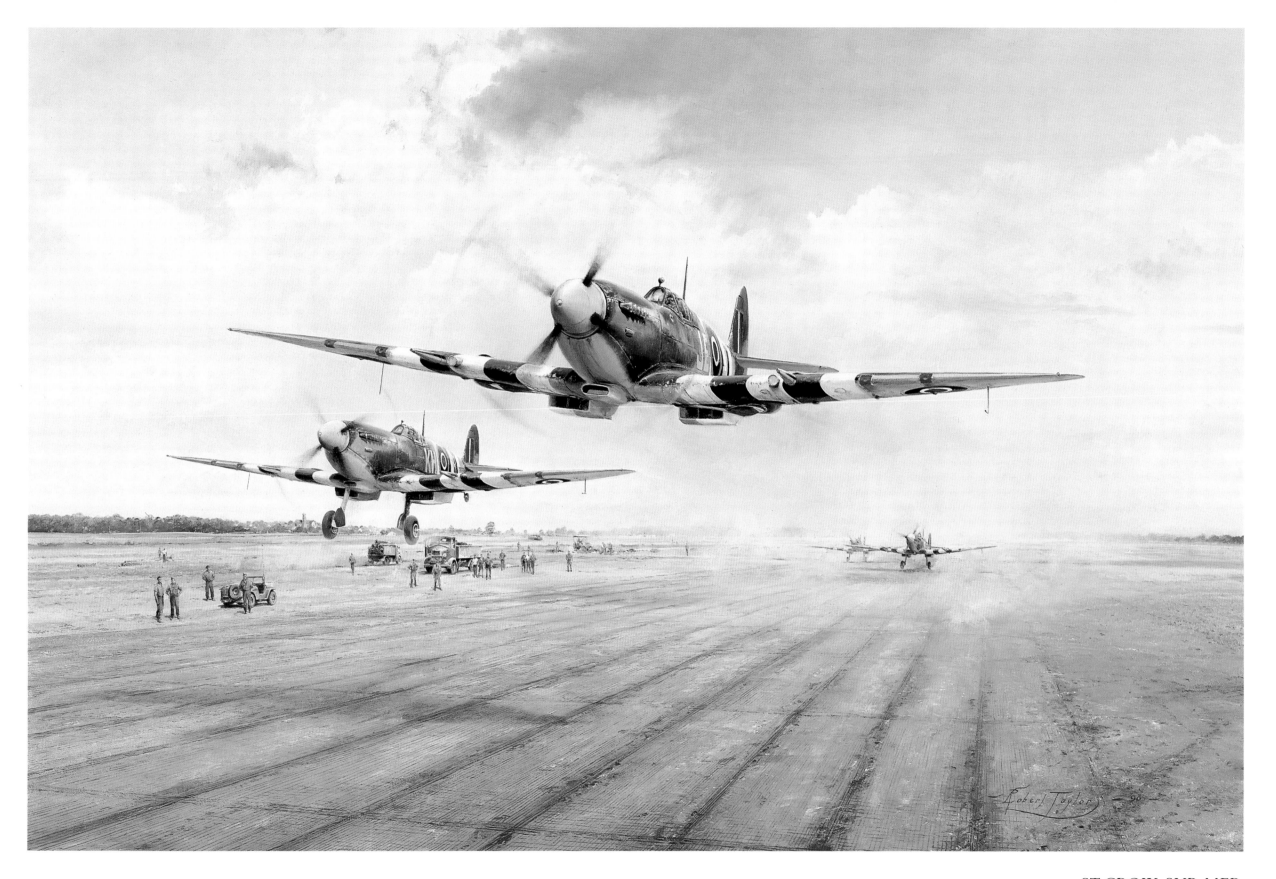

ST CROIX-SUR-MER

In the collection of Wings Fine Art

THE ABBEVILLE BOYS

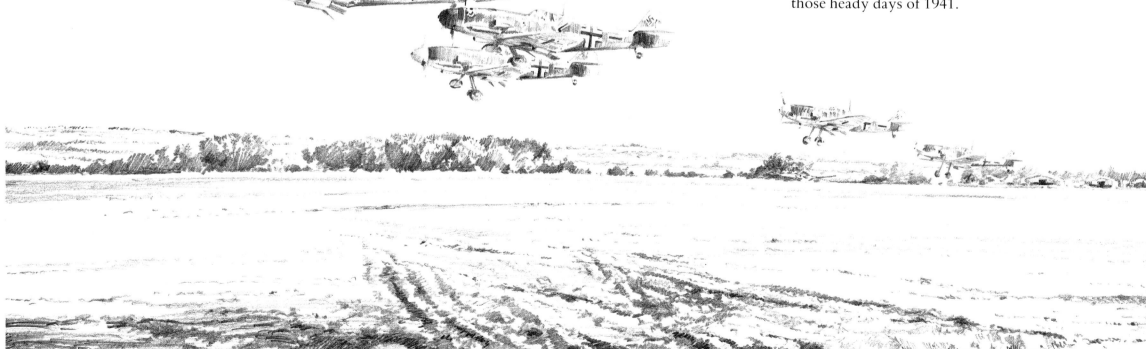

Abbeville is a small town in northern France, just a few miles from the estuary where the Somme flows into the Pas de Calais. In 1940 its grass airfield became the headquarters of what was at the time the best-known Fighter Wing in the Luftwaffe – Geschwader-26. Its brilliant Kommodore, Adolf ('Dolfo'), Galland, at the peak of his career as a combat pilot, arrived at the small grass airfield with his Messerschmitt Me109s and an élite band of fighter pilots. Having contested the Battle of Britain, Galland already had fifty-eight air victories to his credit and was clearly destined for high command; in his Wing he had some of the most experienced and highly trained fighter pilots on the Channel Front.

Just a few weeks after the arrival of JG-26 at Abbeville, the little airfield received another visitor in the shape of the Führer himself. Galland recalls the visit in his biography *Fighter General:*

Hitler spoke to us pilots promising a strengthened and revitalised Fighter Arm on the Channel Front and a renewed and even bigger offensive against England in the New Year. He departed wishing the pilots a Happy New Year. For many of them it would be their last.

In the new year the opposite to that which the Führer had promised happened: the RAF came across the Channel on the offensive and in strength, giving the fighter pilots of the Luftwaffe a period of intense air fighting that Galland remembers as the most exhilarating of his life. It was the RAF pilots who gave Galland's élite Wing the name 'The Abbeville Boys'. Nobody ever came up with a better title for an aviation painting!

I made the sketch below after talking to General Galland about this period of his life. Clearly from our conversations, the days when he led his beloved JG-26 Fighter Wing in regular combat with the pilots of the RAF were the most memorable days of his combat flying career. Abbeville was an exhilarating place for 'Dolfo', so I wanted to feature the airfield in the painting and chose a take-off sequence showing Dolfo powering his Me109 out of the field at Abbeville, his pilots eagerly following him.

The drawing on the right shows the pilots and ground crew of JG–26 – 'The Abbeville Boys' – in those heady days of 1941.

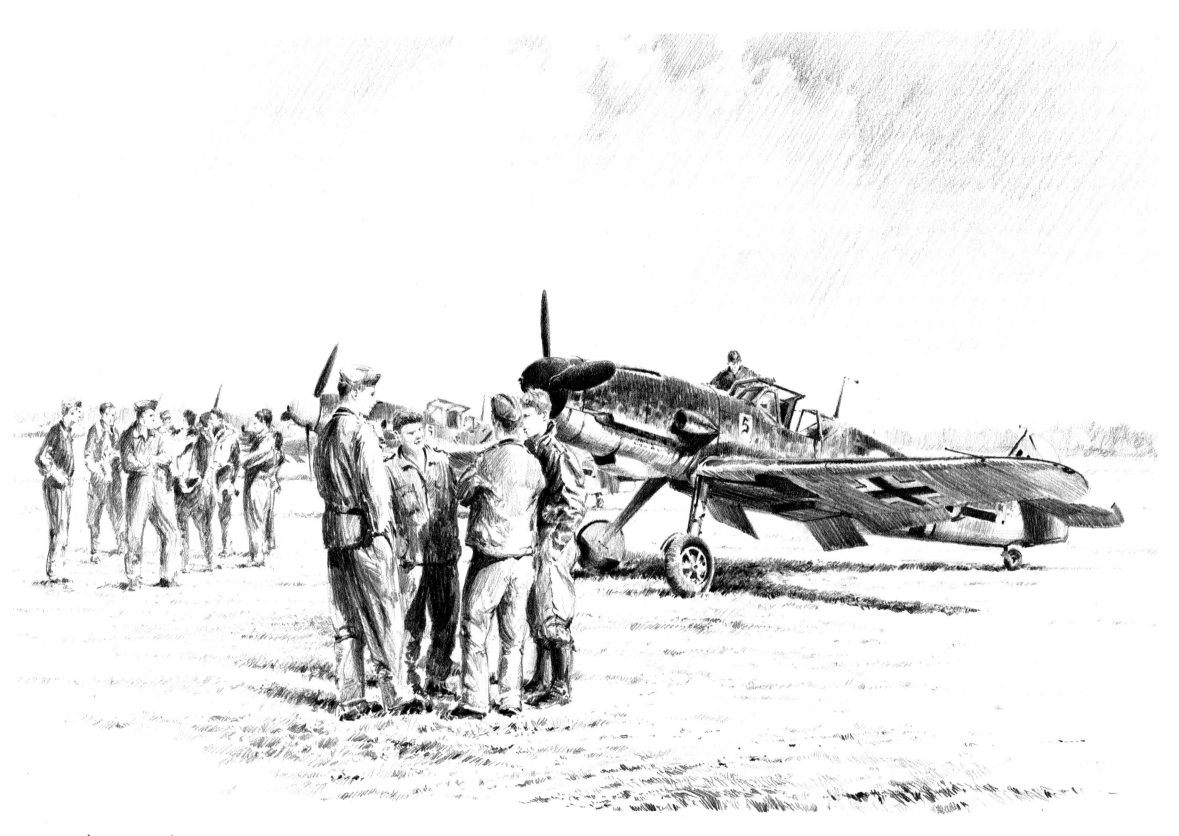

'The Abbeville Boys' 41.

Airfields are always wide open, shapeless areas, and when an artist comes to paint one there is always a problem of trying to find a way to create some interest in this vast expanse. The difficulty doesn't arise where aircraft are to be viewed on the ground, but in a painting where the scene shows aircraft taking off, landing or overflying an airfield, some special creative thinking must go into the composition of this part of the painting.

It is always possible to place vehicles, people, bicycles, trolleys and other paraphernalia in the foreground, but this requires great care if the painting is to remain uncluttered. In a picture such as *The Abbeville Boys*, where the main thrust of the painting is centred upon the aircraft taking off, too much interest placed in the foreground would divert attention from the aircraft and thus dilute the effect. But one has to do something, otherwise the lower half of the picture would become featureless, giving a bland feeling to the whole.

In this case the muddy wheel-tracks that I placed in the forefront of the picture are there to break up the large expanse of grass, and the direction of the tracks is carefully designed to help the general flow of the painting from right to left. Some rain water still lying in the ruts enables the introduction of a change in colour too, as the blue of the sky reflects in the puddles that are poached into the rich brown soil. The general direction of these wheel marks also aims to lead the eye into the picture and towards the other side of the airfield where there is plenty of activity.

To emphasise the aircraft I have done two things. First, I have introduced strong sunlight from above so that there is plenty of light and shadow on the Me109s. Secondly, I painted a powerful cloudscape covering about two-thirds of the canvas, using strongly contrasting colours. This also helps to lead the eye into the painting and away towards the horizon.

The positioning of the aircraft took much trial and error. It is quite difficult to paint aircraft 'touching' each other on the canvas – not only from the technical aspect, but to make this work in a visually pleasing way. I don't like to make my combat aircraft look too organised, as if they are 'flying by the manual'. That may be how it was supposed to be, but it is not how it was! It is easy to paint aircraft in 'air-show precision' formations, but if one does so, the painting tends to look contrived and unreal. There has to be a carefully constructed air of informality about the grouping of aircraft to get an atmosphere of reality into a painting.

I have spoken elsewhere about the need for an aviation artist to spend time on that part of the painting which is *not* aircraft; this is something which I feel strongly about. A test I always make with a painting before I consider it completed is to find a way of 'removing' the aircraft for a moment so I can view and evaluate what remains. I ask myself whether I am left with a picture that would stand up on its own without the aircraft. If it fails my test, I go back to work on the canvas.

I made an interesting calculation after completing *The Abbeville Boys* which told me that less than 10 per cent of the total area of the canvas actually contains aircraft.

Me109

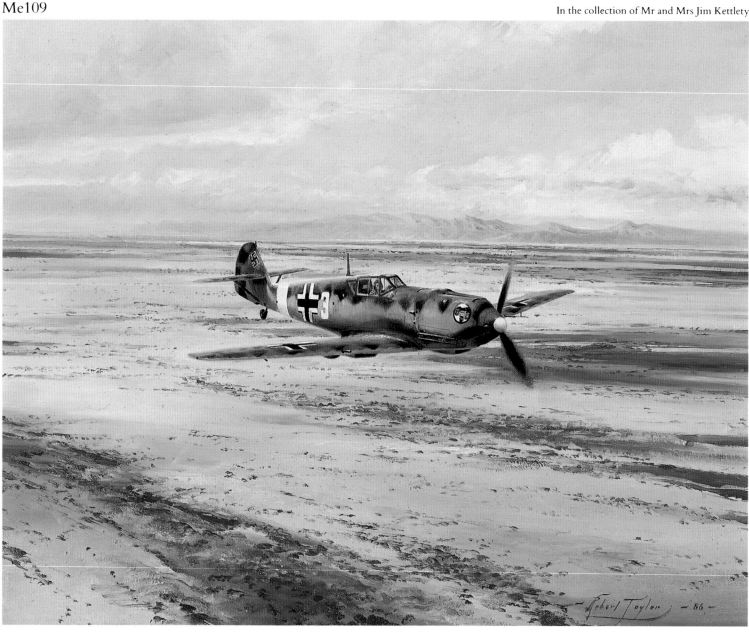

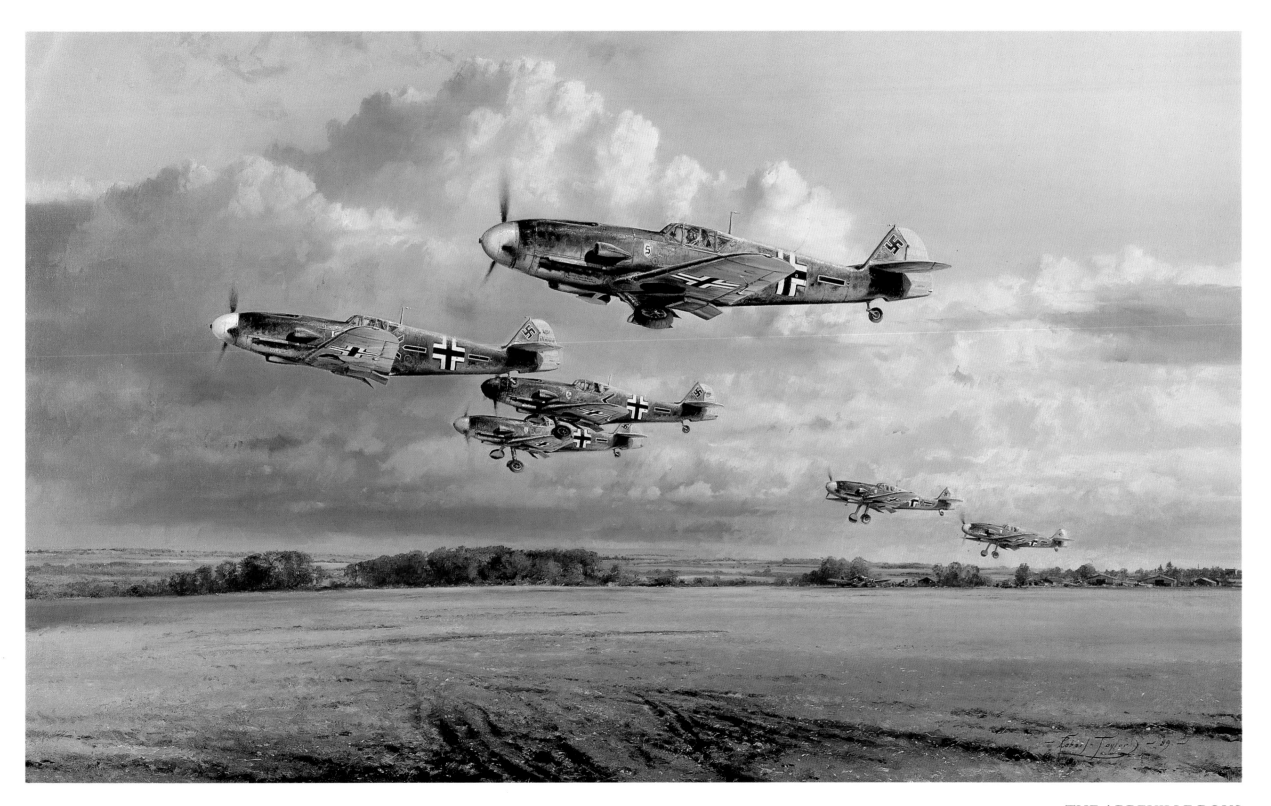

THE ABBEVILLE BOYS

In the collection of Mr and Mrs Dennis Greene

DAWN PATROL

I began my professional career as a marine artist, my first love being the majestic Tall Ships which were plying their trade about the world before and just after the turn of the century. These wonderful old sailing ships, constructed almost entirely of wood, canvas and rigging, have always held a special fascination for me. In many ways World War I aircraft have similar qualities: they were made largely of the same materials, were constantly at the mercy of the elements, and, like the old sailing ships, were tiny frail forerunners of their modern counterparts.

Perhaps the most attractive of all World War I fighters was the SE5A. Although it was slower and less manoeuvrable than others of the era, such as the Sopwith Camel, the SE5A was beautifully proportioned and had enormous character. Best of all from an aesthetic point of view was the lovely dihedral configuration of its wings.

Aerodynamic computer design is, I suppose, what is responsible for most modern jet aircraft looking fairly similar, all their vital parts concealed within highly streamlined space-age bodies. The march of progress, it seems, removes much of the individual personality of machines, which is rather sad. All the old aircraft had distinct shapes, each was quite different to look at and instantly identifiable, its individual character enhanced by its own unique appearance.

Like an old sailing ship, you can look at the SE5A and see almost everything that makes it work. Virtually everything of any significance is fully on view, including the crew! There is something eminently satisfying about painting these old aeroplanes, and it has often occurred to me that the very same material that I paint upon – canvas – was the clothing for those frail, manoeuvreable early

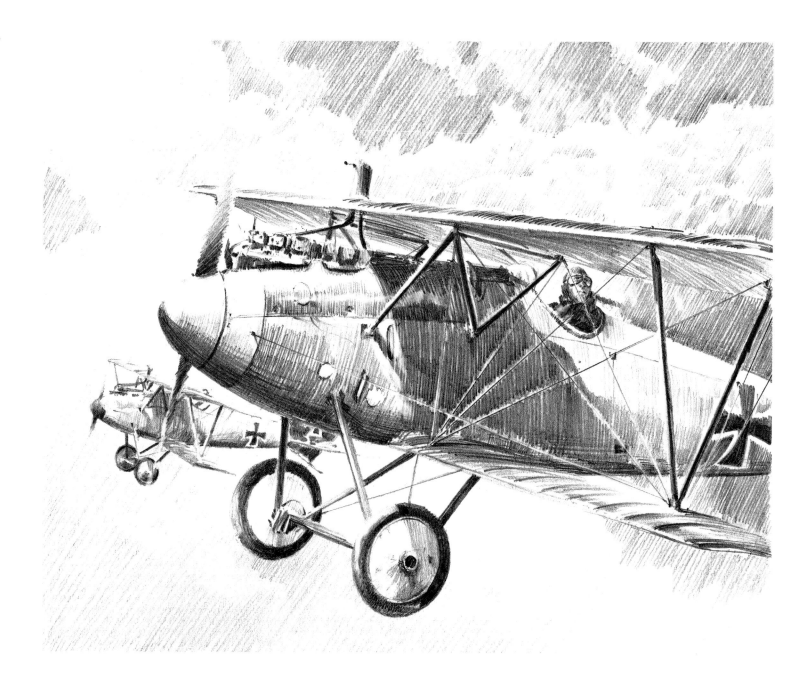

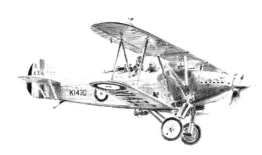

fighters. Striving with oil paint to achieve the effect of taut canvas over a spruce airframe is a pleasant challenge for me, and as I add the highly tuned rigging lines (usually painted in almost last), I get the feeling that I am preparing my aircraft for flight. The brief for this commission was a simple one: to paint an aviation scene from World War I. I had great fun deciding what to paint, and drew many sketches of these wonderful old bi-planes, before I chose the SE5A.

The drawing on the opposite page shows the Albatross of Jasta II, the aircraft of the Red Baron in which he was shot down and wounded over Belgium on 6 July 1917. It was a fine aircraft, superior to most Allied fighters of the day, and was flown by many of the German Aces.

The drawing to the right shows a Bristol fighter of the RAF's 22 Squadron which is under attack from a pair of German Albatross fighters. The Bristol fighter, affectionately known as the 'Brisfit', was the first British two-seat fighter to enter service in World War I. Compared with single-seat fighters such as the Pup, the Camel, and indeed the Albatross, the Bristol fighter was immense, having a wing-span of almost 40 feet. It was nevertheless fast and manoeuvrable and proved to be a formidable opponent. It remained in production long after the end of the war, being built in both British and American factories, and flew with the RAF until as late as 1932.

The small sketch above shows a Hawker Hart, a pacy bi-plane in service with the RAF between the wars and unmistakably recognisable as the fore-runner to the Hurricane.

After all my deliberations, and influenced by the sheer beauty of the SE5A, I chose this aircraft for my painting.

Dawn Patrol shows a flight of SE5As of the RAF's No 85 Squadron climbing to 8,000 feet above Armentières, northern France, in June 1918. In the foreground is the aircraft of the tough Canadian, Major Billy Bishop, VC, who survived the war as one of the RAF's top scoring pilots.

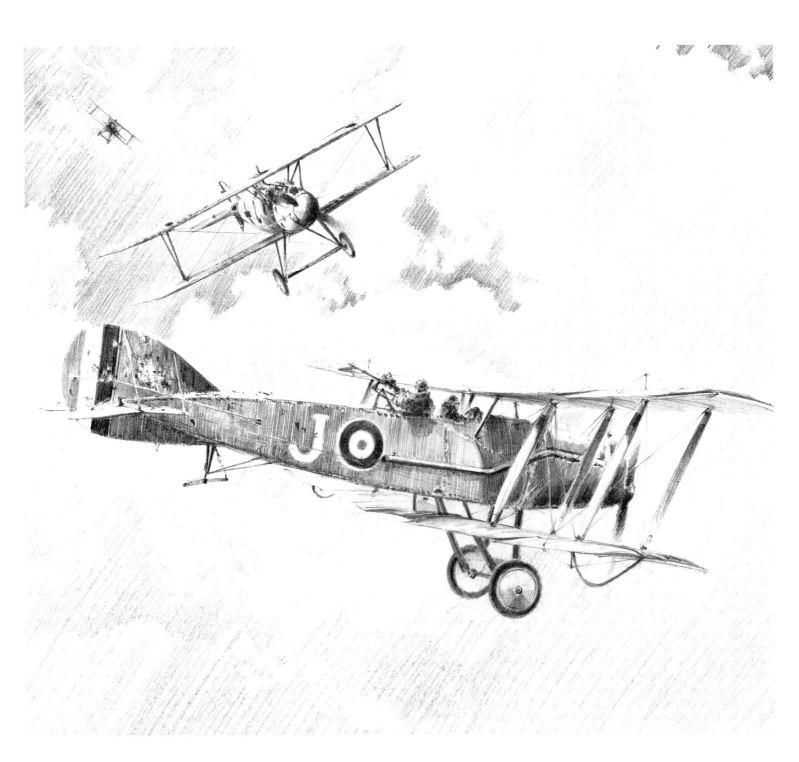

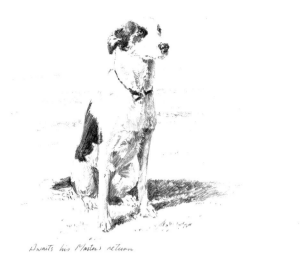

To witness the glory of dawn breaking from high above the clouds surely cannot fail to move the most unemotional of beings. The glow of a crimson horizon turning through pastel shades of orange and yellow to the pure azure blue of the morning sky is a phenomenon so beautiful it defies description. To portray on canvas a moment of this ethereal environment presents a continuing challenge to all my artistic senses which never fails to excite me. An aviation painting is all about the huge dimensions in which aircraft fly. A world of constantly moving patterns of light and dancing shadows, ever-changing in shape and colour, towering cloud formations and huge halls of air: a world of limitless horizons. It is into this world that I immerse myself when I paint a picture like *Dawn Patrol*.

Below is a detail from the painting.

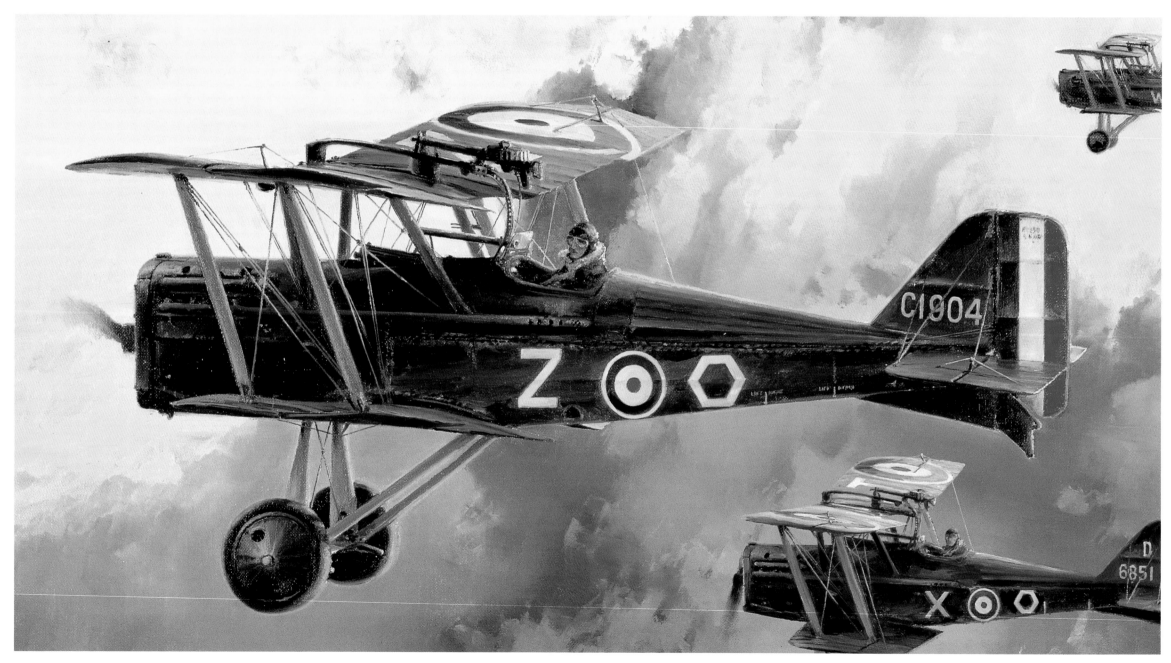

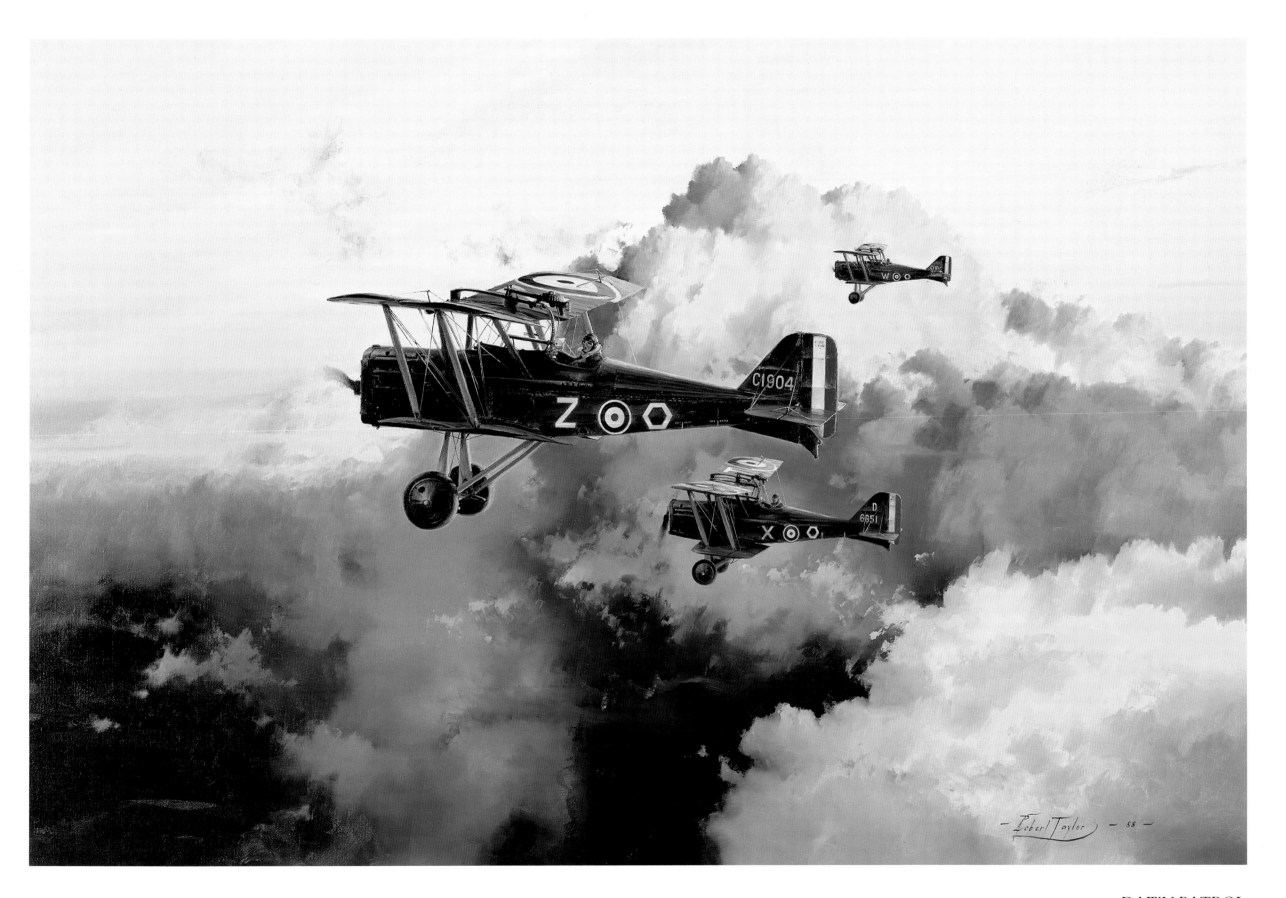

DAWN PATROL

In the collection of Mr Nick Maggos

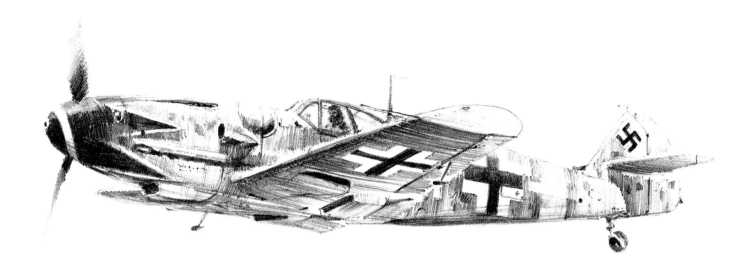

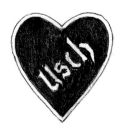

ACE OF ACES

Talk to all the top-scoring World War II fighter pilots about their personal approach to combat and their individual air-fighting techniques and one common tactic always emerges: without exception they all advocate the importance of getting in close to the opponent before they open fire.

Some pilots, using raw courage and great flying skill, were able to fly their aircraft with confidence directly at an enemy plane, closing to within a few feet, their aerobatic skill and infinite sense of timing saving them from the mid-air collision which a lesser pilot would suffer. Others relied less on the extreme of a close encounter, depending more on their skill and judgement in the art of deflection shooting.

Whatever their personal technique, all the great Aces are agreed about the need to avoid opening fire at too great a range. 'The most common fault of the young fighter pilot was to start shooting too soon at too long a range,' Gunther Rall told me in a recent discussion. 'There is no rule dictating the range at which to fire. The circumstances dictate the decision and the judgement of the precise moment comes with experience.'

Erich Hartmann shot down 352 enemy aircraft. No other pilot in history had greater success and it is a record that is unlikely ever to be surpassed. Hartmann attributes his astonishing number of air victories to his dictum 'Get in so close to your opponent that you simply cannot miss.' He practised what he preached: of the sixteen times he was brought down in combat, eight were caused by flying debris from the aircraft he had destroyed.

The subject of air-fighting is not the domain of a mere aviation artist and I am at pains to say that I am no authority on the subject, but as a painter of air combat scenes I am a keen student of the techniques involved and have had the privilege of countless discussions with experienced pilots from both world wars. I have drawers full of notes, diagrams and actual combat reports that I have collected over the years, most of them obtained from, and discussed at first-hand with pilots. This mass of information has helped me tremendously and is constantly referred to when I am painting combat scenes.

Occasionally, when I have painted a combat scene in which two aircraft are shown in very close

proximity, I have received letters telling me that fighters never got that close during air-to-air fighting. I usually politely suggest that the correspondents take a look at the combat reports of Erich Hartmann, or Alan Deere, or Douglas Bader, or Gabby Gabreski, or any other high-scoring fighter Ace for that matter.

I have twice been commissioned to paint pictures featuring Erich Hartmann. One painting dictated a non-combat scene showing a study of the great Ace with his wingman on the point of taking their Me109s into combat. The second portrays the moment of demise of one of Hartmann's 352 victories and features a Russian Ilyushin. Both are illustrated overleaf.

Erich Hartmann maintains that his massive score of air victories was a result of his tactic of waiting for the precise moment of advantage and pressing home a high-speed attack almost to the point of collision. In *Knights Cross*, I have attempted to emphasise this tactic by showing the Ilyushin, already doomed, just seconds after the attack, with the position of the two aircraft such that they have obviously passed very close to each other.

By contrast *Ace of Aces* demanded one of the more serene moments during one of Erich Hartmann's 1,400 combat missions, and shows the great Ace with his wingman, at the precise moment of the commencement of the attack. Hartmann is looking over his left shoulder at his chosen target way below, as he manoeuvres his Me109 into position. I shaped the pattern of the sky to help the lateral movement of the painting, the sun being placed fairly low and to the right of the view, which enabled me to include some nice areas of light and shadow on the two nearest aircraft. The badge on the nose cowling is the JG-52 emblem and the 'bleeding heart' symbol just below the cockpit was Erich Hartmann's personal insignia. In it was painted his childhood sweetheart's name Ursel. They married during the war and today live happily together in Germany.

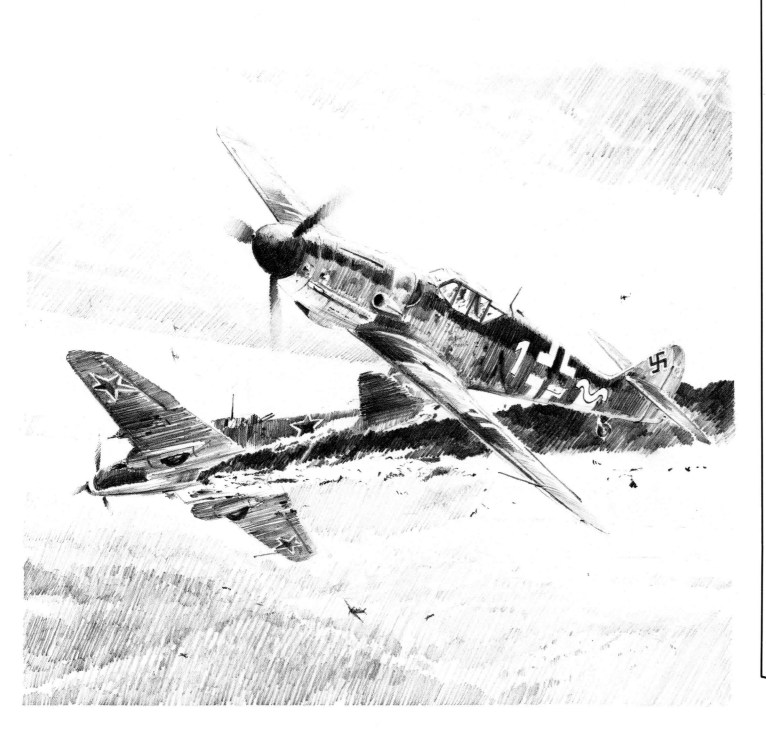

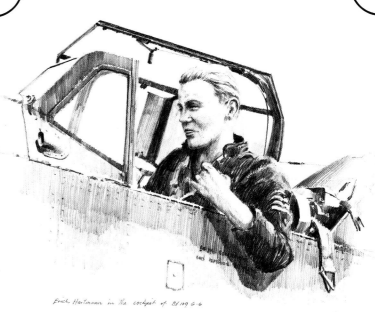

Erich Hartmann in the cockpit of Bf 109 G-6

THE BLOND KNIGHT

Erich Hartmann became a qualified Me109 pilot on his twentieth birthday, and August 1942 saw him join what was to become the most successful Fighter Wing in history. Led at the time by the popular and highly respected Dieter Hrabak, Jagdgeschwader 52 was based in Russia and was home to some of the leading Luftwaffe Aces of the day.

Initiated into the arena, the young 'Bubi' Hartmann had the good fortune to be assigned as wingman to the high-scoring Ace Walter Krupinski. After an inconspicuous start, he notched up his first ten victories flying with Krupinski. His tactics were simple, bold and fearless. He would quickly assess a situation, then make a decisive attack, flying directly at his opponent 'Until his aircraft filled my windscreen', firing a short burst at very close range. As he became more skilful and experienced as a pilot, so he became even more daring with his attacks, flying ever closer to his opponent, often not opening fire until he was well within 100 yards.

Erich Hartmann flew 1,425 missions, involving over 800 dog-fights with enemy aircraft during his combat career. He suffered many accidents and equipment failures, resulting in several crash-landings and one parachute escape. By the end of the war he was credited with 352 air victories, more than any other fighter pilot in history.

Below is a detail showing the central section of a painting entitled *Knights Cross*, which depicts the combat described on the previous page. I painted Erich Hartmann in the cockpit of his Me109 coolly looking across at the stricken Ilyushin, its gunner already baling out. The symbol behind the cross on the fuselage indicates that Hartmann is flying an

Me109G of III Gruppe, JG-52.

The Me109s in *Ace of Aces*, the painting to the right, are also 'G' models, but here the armoured plate behind Hartmann's seat has been removed with the introduction of the Erla Haube canopy. Becoming known as the 'Galland canopy', this provided all-round armoured glass and afforded

much greater visibility. The arrow-head and the bar on the side of the fuselage signifies the aircraft of the Gruppen Kommandeur, II Gruppe, JG-52.

The 'Black Tulip' nose decoration was painted on Hartmann's personal aircraft, but he later had this removed: such was Erich Hartmann's reputation by this time that when Russian pilots saw it they fled.

KNIGHT'S CROSS (detail)

In the collection of Mr and Mrs Dennis Greene

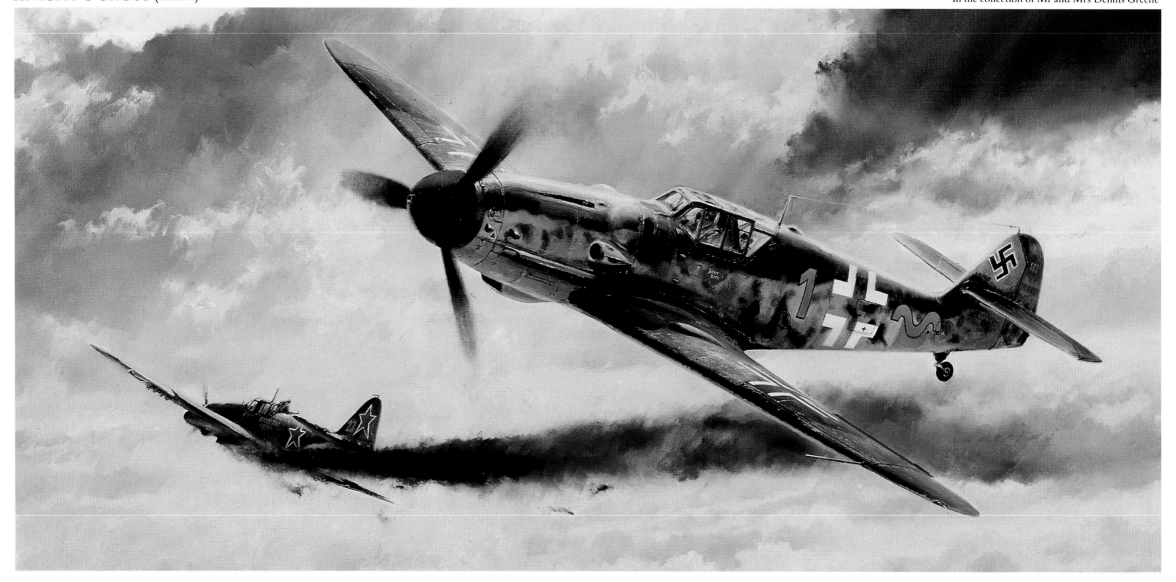

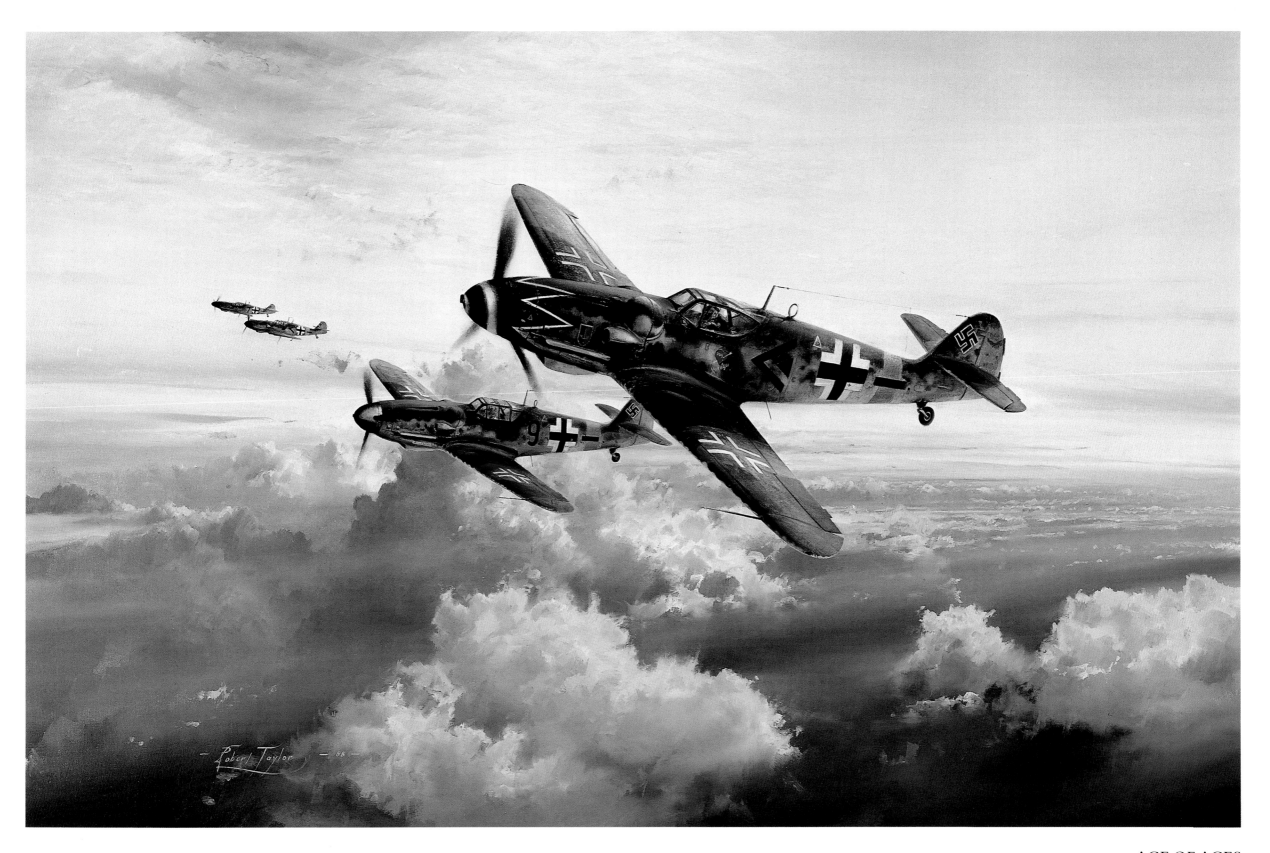

ACE OF ACES

In the collection of Mr Edgar Leicher

LOW HOLDING

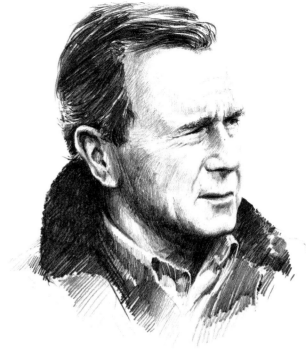

Museums provide a vital source of information for artists, their historians going to endless trouble to assist in uncovering facts which are such an essential part of painting military pictures. It is therefore always pleasant to become involved in projects which are designed for their benefit. Over the years I have been involved in a good many fund-raising exercises organised by my publishers, The Military Gallery, for the benefit of service museums and charities, and one of the most successful of these involved the President of the United States, George Bush.

John Toomey, an ex-naval pilot and trustee of the US Naval Aviation Museum Foundation at Pensacola, Florida, had the idea of putting together a project to raise funds for the museum's building fund. A limited edition would be signed by another ex-naval aviator, who happened to be at the time the Vice-President of the United States, and the proceeds would go to the museum.

Virginia Bader, who runs a well-known aviation art gallery in Alexandria, just outside Washington DC, was approached by John to recommend a publisher and artist, and to my good fortune she kindly recommended The Military Gallery and myself. My first reaction when I heard about the project was one of surprise, as I had been unaware that Vice-President Bush was an ex-service flier. My surprise was no doubt nothing by comparison to the Vice-President's when he was told that one Robert Taylor was to paint his aircraft, for I am quite sure he had never heard of me! George Bush was Vice-President when we started the project and became President after the print was published – but I make no claims!

In 1943, aged 18, George Bush was the youngest commissioned pilot in the US Navy. He served as a carrier pilot and fought in the Pacific until September 1945. After training he was assigned to the USS *San Jacinto*, a cruiser converted to a small carrier. Piloting a TBM Avenger of the *San Jacinto's* VT-51 George Bush flew his first combat mission in a raid on Wake Island on 23 May 1944. Before the war was over he would log 1,228 hours, make 126 carrier landings, fly 58 combat missions, and survive a ditching with a full load of ordnance. On the 2 September 1944 during an attack on a radio tower at Chichi-Jima, his aircraft was hit by intense ground fire. In spite of fire and smoke in the cockpit he continued his attack, scoring hits on the target before being forced to bale out, an act for which he was awarded the Navy's Distinguished Flying Cross.

After the painting was completed and the prints published, John Toomey's associate, Paul Vander Myde, who formerly worked for the President when he was a Texas Congressman, had the difficult task of co-ordinating the project, which included getting the prints signed by President Bush. With the President's heavy schedules this involved a feat of no mean logistical expertise: some of the prints were signed at the White House, some at Camp David, and some on board Air Force One!

The project came to a very satisfactory conclusion, raising in the region of half a million dollars for the museum, most of the credit for which goes to John Toomey, President George Bush, Rear Admiral 'Skip' Furlong, Paul Vander Myde and the staff at the National Museum of Naval Aviation in Pensacola.

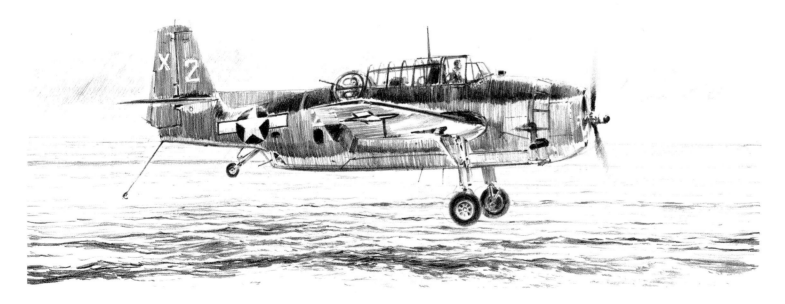

I made several drawings for the painting once I had decided upon the general concept of the picture. The first, below, shows a TBM Avenger making a climbing turn, having just launched from the *San Jacinto*. This provided a good view of the carrier, and showed the SBD at a nice angle, but I thought the composition, which showed just one Avenger, placed too much emphasis on George Bush's aircraft, which I guessed he wouldn't like. I also felt that this composition had too much of a marine feeling about it and as I was seeking to paint an aviation scene, I decided I would need to get up a little higher, and include some more aircraft.

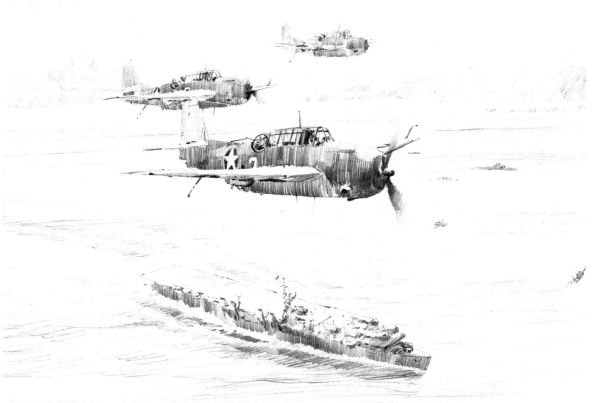

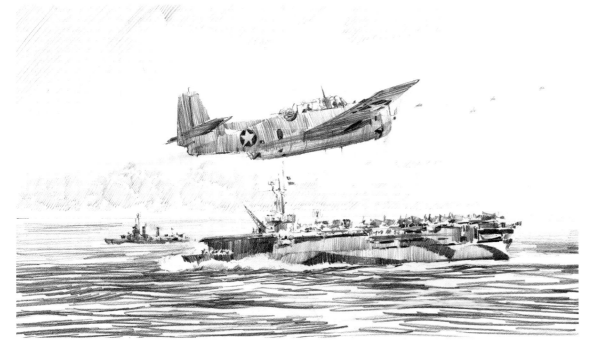

The second drawing, above, came much closer to the feel I was looking for, and it was after I had made this drawing that I decided to back-light the painting. Having the light behind the main subject of a painting, although not without its problems, is a very effective technique in helping to create atmosphere within a composition.

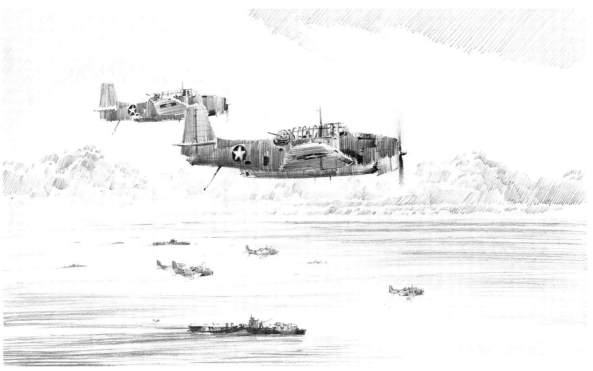

The third drawing, on the right, gave me the angle I wanted for George Bush's aircraft, but as he wasn't leading the section, I had to move the lead aircraft up ahead and a little higher. I was not happy with the top-side view of the *San Jacinto* and so moved the carrier further away, changing its direction slightly to give a more harmonious flow to the painting.

One of the worst fears of the naval pilots in the Pacific was the ever-present possibility of ditching in the ocean, either through combat damage or shortage of fuel. The vast expanse of sea over which that war was fought precluded any organised air-sea rescue service, and if an aircraft was forced down anywhere other than in the proximity of the fleet, the crew's chances of survival was very slim.

I wanted this painting to have a good feel about it, and decided that I would show a group of TBMs flying a low-holding pattern in preparation to landing, having returned from a combat mission.

The TBM Avenger was a splendid-looking aircraft. Its great radial engine was nicely streamlined into a bulky but attractively shaped fuselage, and, most satisfactory of all for me, it was blessed with a huge glass canopy complete with gun turret. Plenty of glass gives an artist the opportunity to introduce all kinds of reflected colours and, best of all, the chance to paint more than just the top of a pilot's helmet.

I was influenced to back-light the painting by the large areas of glass atop the Avenger, and, being aware of the lack of haze in this area of the Pacific, the clear view to the horizon. Looking against the sun over such an expanse of water would introduce, I thought, a slightly romantic feeling to the ocean.

The *San Jacinto*, shown below in a detail from the painting, was a top-heavy, thin-skinned lightly armed converted cruiser which carried thirty-four planes.

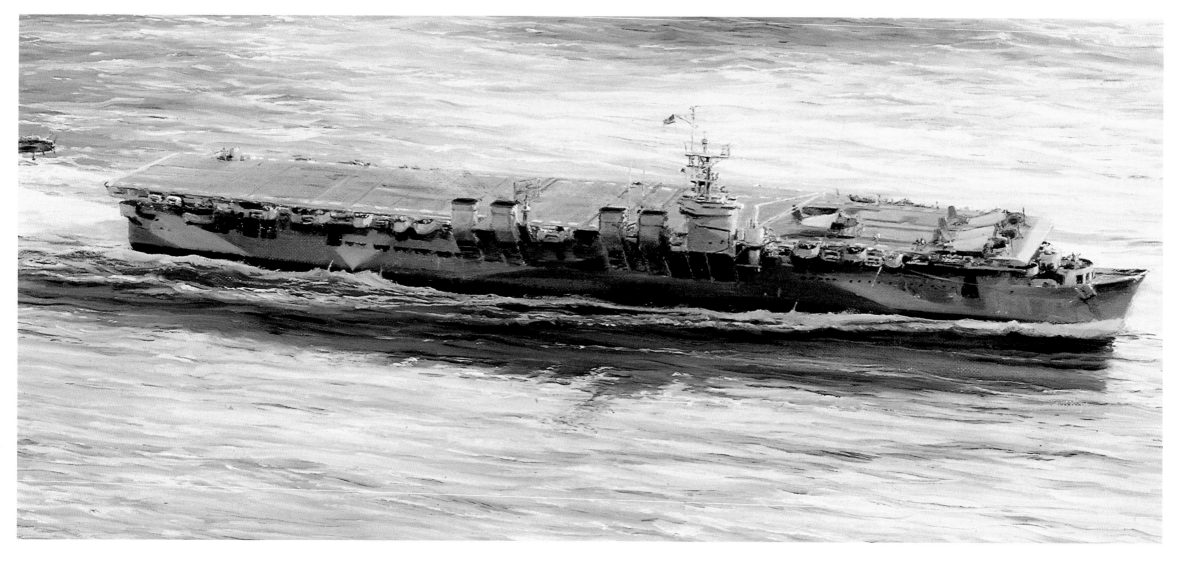

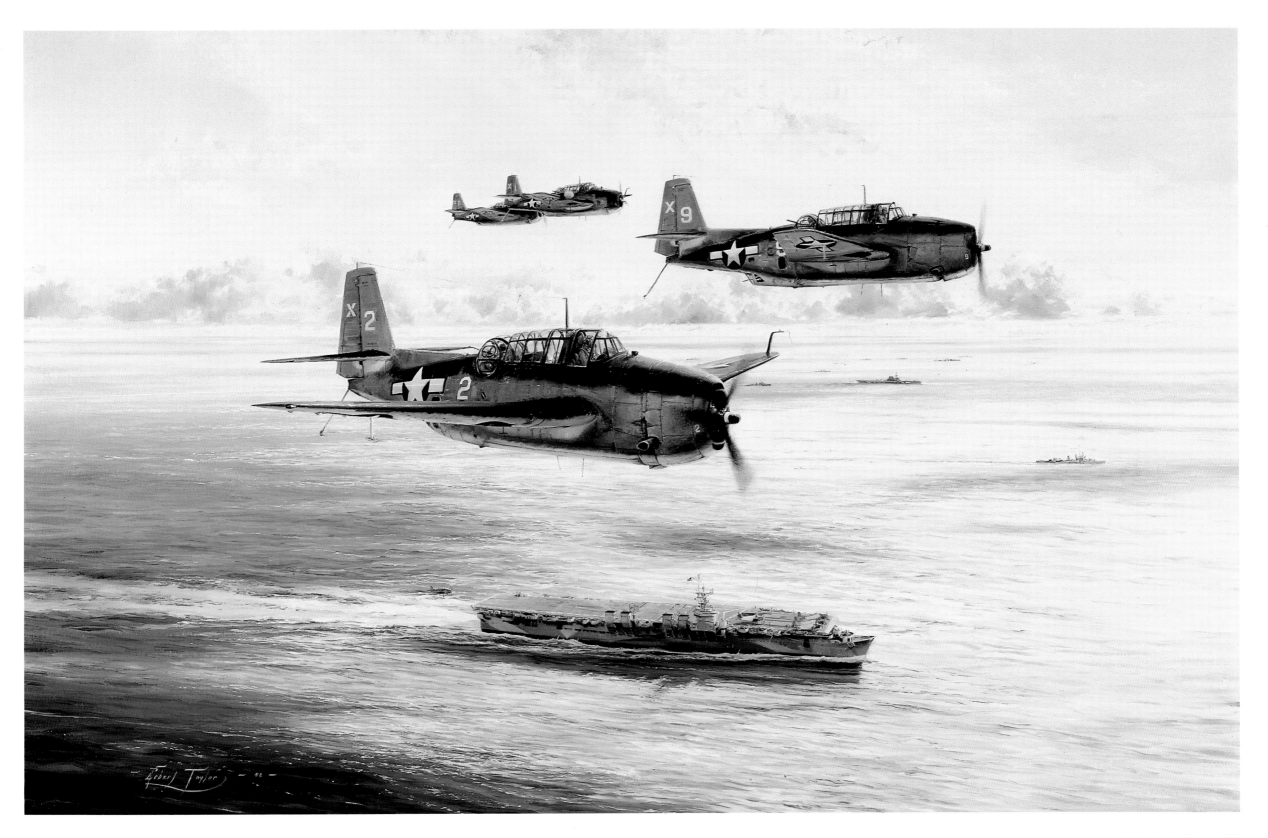

LOW HOLDING

In the collection of The Military Gallery

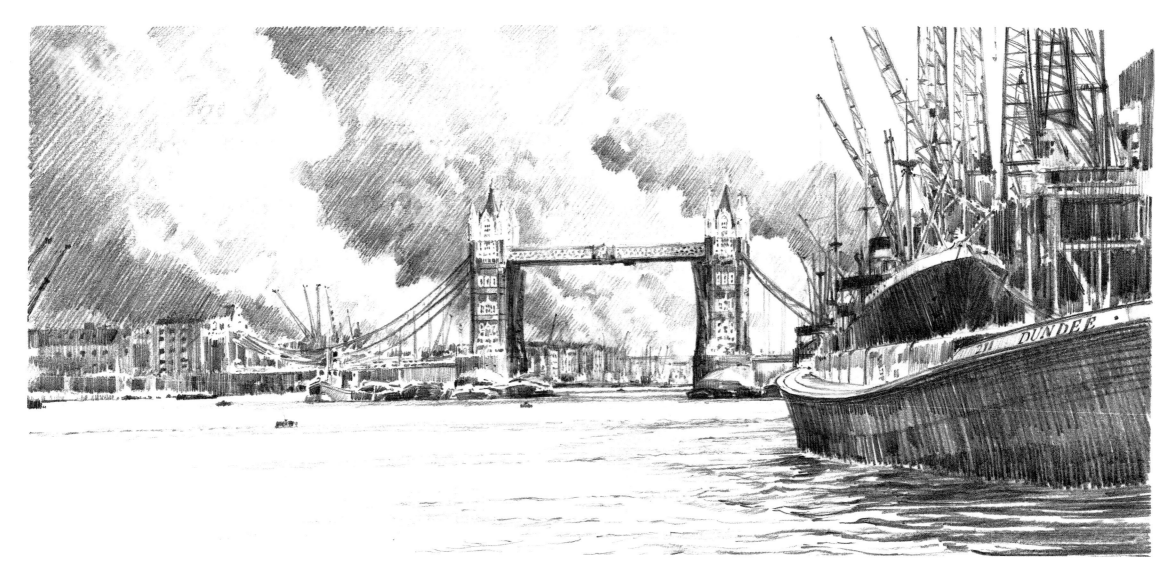

COMBAT OVER LONDON

The main operational runway of virtually every airfield in Britain runs approximately east to west. To be more precise, the actual compass heading is usually 240°, because that is the direction from which the prevailing west-south-westerly winds blow in from the Atlantic.

London's Heathrow airport is situated about 15 miles almost due west of London, and it is for this reason that most passengers arriving at Europe's busiest airport have such a good view of London as they descend the glide-path to one of Heathrow's two main runways. On 15 September 1990, the airport was closed for nearly half an hour to allow the RAF to stage one of the most spectacular and emotional fly-pasts ever seen over London. Instead of seeing a steady stream of descending commercial airliners, the hundreds of thousands of people who had gathered from all over the world watched a dazzling fly-past of military aircraft. Proudly led by a gaggle of Spitfires and Hurricanes, the Royal Air Force paraded all its front-line aircraft, one immaculate formation following another, culminating with a solitary pair – a Spitfire and a Hurricane – flying a tribute to the men of the Battle of Britain. Below, in the courtyard of Buckingham Palace, with the Queen taking the salute, were the survivors of the epic battle, Churchill's Few, bemedalled and proud. It was an occasion of great emotion.

With the unforgettable roar of the Merlin engines still hanging in the air, and before anyone had said a word to each other, almost as if part of the carefully staged aerial pageant, three magnificent white swans flew over the palace in perfect 'vic' formation. One veteran remarked 'It was an entirely appropriate ending to the display – a sort of symbol of peace. That's what we were all fighting for fifty years ago, and what so many gave their lives for.'

The Battle of Britain was fought in three distinct phases. The first saw mass aerial attacks against the south coast ports and these were followed by bombardment of the fighter airfields. The final phase was the one that is most remembered, for it affected most people. Here the fighter pilots flew in defence of their capital city, and day after day the citizens in the streets watched the battle reach its climax high above them in the late summer sky.

I painted *Combat Over London* for a limited edition print which was announced on Battle of Britain Day.

REMINISCING –
SPITFIRE AND MESSERSCHMITT

By

Air Commodore Alan Deere DSO, OBE, DFC

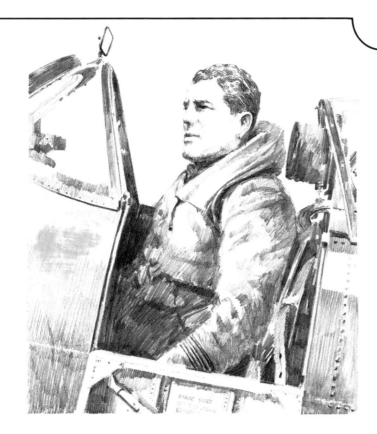

On the morning of 23 May 1940, during the Dunkirk operations I perhaps earned a small place in history when I shot down a Messerschmitt 109, becoming the first Spitfire pilot to do so. The victim was one of the two 109s which I encountered, but the prolonged dog-fight with the second one, although inconclusive, was, I think, of great significance since it provided the first basis for comparison of these two great fighters. The incident was, therefore, worthy of the telling.

The second 109, its sleek grey body entrancingly silhouetted against broken white cloud from which it had emerged, flashed in front of me just as I broke from the first engagement. The pilot must have spotted me, for immediately he went into a steep turn clearly intent on getting on my tail. But I had other ideas. I easily maintained my position behind by turning inside him and although out of range I let him have a quick burst – a sort of warning. He reacted instantly as violently he hurled up in a steep climbing turn. Suddenly, he levelled out and as he did so he bunted over into a dive. Unlike the 109, the Spitfire lacked direct injection and I was unable to follow this unexpected play. Quickly I rolled onto my back, and pulling hard through the subsequent dive, I followed, now somewhat behind. With throttle fully open and though the gate on extra boost, I gradually closed in again. Clearly the fleeing 109 pilot had his eye on me because as soon as my

closing Spitfire threatened he commenced a series of violent evasive manoeuvres. The adrenalin now in full flow, I hung on grimly.

I could now clearly see the pilot's face as his helmeted head darted from side to side, intent on keeping me in sight. Again I tried a burst, hopefully, but it was just not possible to bring my guns to bear as, weaving and yawning, he flung his 109 about the sky. And so it went on until, sweating from exhaustion, I was forced to accept that I was not going to kill this bird. Also by this time I was a long way from home; I was low on fuel and I had no wish to have to land in France. Reluctantly, I broke off combat mouthing a silent salute to the worthy opponent as I did so. (I landed back at Hornchurch having been 2.15 hours airborne, about the maximum for a Spitfire in combat.)

Undoubtedly, the 109 in the hands of a good pilot was a tough nut to crack. Initially, it was faster in the dive but slower in the climb; the Spitfire could out-turn it but was at a disadvantage in manoeuvres that entailed negative 'G'. Overall, there was little to choose between the two fighters. And this proved to be so in the fighting that followed, the improving versions of each aircraft continuing to march in step. But in mid-1943 the Spitfire IXB entered the arena to become 'cock of the walk', remaining so for the rest of the air war in Europe, totally outmatching its counterpart, the 109G.

Painting two aircraft in direct combat always poses a problem, particularly where the aim is to show one of them shooting at the other. The difficulty arises with the positioning of the two contesting aircraft. There is usually at the minimum several hundred feet between aircraft in combat, which means that in order to get both of them on the same canvas, the aircraft have to be shown either coming fairly directly towards the viewer, or going away. Whichever the choice, one of the aircraft has to be painted much smaller than the other.

One could widen the angle, of course, and paint both aircraft very small on the canvas, but people who appreciate and enjoy aviation art prefer to get a good look at the aircraft in a painting, so the artist has to find other ways of portraying the combat realistically.

One solution is to portray a head-on attack, the manoeuvre depicted in *Combat Over London*. The head-on attack was a tactic sometimes employed by fighter pilots, often with spectacular results. Alan Deere described one such attack to me. Neither he nor his opponent had been prepared to give way to the other, with the result that they collided in mid-air. Miraculously Alan survived.

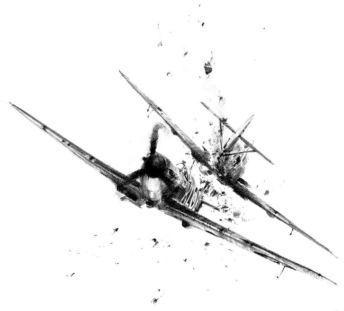

I had already previously painted a trilogy of pictures to commemorate the fiftieth anniversary of the Battle of Britain which featured individually Spitfires, Hurricanes and Me109s. Although each painting showed a combative scene, none showed opposing fighters actually in combat with each other, and it

HEAD ON ATTACK

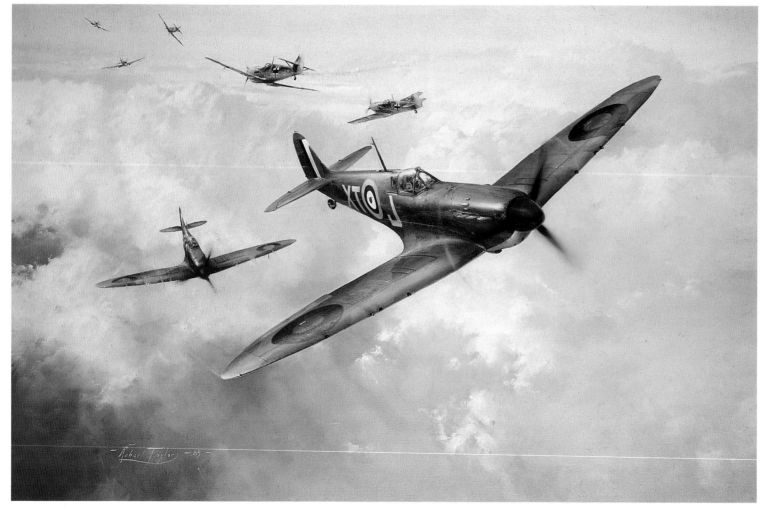

seemed appropriate that to complete my contribution to that historic anniversary year I should paint a dog-fight.

I had the difficult task of choosing whether to paint a Spitfire or a Hurricane to go into combat with the obvious opponent – the Me109. I am fond of painting the Hurricane and originally planned to in this case, but changed my mind at the drawing stage. I decided at the outset to make this a high-level dog-fight but I wanted viewers to be able to pick out some identifiable landmarks 28,000 feet below.

Even if I paint an aviation picture containing no ground reference at all, I can usually tell anybody who asks me the location of my aircraft and what the terrain is below. I always like to know!

At first I intended to show the south coast port of Dover with the adjacent white cliffs, which would have dated the painting to the early part of the Battle when the Luftwaffe were attacking the south coast sea ports. I decided, however, that as this was to be my final painting for the Battle of Britain's fiftieth year I would show a combat late in the conflict, when the Luftwaffe were attacking London. Once the location was decided, I made a few thumb-nail sketches in order to decide what would be happening in the dog-fight. I had painted a head-on attack some years ago based upon a particular combat described by Air Vice-Marshal David Scott-Malden which had worked quite well (this painting is seen on the left) and inspired by Alan Deere's account of one of his head-on attacks I decided that this would be right for this picture.

When I made a full-size working drawing, I was really happy with the size and angle of the Me109, but the Hurricane, being a more bulky aircraft than the Spitfire, dominated the picture too much, detracting from the Me109. The Spitfire's sleeker lines evened up the balance of the painting so the poor old Hurricane, not for the first time, got pushed out of the limelight. I apologise to all Hurricane pilots.

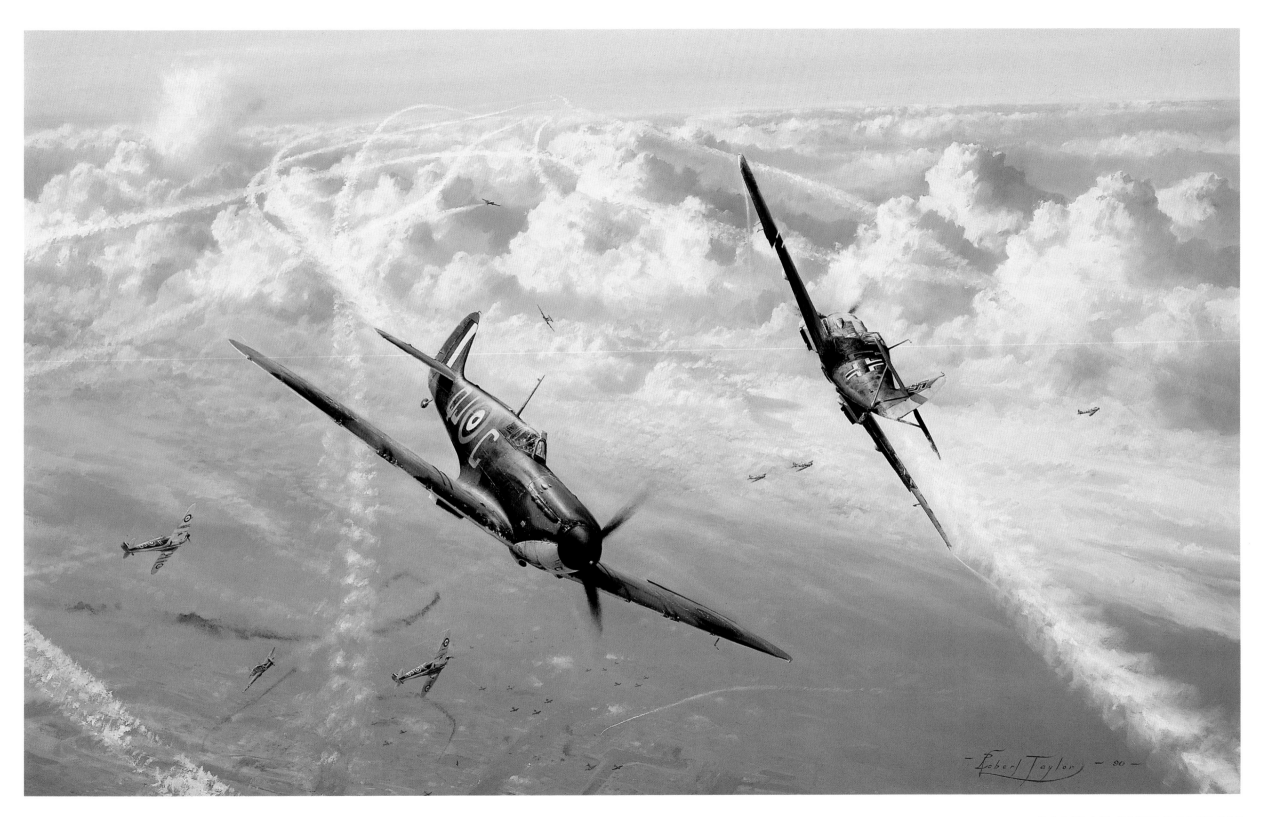

COMBAT OVER LONDON

In the collection of Wings Fine Art

JV-44

Squadron of Experts

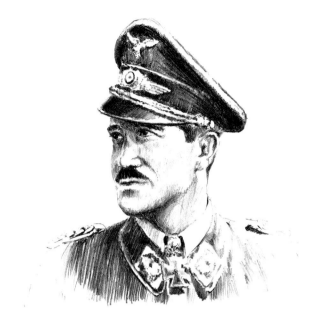

I am not sure exactly what it is about the Me262 that arouses so much interest in people. Maybe it is because when it first came into service it was an aircraft ahead of its time; perhaps it was its revolutionary appearance and design, or even the debate as to how it might have changed the pattern of aerial supremacy had it appeared earlier in World War II. There again, its legend may be due to that extraordinary group of fighter pilots who assembled in General Adolf Galland's specially formed Wing to fly this remarkable aeroplane. In truth, I suspect it is a combination of all these things which provided a niche in aviation history for Willie Messerschmitt's glamorous jet fighter.

Having been made a scapegoat by Goering and deposed from his position as Inspector of Fighters, and as the Allied Forces drove inexorably towards Berlin, Adolf Galland assembled around him a squadron which contained some of the greatest surviving fighter pilots in the Luftwaffe to operate the new twin-jet fighter. It was to be a last-ditch attempt to stem the tide. The combination of Galland's mercurial leadership and the revolutionary new fighter aircraft became a magnet to the Luftwaffe's élite, drawing a host of colourful high-scoring fighter Aces together for a 'last fling' in combat, flying the new jet fighter.

So outstanding were the assembled pilots recruited by Galland that the coveted Knight's Cross was often referred to as the squadron badge, and the group became known as Galland's Squadron of Experts. Designated JV-44 (Jagverband 44), the inspirational force which Galland had put into the entire Fighter Arm was now concentrated into one squadron, and enthusiasm and morale soared to heights not experienced since the early days of the war.

The combination of skilled, experienced pilots, and an aircraft vastly superior to anything else in the air, gave the squadron immediate though short-lived success. But already it was a lost cause: the Me262 had come too late to change the course of events and almost as suddenly as it had arrived, it slipped into history.

The Me262 was vastly quicker than anything else in the skies of Europe in 1945, having a diving attack speed in excess of 560 miles per hour, and it was this aspect that I felt I should try to bring out in my painting. The use of a solid bank of cumulus cloud was designed to help give the impression of the speed of the diving Me262s, and this was helped by the angle of the aircraft and their smoky trails of jet exhaust. The clouds were also constructed to help place the aircraft at altitude, thus adding some dimension to the painting.

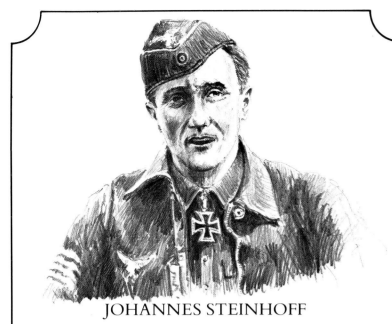

JOHANNES STEINHOFF

Johannes 'Macky' Steinhoff is one of the most remarkable men I have met. He flew and fought throughout the war, seeing action on most of the European and Eastern Fronts. An outstanding fighter pilot with 176 air victories, he was above all a courageous and popular leader, often risking his position by ignoring what he considered to be stupid tactical orders. Together with Guenther Luetzow he had survived a risky attempt to persuade Hitler to remove the incompetent Goering as Luftwaffe Supreme Commander. He was one of the highest scoring, most highly decorated and senior ranking officers to join Galland's Squadron of Experts.

On 18 April 1945, when taking off with Galland's JV-44 squadron, with a full load of twenty-four rockets, Steinhoff's Me262 hit a small crater in the airfield; the aircraft crashed and exploded in flames. Although he was badly burned, somehow Steinhoff survived, but the crash ended his wartime flying and Galland lost one of his most trusted and brilliant fighter leaders. After the war General Johannes 'Macky' Steinhoff became one of the formative officers in the New German Air Force, rising ultimately to become its Chief of Staff.

Macky Steinhoff was one of a group of famous fighter Aces who travelled to the opening of my exhibition at the National Air and Space Museum in Washington DC in 1987. En route above the Atlantic I discovered another of his many talents when he presented me with a caricature drawing of himself in his F-104 Starfighter. In fact, he is an accomplished watercolourist.

The drawing below was a first attempt for the painting, and perhaps demonstrates the need for much planning before the commencement of placing oil on canvas. I drew the largest Me262 first, selecting an angle which I thought showed off the aircraft at a good angle. Next I drew in the wingman below, and roughed in some cloud tops. At this point I had not included the two smaller 262s, but already I could see that the composition would not convey the sort of speed I was looking for. The ultimate composition, showing the Me262s slanting down and across the canvas, with the cloud bank angled away in the opposite direction, provided the effect I sought.

I had read somewhere that when asked why they had fought on so doggedly to the end, even when the war was obviously lost, the Luftwaffe pilots replied 'For the honour of the Squadron'. Although I never intended it, after the painting was completed I thought that perhaps it had caught something of that spirit.

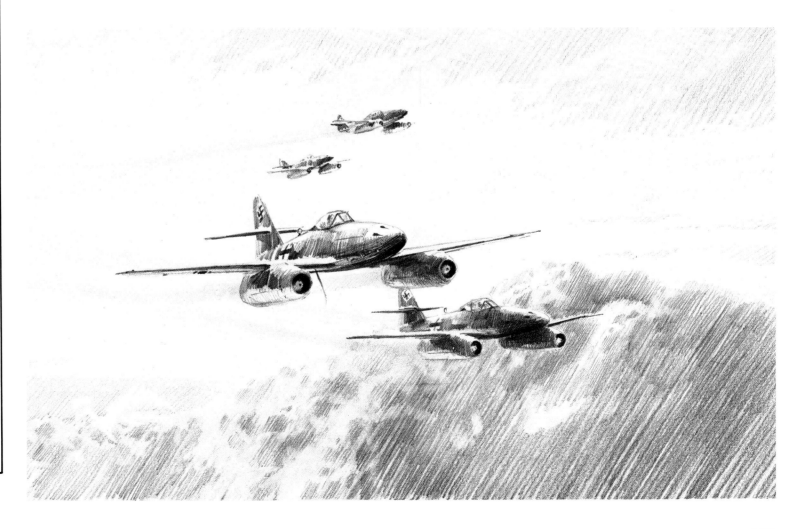

Combat aircraft are in reality never the flawlessly painted machines that the carefully airbrushed technical illustrations would have us believe. Even when they are brand new, body panels are often slightly uneven, pinched where the rivets hold them to the airframe, and of course the more action an aircraft sees, the more the dents, bumps and paint chips become prevalent all over its bodywork. All this becomes accentuated when the sun reflects off the paintwork, and to make the point I have carefully inserted a certain amount of wear and tear in the fuselages of the Me262s of JV-44 as they come slanting out of the sun. The enlarged detail from the painting seen below helps to illustrate this.

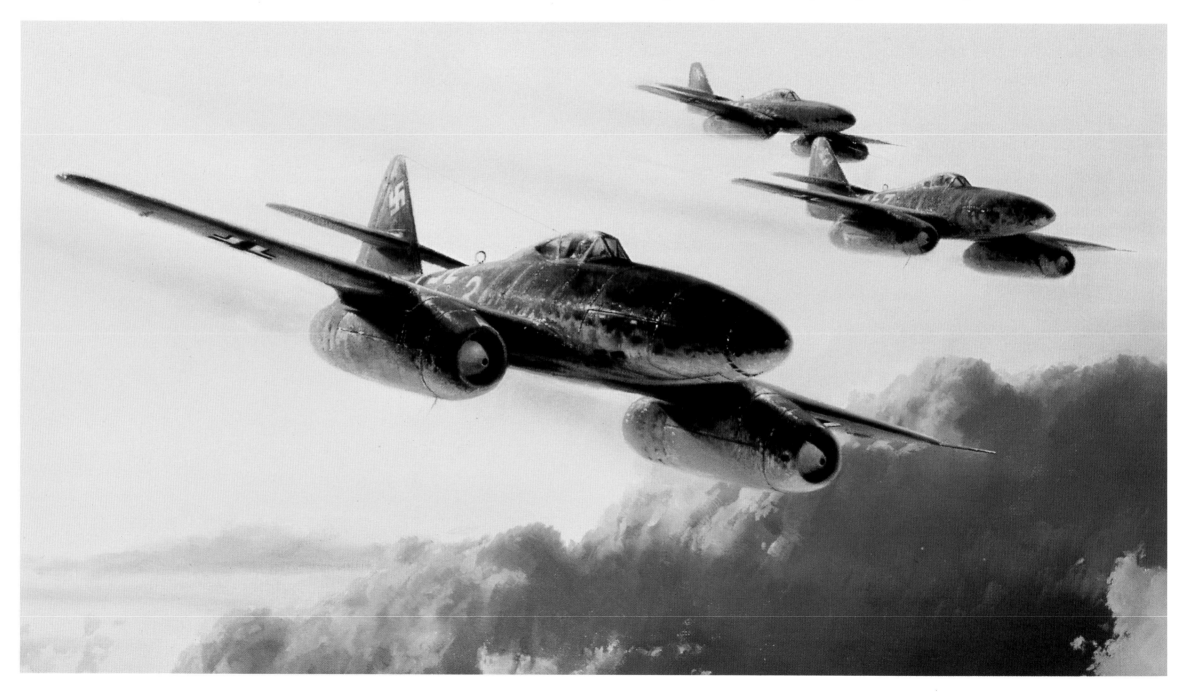

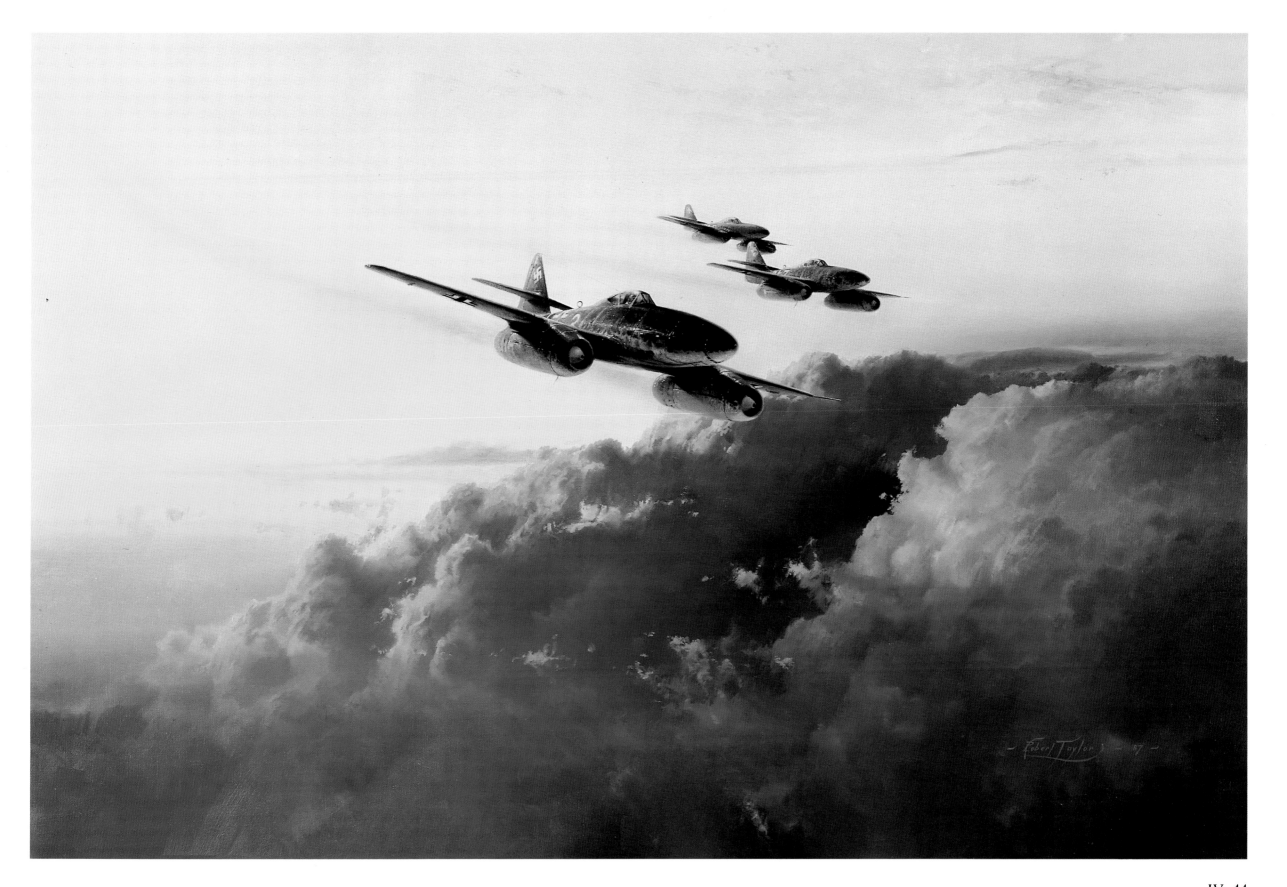

JV–44

ZEMKE'S WOLFPACK

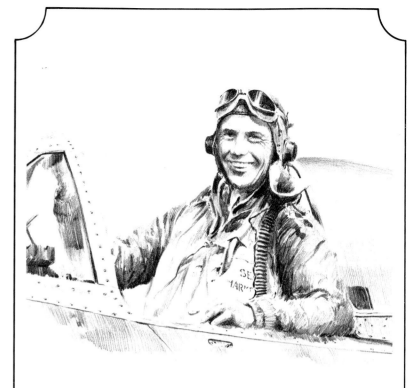

I sat up the best part of one night talking to Hub Zemke. In fact, if I had not been jet-lagged at the time, I am sure that neither of us would have gone to bed at all that night. We were staying with Pat and Judy Barnard in California; Hub had driven down from his almond ranch near Sacramento to discuss a painting featuring his famous 56th Fighter Group. His new book *Zemke's Wolfpack*, with Roger Freeman, was due out shortly after our meeting and Hub had the entire manuscript with him – I know, because we went almost right through it that night. After some ten hours of non-stop chatter, we were knee deep in sketches, diagrams, notes and quotes; I felt as if I had just returned from a Zemke mission!

After a couple of hour's sleep, I staggered down to breakfast, quite sure that the veteran fighter Ace would be catching up on his slumber, to be welcomed at the foot of the stairs by a cheerful 'Good morning Robert. What kept you?' – I should have expected it. All the fighter pilots I have ever met rise at the crack of dawn and can't wait to get going. Most of them can give me a good thirty years and I still have to run to keep up!

I had met Hub a few times before. I knew that he was considered to be one of the greatest American fighter leaders of the war, and I had wanted to paint a scene featuring his famous 'Wolfpack' for some time. What Hub did for me during this memorable meeting was to provide all the necessary information needed to paint *Zemke's Wolfpack*; he also kindly offered to write some notes about the P-47 for my book. I accepted both, gratefully.

COMBATING THE P-47 THUNDERBOLT
By Colonel 'Hub' Zemke

Arriving on the European scene as the new 56th Fighter Group Commander in mid-August 1942, found me deeply disturbed with the actual performance of our aircraft, the P-47 Thunderbolt. Fully loaded, the 'Jug', as it had been labelled, now topped out for take-off at 14,600 pounds – a far cry from the nimble streamlined 'Spits' and Me109s that tangled daily over the English Channel.

The 2,000 horse-power machine didn't leap with glee on take-off. Acceleration gave no indication of shifting gears and it took 10 minutes to climb to 17,500 feet. At this altitude and above, the efficient exhaust gas-driven supercharger took hold, enabling the huge kite to perform with some semblance of a thoroughbred. Above 20,000 feet the Jug strained at its laces and started whipping around like something expected of a fighter.

Having proved its high-altitude ability, the next tactical problem was how to keep the P-47 at altitude for most of its combat time. Fortunately, most of the B-17 and B-24 bomber formations flew between the altitudes of 20,000 and 24,000 feet and so the Luftwaffe had to climb to these altitudes to engage. We soon found that by flying the P-47 at between 25,000 and 27,000 feet made the Luftwaffe

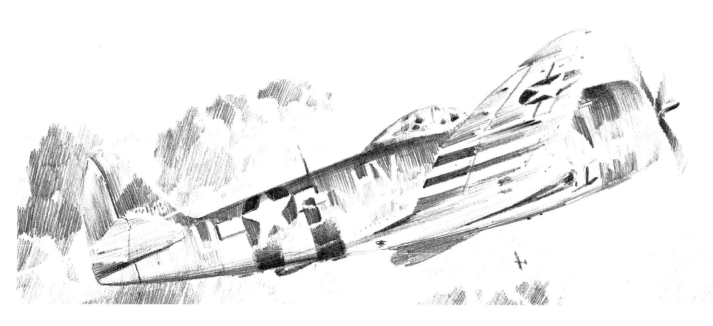

fighters play into the hands of the waiting Thunderbolts, the added 2,000 feet giving us the advantage of a good attacking diving speed. This edge presented a continued nemesis to the Luftwaffe fighters.

Acceleration and top speeds in dives were astronomical. Stick and rudder controls were light and positive. Recovery in a zoom could rocket this 7-ton mass back to its original altitude, a tactic which was continually employed in the days to come.

Though free of violent stalls and spin reactions, the radius of turn at slow speed was such with this obese single-seater that entering into the classic turning, twisting dog-fight was a 'No', 'No'.

Recognising the aircraft's qualities, the Wolfpack's tactics soon evolved into a series of dive and zoom manoeuvres. With the emphasis on keeping the Jug's flying speed up and with much training, the tactic soon involved an entire flight, and ultimately a complete squadron, in the attack. The word of the day was 'If you can't take the target out on the first pass, set the situation up for the following flight or squadron to make the kill.' It became a team effort.

April 1943 found the role of the P-47s changed from the defensive interceptor to offensive escort-fighter, and later the sturdy old Jug took on a close-support role, when bombs and rockets were added to the arsenal of junk hung beneath the wings and fuselage.

With the less vulnerable air-cooled engine, the P-47 became the mainstay of the surging American army, and the brunt of the close support work now fell to the durable Jug. Reallocation of fighter aircraft found the entire 8th Fighter Command converting fourteen Groups to the long-range P-51D for strategic escort. Only the 56th Fighter Group retained the stoic P-47.

Undaunted by certain limits of fuel range and eventually up-graded with greater horsepower and propeller efficiency, the lieutenants of the 56th Fighter Group brought their P-47 Fighter Group through two years of rousing combat to finish World War II as the top accredited American Fighter Group in the European theatre, with 667 aerial wins.

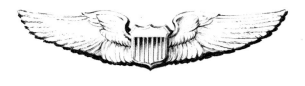

The drawing below was one of a few made before my late night session with Hub Zemke. It was my intention to show a P-47 diving through a formation of German Fw190s, but the angle of the P-47 was too shallow to demonstrate the dive and zoom tactic. I could have cured this by tilting the horizon steeply from left to right, but there was an additional problem in that there were too many Fw190s in the picture to make it likely that this particular Thunderbolt would survive. I could have changed this too, but after talking to Hub I decided upon another approach.

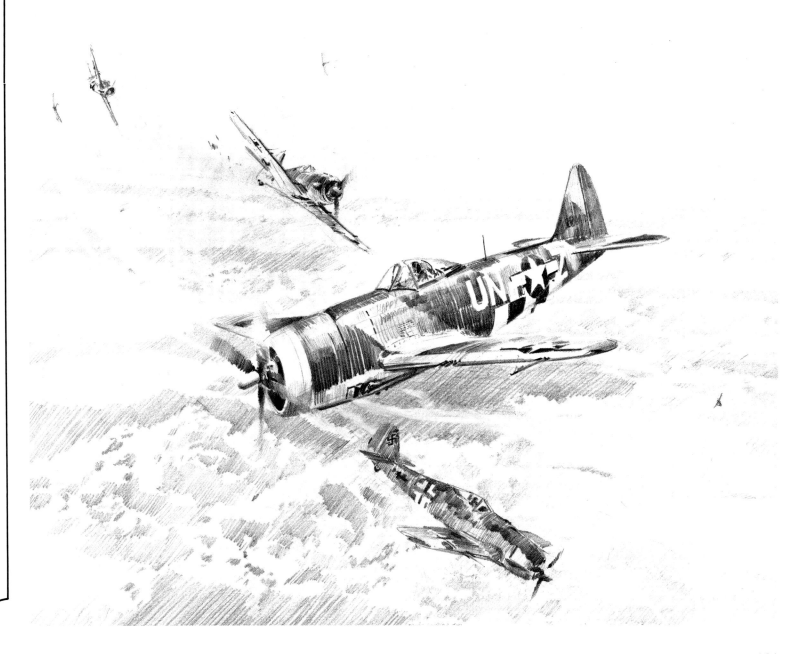

The P-47 Thunderbolt was never a pretty aeroplane. Its huge air-cooled engine and bulky fuselage gave it a pedestrian look, and it is difficult to find an angle that flatters the aircraft. The big advantage it had over its adversaries was its ability to dive at great speed, maintaining a steady gun platform as it hurtled down. I wanted to find a composition that would in some way place some emphasis on this quality, and at the same time to show a good view of the aircraft. Hub Zemke had

P–47 THUNDERBOLT

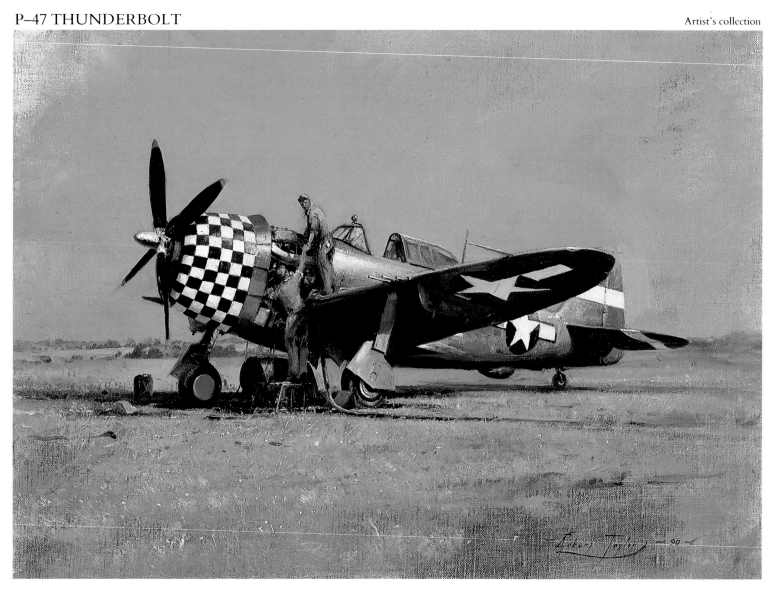

described in detail so many combats to me, but the one which coloured my imagination most was a peel-off sequence which would give the painting plenty of movement. A damaged straggler B-17 under attack by Fw190s would provide drama, but I had two other problems to resolve before I had the making of the painting I was looking for. The first was the difficulty created by the garish colour scheme of the aircraft – the P-47s were metallic silver with a cherry-red nose and tail decoration, and black and white invasion markings: a really unpleasant conglomeration of colours which I would somehow have to overcome. The second problem was to find a way of creating height in the painting so as to emphasise the diving capability of the P-47.

To introduce more interesting colours into the aircraft I placed the sun low on the horizon and to the right of the picture. This enabled me to bounce yellow and orange light off the fuselages and undersides of the wings, toning down the bright cherry red paint, and to reduce the sharply contrasting black and white invasion stripes, giving a little uniformity to the balance of colours.

The feeling of height was achieved by the positioning of the two leading P-47s, Zemke and his wingman, and their relation to the two nearest aircraft. The position of the B-17 and the Fw190 nearest to it took a lot of working out, and their final positions were decided after much trial and error. I placed the attacking Fw190 right above the tail of the second nearest P-47 to draw attention to it, because it was crucial to the drama of the painting. The two other Fw190s approaching from the right add to the drama, and were also placed close to the nearest P-47 to ensure that they were not easily missed: they add considerably to the threat upon the damaged B-17.

Finally, I constructed a big cloud scene to provide depth and distance to the painting, the two small Fw190s that are furthest away helping this aspect.

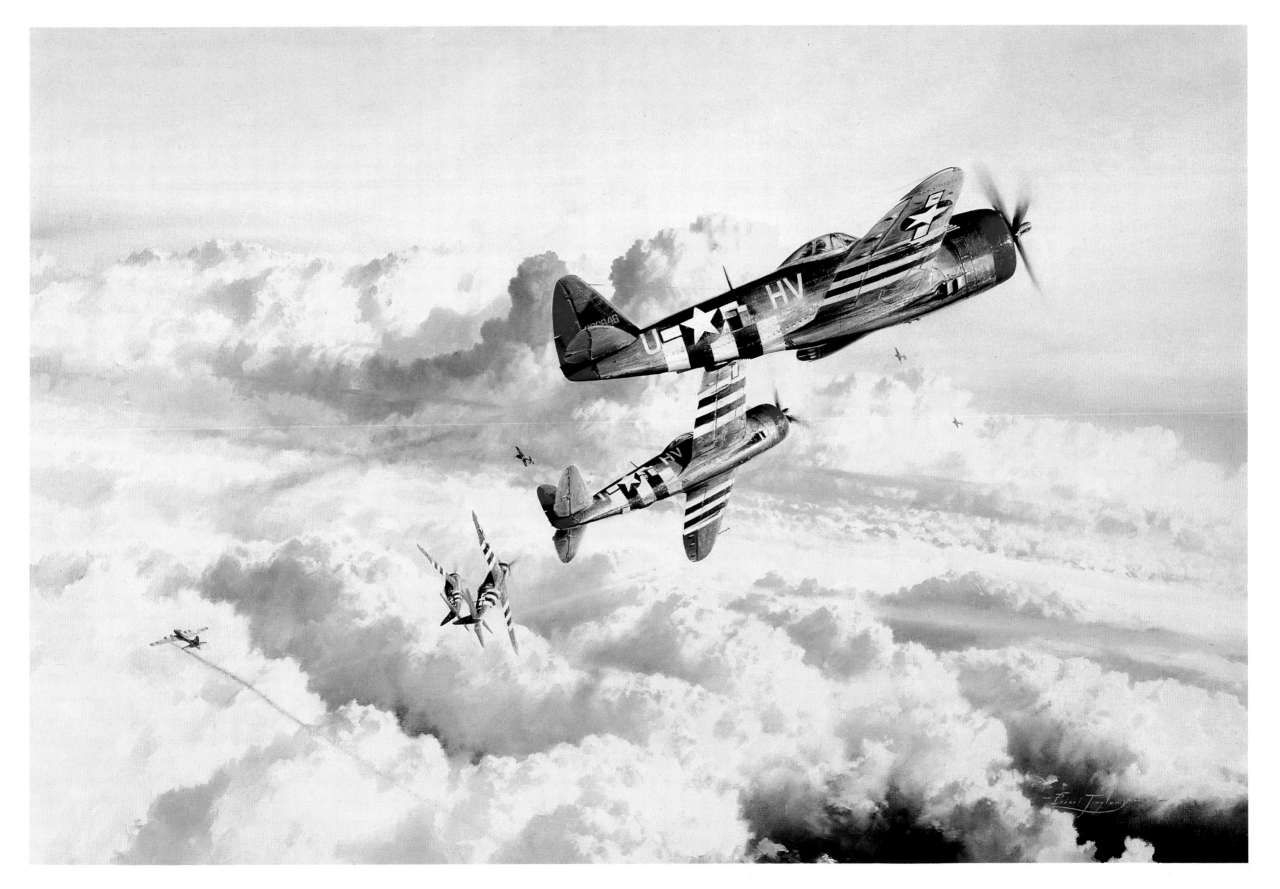

ZEMKE'S WOLFPACK

Private collection

BADER'S BUS COMPANY

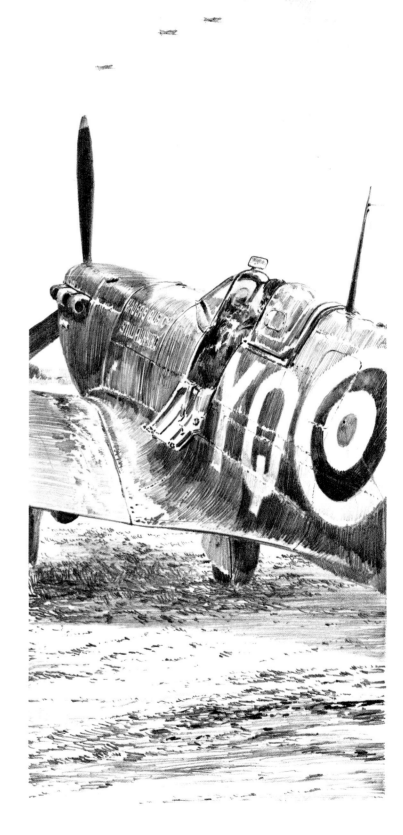

The legend of Douglas Bader lives on. He is remembered not so much because he was a fighter pilot who had no legs, but for his indomitable spirit and leadership. I have heard it said many times by the pilots who flew with Bader that he taught them, as young pilot officers, how to conduct themselves in war. He imbued in them a spirit of aggression, determination, and self-confidence. He was himself as if indestructible. He had led 242 Squadron through the Battle of Britain and was later

to take the fight to the enemy for the first time, leading the newly formed Wing at Tangmere on the south coast of England. There he built up as fine a fighting unit as there ever was, three squadrons of pilots who would have followed him into hell. When he failed to return from a dog-fight over the French coast between Boulogne and Le Touquet on 8 August 1941, the whole of the station at Tangmere went into a state of disbelieving shock.

Cocky Dundas who had flown over sixty missions with Bader and who, with the other Tangmere pilots, had just returned from the combat, organised an immediate search of the area. Accompanied by Johnnie Johnson, Geoff West and Nip Hepple, they flew their Spitfires at wave-top height under the noses of the shore batteries, searching the French coastline in the hopes of finding their fallen leader. Their fruitless, if courageous, mission ended with their return to a Tangmere desolated by the thought that their mercurial Wing Commander was no more.

When, a few days later, the news came through that Douglas Bader had survived and was held prisoner, a huge wave of relief spread throughout the station. All the fighting spirit instilled by Bader returned, and the pilots took up the fight against the Luftwaffe squadrons based on the Western Front with renewed vigour and determination.

It had been Douglas Bader's usual routine, mindful of the need for minimum use of radio, to announce his arrival over the French coast with the brief transmission 'Bader's Bus Company on time'. The welcome news of Bader's survival prompted Johnnie Johnson and other pilots at Tangmere to paint their Spitfires with the message 'Bader's Bus Company still running'. This gave me the idea and the title for the painting.

I had the good fortune to know Sir Douglas Bader quite well during the last decade of his life. He took an interest in my painting, and was a continuing source of encouragement and inspiration to me. He was also a great stickler for accuracy and would often remind me that the present generation of artists painting the events of World War II had the advantage of being able to talk to those who took part – an advantage which future generations of aviation artists will not have. 'You have got no excuse for getting it wrong, old boy' he used to say, with a great grin on his face.

When working on ideas for Bader's Bus Company, I knew I wanted to paint a kind of memorial to Douglas Bader. In the event the painting and the prints subsequently published from it were in part used to raise money for The Douglas Bader Foundation, an organisation which devotes itself to the rehabilitation of people who have lost limbs.

The painting needed to have a symbolic feeling about it, so I painted the aircraft of Cocky Dundas, Johnnie Johnson, Denis Crowley-Milling, Ken Holden, Geoff West, Nip Hepple, and other Tangmere Wing pilots embarking on an operational sortie, their inspirational leader no longer with them. The idea was that the painting should convey an optimistic feeling showing the Tangmere Spitfires leaving the south coast of Sussex behind them as they climb into the morning sun.

In order to create the feeling of space I was looking for, I painted a really big cloudscape. I spent a good deal of time just working out the lighting for the picture, taking care not to allow the aircraft to

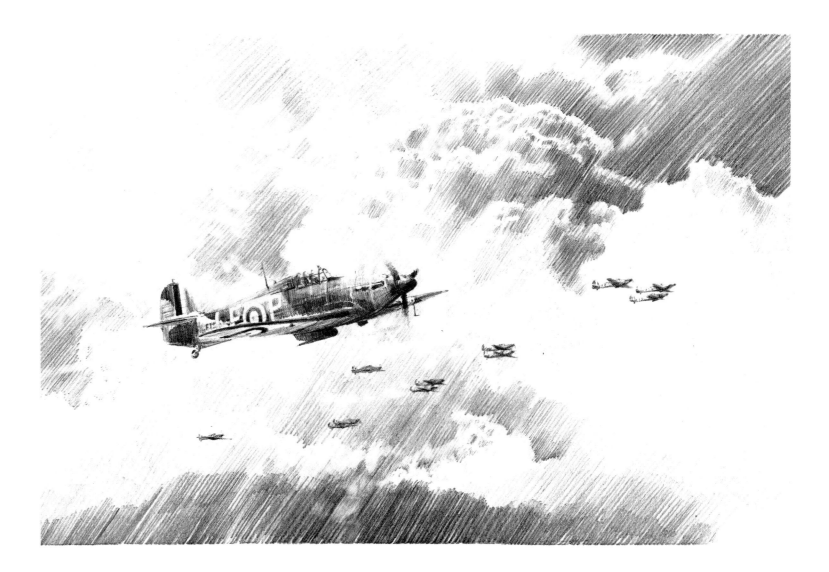

dominate the composition. I was really happy with the result, but the first letter I received about the painting after the print was published asked me why I had made the Spitfires so small!

There is often a temptation for the aviation artist to paint his aircraft too large and his skyscape, or other background, too small. I find that, much as I enjoy painting aircraft with all the detail that this involves, one has to find a happy compromise between the size of the aircraft and the area devoted to the rest of the composition, if the painting is to become more than a simple aeroplane portrait. In fact, if pressed to say which part of an aviation painting is the more important, the aircraft or the scene in which it is set, I would have to say that for me they come out about equal.

No matter how well one succeeds in painting an aircraft, it doesn't really start to 'fly' on the canvas until it is placed in a carefully constructed and complimentary environment. There is no substitute for careful planning and in my experience, there are no short-cuts!

It is one thing to paint an aircraft in flight and, as I have found over the years, quite another to arrange a really good background so as to make the aircraft portrayed look as if they are really moving.

A substantial part of the planning for each painting I do revolves around the choice of background which will support the main aircraft in the painting. One is usually looking to obtain the ingredients that will emphasise height and movement. There are a number of techniques which I find useful in this respect; however, almost all the desired effects can be achieved with careful composition of the background. Although the attitude of the aircraft in a painting is important in conveying movement, the positioning of the aircraft within the overall composition of the picture is just as crucial. And the construction of the background is vital. The combination of all these factors is what gives a painting its perspective.

The most obvious way to obtain the desired perspective is with the careful use of clouds. Fortunately, we artists have much latitude here because clouds are random ever-changing shapes, but care must always be taken to ensure that the particular cloud formations employed are authentic. Most pilots are expert on the subject of clouds because they are the indicators of weather, and weather is all-important to pilots. As pilots make up a good portion of the viewers of aviation art it is as well for us aviation artists to study and to understand the natural environment of the aircraft.

I have an extensive library of reference books about aircraft and ships, and over the years have also collected a large amount of material on the subject of weather and the elements. There are many different types of cloud formations, and meteorology dictates that some cloud types never appear at the same time as others, so a fundamental knowledge of meteorology is fairly essential for an aviation artist.

In arranging one's clouds, an important dimension to consider is lighting. The varying use of light and shadow with colour provides the dimensions of space, distance and height. Where a feeling of height is of critical importance to a particular picture, this can be accentuated by the introduction of ground reference. This need only be a fleeting glimpse through a gap in the clouds, but sufficient to indicate whether the aircraft is at 5,000 or 25,000 feet.

The position of the sun relative to cloud formations is what affects their colour. As the sun rises, travels through the heavens and sets, it shines through a constantly varying amount of the earth's atmosphere. The density, or the amount of moisture in the atmosphere, is what governs the different hues that fall upon the clouds, giving them their colour.

The sun is white hot. When it is directly overhead on a crystal clear day its light is nearly white. Just before sunset it is often possible to look directly at the sun, a deep red ball of fire, one's eyes protected by the sheer volume of atmosphere through which it glows.

We artists are blessed with this eternal light which obligingly provides a constantly changing array of colour and allows us to illuminate our paintings almost any way we choose. One of the great joys of painting is to be able to immerse oneself in this wonderful spectrum of colours, and to find ways of bringing them to the canvas.

The painting on the left shows the Spitfire of Don Kingaby, one of the RAF's most highly decorated fighter Aces, attacking Ju88s over the south coast of England during the Battle of Britain.

FIRST COMBAT

Private collection

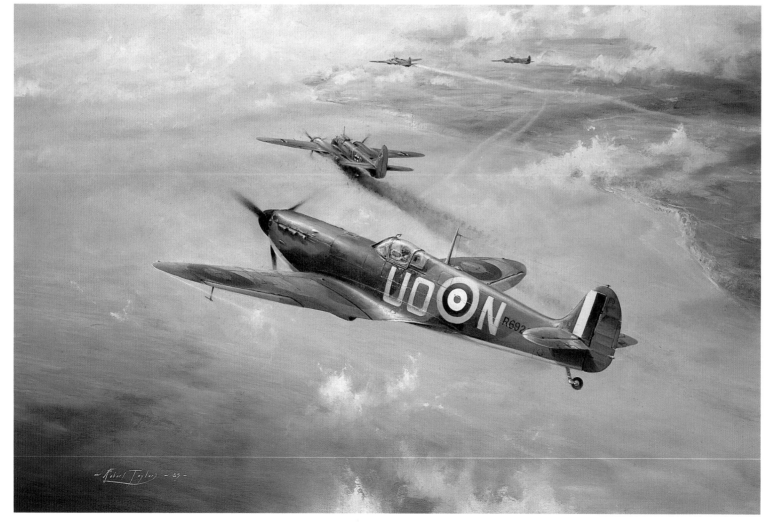

126

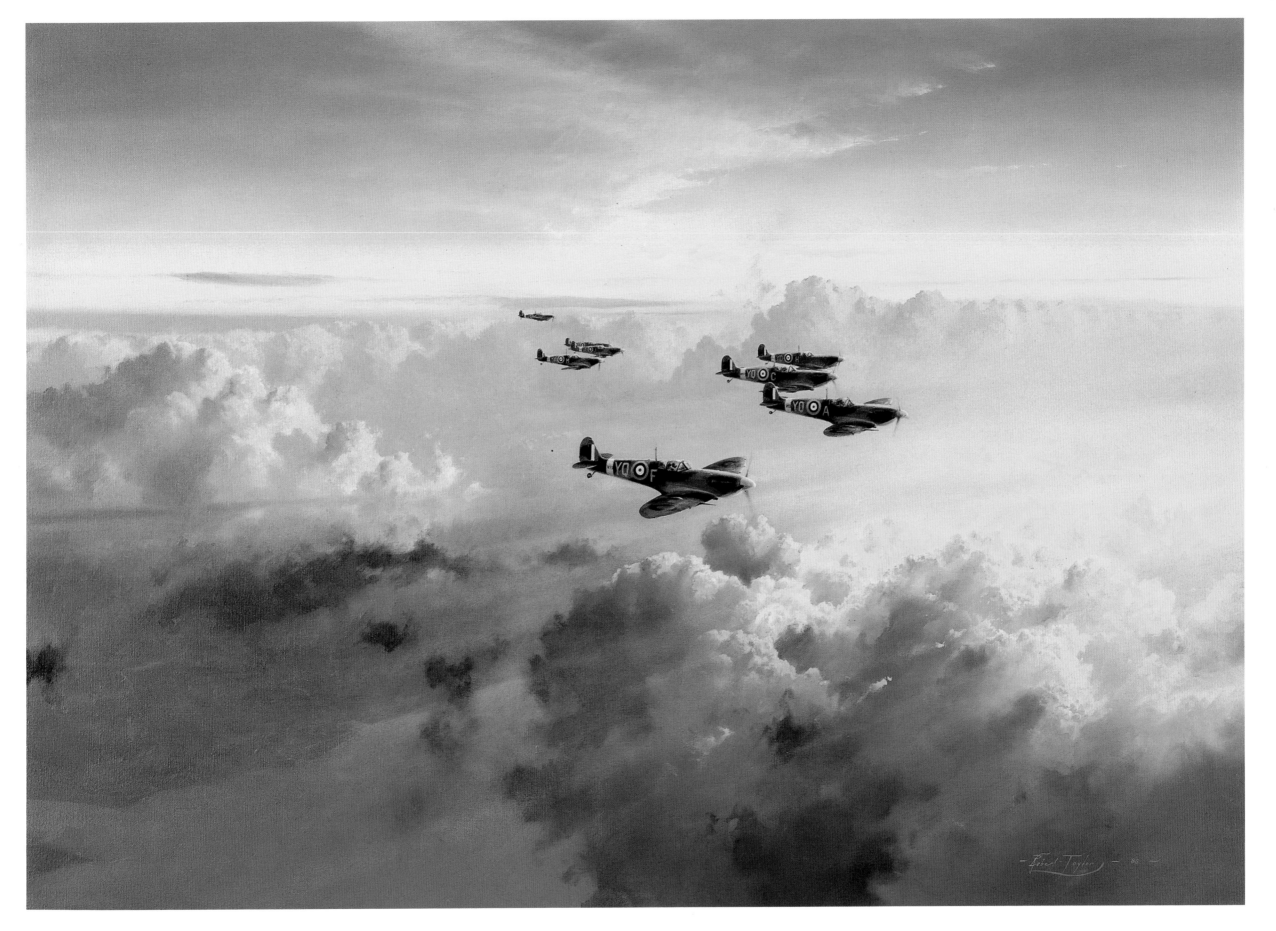

BADER'S BUS COMPANY

In the collection of Mr Ron Mitchell

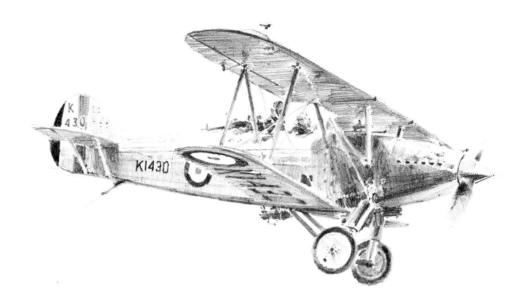

ACKNOWLEDGEMENTS

To publish a book of this kind involves a colossal number of people. In the same way that for every actor you see on the film screen there are dozens who have worked behind the scenes, so it is when publishing a book of this nature. So many people have contributed to this volume, and to the making of the paintings it contains, that I hardly know where to begin with my acknowledgements.

I am proud and honoured that Group Captain Peter Townsend should have written the foreword. He is of course one of Churchill's FEW, having commanded 85 Squadron through the Battle of Britain with great distinction, and today is the well-known author of many books. I shall always cherish his kind words.

I want to thank Charles Walker for writing about me. I appreciate his eloquence and am flattered and slightly embarrassed by his compliments, but appreciate greatly his patience and attention to detail, and the time and effort he has given.

My special thanks to Pat Barnard who, with Mike Craig's help, designed the entire layout of the book, made sure that all the drawings fitted into place, and edited all the text. This was a mammoth task and the section I wrote must have given him nightmares.

The writings of Commander Dick Best, Air Commodore Alan Deere, Colonel Jim Goodson, General Gunther Rall and Colonel Hub Zemke have added great credence to my book. All have helped me with research for my paintings at various times and I value the help and friendship of these distinguished aviators.

I would like to pay tribute to all the staff of my art publishers, The Military Gallery. Over the years we have always worked together as a happy team, and it is largely due to their enthusiasm and dedicated team spirit that this book has been made possible.

I am grateful also to my publishers David & Charles for giving me the freedom to have this book designed and presented the way I wanted it, and to David Porteous who co-ordinated the production with the same skill and consideration which he demonstrated when supervising the production of my first book.

I must express my deep gratitude to Colonel Don Lopez, who is a tower of support, and his assistance with the seeking out of vital research material is of immense value to me. Whilst on the subject of research, I would also like to acknowledge the invaluable help and advice given to me by Air-Vice Marshal Johnnie Johnson, Paul Beaver, the editor of Janes; Roger Freeman, the author; Helen Springhall of the Nimitz Museum, Peter Cooke, Captain Jonathon Bywater, Dieter Stricker and Virginia Bader. All of these people are a continuing source of help to me, and without them and the many other individuals and museums who so willingly provide information, I would have difficulty starting a single aviation painting.

Stephanie Roberts-Morgan typed every word in this book on her word processor, which was a monumental task, and to her go my thanks, as well as to Mike and Rosie Craig who proof-read the text, and John King who photographed so beautifully all the paintings.

Last but by no means least, I offer my grateful thanks to the collectors of my paintings reproduced in this book, whose names appear by the colour plates. I hope they will enjoy reading the stories behind their paintings.

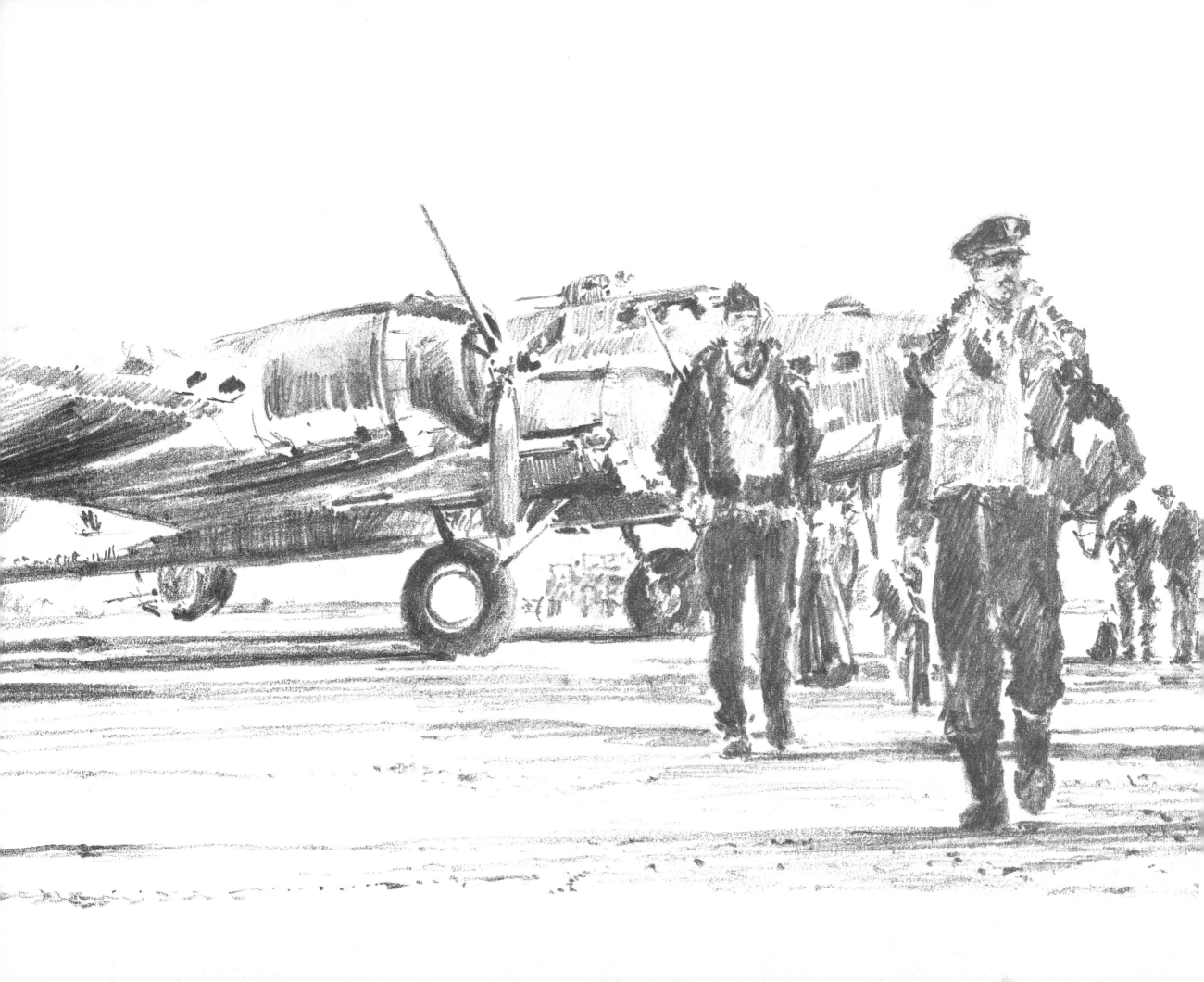